Inside Schools

Routledge Education Books

Advisory editor: John Eggleston
Professor of Education
University of Keele

Inside Schools
Ethnography in educational research

Peter Woods

London and New York

First published in 1986
by Routledge & Kegan Paul plc

Reprinted 2002 by
RoutledgeFalmer, 11 New Fetter Lane,
London EC4 4EE

Published in the USA by Routledge
29 West 35th Street, New York, NY 10001

Transferred to Digital Printing 2004

Set in Times, 10 on 11 pt
and printed in Great Britain
by Hobbs the Printers Ltd, Totton, Hants

RoutledgeFalmer is an imprint
of the Taylor & Francis Group

Library of Congress Cataloging in Publication Data

Woods, Peter.
Inside schools.

(Routledge education books)
Bibliography: p.
Includes index.
1. Education—Research.   2. Participant observation.
3. Action research in education.   I. Title.   II. Series.
LB1028.W64   1986   370'.7'8   85-28285

ISBN 0 415 05 9186

FOR CHARLES AND DOROTHY

Contents

Preface

In preparing this book, I have had three major themes in mind. One is the person of the ethnographer – the most important research instrument within ethnography. Yet while crucial, it is not the easiest thing to study. As Pollard (1985a, p. 231) notes, 'I find it hard to comment in detail on how "the type of person I am" affected the research, although I am sure it did, indeed it was my deliberate intention to use my "self" as a tool in the research process.' However, we are now beginning to get more research biographies to assist us in that task (for example, Burgess, 1984a), and we know that there are certain, almost logical, personal requirements attached to things like the presentation of self in gaining access to an institution, or in the handling of interviews. To these, I add a consideration of the mental states and psychological frameworks within which analysing and writing-up, in particular, are done, and the whole, I hope, helps to build up a picture of the ethnographer's personal kit.

A second theme is 'education'. Hammersley and Atkinson (1983) and Burgess (1984c) have considered the approach as applied to many different aspects of social life. There is equal virtue, I would argue, in examining its application to a particular field, especially when there has been the extent of work as there has been within education. Not only does this deserve consideration in its own right, as an important area of social activity, but it can also give rise to general principles that apply to all areas. For where a number of people engage with inter-related substantive issues, so their methods also inter-relate at a substantive level; and from that comparative base, general principles might arise in the 'grounded' sense of one of the classic texts (Glaser and Strauss, 1967). In this respect, it is important to bear in mind that by its very nature, ethnographic research tends to be individualistic and insular, even within the same area, so that it is difficult to establish such relationships within an actual research study.

There is also a practical benefit in a focus on education for those wishing to study in the area, and a third theme in the book is a particular attention to teachers as researchers. Ethnography has a great deal to offer teachers, and indeed other practitioners, especially at a time of growing interest in the 'teacher–researcher', and in 'action' and 'collaborative' research. It is easily accessible to them, and many of them are, themselves, natural ethnographers. They practise many of the methods in the course of their teaching, and it might be argued that teaching and ethnography are similar art forms. I pursue these ideas in chapter 1.

However, teachers are not the only audience in mind, for the problems of 'getting started' and 'getting in' rehearsed in chapter 2 are fairly universal; the data collection techniques discussed in chapters 3, 4 and 5 can also be applied in different fields, as can the analysis considered in chapters 6 and 7. The 'writing-up' problems examined in chapter 8 are experienced in all kinds of research, and indeed in all kinds of writing. I would hope, therefore, that the book will be of interest to all those wishing to undertake qualitative research in any field, to students of sociology and of research methods. It might also be of interest to those looking for a better understanding of how the ethnographic research studies of recent years were accomplished. Some of these studies have at times been criticized for not saying enough about their methods – a problem of space rather than that they had nothing to say. In a sense, therefore, the book has a validating function, aiming to get behind the neat, polished accounts that we feel bound to try to produce, and to show some of the sweat and tears, as well as subtlety and rigour, I hope, that went into their compilation.

Primarily, however, the book is designed to assist all those wishing to undertake ethnographic research. Such research may be a comparatively small-scale endeavour over very personal and localized matters, or large-scale, where the resources are to hand, over a lengthy period of time, and undertaken, perhaps, with colleagues and/or a professional researcher. Whatever the project, a major message is that it is much more important to internalize the 'ethnographic spirit' rather than to memorize techniques, and I hope there is some of that quality in the book also.

Acknowledgments

For their helpful comments on draft material, my thanks to Pat Sikes, Lynda Measor, Martyn Hammersley, Bob Burgess, Stephen Bali, Andy Hargreaves and Bill Greer. I am particularly grateful to Pat and Lynda for permission to use previously unpublished material of theirs in chapters 4 and 6; and to Martyn for the figure on pp. 140-1.

Chapters 6, 7 and 8 include extracts from two previously published papers ('Ethnography and theory construction in educational research' in Burgess, R. G. (ed.), *Field Methods in the Study of Education*, Falmer Press, 1985; and 'New songs played skilfully: creativity and technique in writing up qualitative research' in Burgess R. G. (ed.), *Issues in Educational Research: Qualitative Methods*, Falmer Press, 1985) and I am grateful to the publishers for permission to use them here.

Mrs Meryl Baker has solved numerous first draft riddles (see chapter 8) with great perspicacity and typed the whole with enviable speed and accuracy.

Chapter 1

Ethnography and the teacher

Teaching and educational research do not have a happy association. To many teachers much educational research appears irrelevant. They have little part in initiating and conducting the research. The issues selected for examination are not theirs. They are defined in ways that take little account of the day-to-day intricacies of the teacher's task, and are dressed up in methodological mystery and incomprehensible jargon. The following comment from a teacher is typical.

> Some of it seems very artificial. It seems to be simply a means to an end. A piece of paper awarded to the person who's done the research, at the end, to prove that he/she has satisfied the examiners. The actual research itself is meaningless, and irrelevant to any working teacher . . . I don't think the teacher in the classroom is ever really taken seriously enough . . . and a lot of theory . . . isn't very relevant to what goes on in a classroom or a school. (Quoted in May and Rudduck, 1983)

One of the main reasons for this gulf between teachers and research is, I suspect, the simple fact that much educational research has not been done for teachers. Rather, it has been generated within a body of knowledge related to one of the disciplines, such as psychology, sociology, philosophy, and its theoretical interests (see also Adelman, 1985). It is not that it is irrelevant to teachers' concerns, but that, if the primary aim of the research study were to be concerned with teacher practice, it would need to be cast in a different way. Also the connecting links would need to be clarified. Teachers might complain that there is too much philosophy and theory, and not enough consideration of how research relates to practice. They might further accuse researchers of not explaining

1

themselves adequately. Researchers might argue that only teachers can interpret the relevance of any study for their classroom practice, for only they are conversant with the many different factors that go towards decision-making within the actual situation. Between them, the practical significance of the work is frequently lost.

The ideal situation in principle is to amalgamate the two functions - the production of knowledge and the demonstration of its applicability to educational practice - within the same person. There has been arguably, some movement towards this from both sides - from the research, academic end in the form of 'teacher educators', and from the teacher end in the form of 'teacher-researchers' (Stenhouse, 1975). However, both of these roles are still firmly located within their own spheres, with all the attendant boundary problems. Can researchers or teacher educators really appreciate teacher practice without continual experience of it themselves? Can teachers or other professionals, without much more generous provision of free time, engage in any worthwhile research? The difficulties are considerable, but the belief that this represents currently the best hope for bridging that gap, underlies this first chapter. Later chapters then aim to help equip teachers, other practitioners and researchers with what I consider to be a particularly useful research approach for that kind of endeavour. To substantiate the point about the potential for synthesis in ethnography, it is necessary first to consider the nature of pedagogical knowledge.

Pedagogical knowledge

First, it is knowledge that teachers - and not educational researchers - have. If research is to be cast in this field, teachers, not researchers, would need to specify the issues, and there would need to be some internalization of research method on the teachers' part, or of pedagogical knowledge on the part of researchers. Second, it is knowledge that both informs and constitutes the practical action of teaching. This involves more than just instrumental effectiveness at 'task'. It includes the whole circumstances surrounding the task. The disciplines inform the theory in these areas; for example, questions of why one is doing it (philosophy), how the child learns (psychology), knowledge of the child's 'presentation equipment' (sociology), skills of communication (linguistics). However, it is its transformation into practice (how all these inputs are put together and brought to bear on particular issues) that makes it pedagogical knowledge. I would argue that, at the moment, the feed-in of academic knowledge to teacher practice in these areas is low, and, in its absence, a great deal of first-hand, anecdotal, 'recipe' knowledge or folklore is employed. Though this contains a fund of wisdom, it is, in more senses than one, undisciplined. It is not an adequate basis for professional action.

Another feature, I would suggest, is that it is not always conscious, or easily articulated. Teachers often act intuitively, but it is an intuition that usually rests on a firm basis of learned knowledge, and which exists in an 'open certainty'. What I mean by this derives from the fact that, in a sense, certainty and knowledge are occupational requirements of a teacher. They are expected to know, and to be able to make many on-the-spot decisions that allow little scope for doubt and reflection before they are made. Teachers typically handle this by advancing on a broad front, recognizing the imperfection of some actions after the event, but seeking to make restitution when a similar occasion recurs. The certainty that teachers need, therefore, to give their professionalism assurance, is a 'strategic' or 'open' one, not a 'closed' omniscience, impervious to persuasion (though there may well be some teachers who display the latter, but I would argue that their 'pedagogical knowledge' is defective).

Pedagogical knowledge, therefore, involves an 'open' certainty and a 'closed' imperfection. The main reason for the imperfection is the host of factors attending the situations teachers confront, which are in constant flux anyway, so that it is difficult, if not impossible, for a teacher to know them all. Some may have to be guessed at on the basis of evidence of variable worth, and on occasions they will guess wrongly. Perhaps the basis of a teacher's skill is the ability to guess right most of the time.

This is why the teacher is the sole owner of pedagogical knowledge. It is synthetic, building up separate elements (for example, from the various disciplines) into a connected whole, which is a teacher's teaching orientation; it involves knowledge of the situation (which includes not just the material environment, but one's own personal resources, and pupils, and an understanding of the purposes within it). Only the teacher is privy to this constellation of factors.

Some have argued that pedagogical knowledge is additive, not cumulative; that it is more of an art, like architecture, than a science, like medicine (Harris, 1976; Shulman, 1984). In the latter, there have been great advances in knowledge, but the former is more a matter of style, subject to prevailing mores, values, economics, etc., as well as personal whim and predilection. I believe, however, there are elements of both in teaching, but that the scientific advances made in, for example, our understanding of how pupils learn, how cultural forces influence their motivation, teacher socialization, how subjects develop, and so on, are, so far at any rate, inadequately and ineffectively incorporated into pedagogy. Consequently the old mystique about teachers being 'born not made' continues to carry considerable point, for they are thrown back on their personal resources of, for example, the power of story-telling, the ability to speak to and relate to people, dramatic skills, caring and other vocational feelings, the ability to explain and organize, enthusiasm, drive and industry. Somebody scoring high in these areas would probably be considered a good teacher in today's schools. However, some might argue that the kind of individualistic charisma such a combination would produce is actually suppressed by our current system of teacher training, by the way educational research is communicated to teachers, and by the situation teachers are required to face in our schools. We are possibly in a situation, therefore, where the science and art in pedagogy, far from complementing each other to the benefit of both, are acting against each other to their mutual detriment.

Ethnography

Ethnography, I would argue, is particularly well suited to helping to close the gulf between researcher and teacher, educational research and educational practice, theory and practice. The term derives from anthropology, and means literally a description of the way of life of a race or group of people. It is concerned with what people are, how they behave, how they interact together. It aims to uncover their beliefs, values, perspectives, motivations, and how all these things develop or change over time or from situation to situation. It tries to do all this from *within* the group, and from within the perspectives of the group's members. It is *their* meanings and interpretations that count. This means learning *their* language and customs with all their nuances, whether it be the crew of a fishing trawler, a group of fans on a football terrace, a gang of gravediggers, the inmates of a prison or a religious seminary, a class of five-year olds beginning school, a particular group of deviant pupils or conforming ones. These have each constructed their own highly distinctive cultural realities, and if we are to understand them, we need to penetrate their boundaries, and look out from the inside, the difficulty of which varies according to our own cultural distance

4

from the group under study. In any event, it will mean a fairly lengthy stay among the group, first to break down the boundaries and be accepted, and second to learn the culture, much of which will be far from systematically articulated by the group.

It is, thus, no ordinary picture. A snapshot gives merely surface detail. The ethnographer is interested in what lies beneath – the subjects' view, which may contain alternative views, and their views of each other. From these, the ethnographer may perceive patterns in accounts, or in observed behaviours, which may suggest certain interpretations. The social reality is thus seen to be composed of layers. Moreover, it is also recognized that it is constantly changing. Group life may have certain constant properties (which, of course, one is concerned to detect), but it is also in flux, a process with oscillations, ambiguities, and inconsistencies. The tendency of our mental set is to try to resolve these when it comes across them, but they are the stuff of life, to be understood, rather than resolved and thus dissipated.

The ethnographer thus aims to represent the reality studied in all its various layers of social meaning in its full richness. It is also a holistic enterprise in another sense, for, within the limits of one's own perception and ability, the aim should be to give a thorough description of the relationship between all the elements characteristic of a single group, otherwise the representation may appear distorted. For example, in a study of pupil culture, a great deal would be missed if just the classroom situation were studied; or in a study of teacher careers, if just a segment or section were selected for examination. This is not to say that limited studies cannot be done, but that they should be seen within a holistic framework. Typical ethnographies, therefore, are highly detailed, and rich in the sense that they penetrate the swards of meaning that enwrap any culture.

Ethnographers thus try to rid themselves of any presuppositions they might have about the situation under study. They go into the 'field' to 'observe' things as they happen in their natural setting, frequently 'participating' themselves in the ongoing action as members of the organization or group. Whether one is studying people in classrooms, nude beaches, public conveniences, staffrooms, city streets, clinics, hell's angels' chapters – wherever it may be, ideally one has to get in there and 'do it with them'. It will be seen that ethnography can be great fun at times – but it can also be very risky! Either way, it carries the excitement of engaging in a voyage of discovery toward new territories, and the basic human interests of seeking to understand the people that we encounter in them.

The idea of participation, of course, is both to improve one's own empathic insights and to guard against possible contamination of the scene by outsider influences. The same principles underlie their interviews, which are 'unstructured', 'in depth', 'ongoing' in the sense that they may take place on numerous occasions, and are almost part of their natural conversation.

The usefulness of ethnography to teachers

There are certain parallels between ethnography and teaching that make them eminently suitable co-enterprises.

In the first place, they are both concerned with 'telling a story'. Both research, prepare their ground, analyse and organize, and present their work in the form of a commentary on some aspect of human life. Then, ethnography, too, like teaching is a mixture of art and science. Ethnographers have a great deal in common with novelists, social historians, journalists and the producers of documentary television programmes. Geoffrey Chaucer, William Shakespeare, Charles Dickens, Henry Mayhew, D. H. Lawrence, Paul Scott, Thomas Keneally – such as these show superb ethnographic skills in the acuteness of their observation, their keenness of ear, their sensitivity for feeling, their depth of insight through the layers of reality, their ability to get inside the skins of their characters without losing the ability to appraise them objectively, their power of expression, their ability to re-create scenes and cultural forms and to 'bring them to life', and their ability to tell a story with an underlying structure. Ethnographers try to cultivate all these skills. They are not trying to write fiction, of course – that is where the science comes in, in validating procedures and analysis. However in seeking to represent cultural forms as they are lived by their owners, they have a common purpose with some novelists. How these are identified, comprehended and processed is more a matter of style, perception, interpretative processes, 'feel', sensitivities, an ability that is difficult to pin down but that involves empathizing with others, an ability to 'understand' – essentially artistic properties – than a product of scientific method. Some might consider these useful attributes for the teacher. In that they are both artistic and scientific pursuits, ethnography and teaching, therefore, have a certain basic affinity.

Teachers themselves have considerable experience as participant observers and as interviewers on this kind of basis (see Pollard, 1985a). A little knowledge of the possibilities and limitations, the checks and balances, in other words the *science* of the enterprise, together with some spare time and a reflective disposition to achieve, on occasions, some social distance from the teacher role, would enable many teachers to engage in fruitful ethnographic work. It is therefore more *accessible* to them than some approaches. They require no expensive, sophisticated equipment (other than their own mind), no knowledge of statistics, no controlled experiments. They do not need to be steeped in theoretical and methodological knowledge (though this is not to deny its value, as I shall explain later). Once they have recognized and begun to identify with the ethnographic idea, they will grow into it as the research work proceeds. It is not a matter of massive prior book learning. It would be a mistake to conclude that this makes it *easier* than other methods, but it does make it more available to teachers, and it gives them more scope for understanding the criteria by which the truth of any of their research would be judged.

Second, the approach does promise to yield results that are *newsworthy*, and which cannot be acquired in any other way. It is only over the last decade or so that school processes have been studied in any consistency and depth. Ethnographers have explored teacher and pupil perspectives, cultures, strategies and careers (see Woods, 1983, for an account of these), and would claim to have cast new light on these areas. They have, for example, demonstrated the strategical (as opposed to pedagogical) orientation of much teacher activity (for example, Edwards and Furlong, 1978; Ball, 1981; A. Hargreaves, 1977); the structured, meaningful nature of some apparently 'wild' and meaningless pupil behaviour (for example, Rosser and Harré, 1976; Beynon, 1984); the social construction of school knowledge (Hammersley, 1977b; Goodson, 1981; Ball, 1982); the functional properties of pupil culture (Willis, 1977; Davies, 1982); the routine but unwritten rules that guide teacher action (Hargreaves *et al.*, 1975); the meaning behind some apparently inconsistent pupil behaviour (Turner, 1983; Fuller, 1980; Furlong, 1976). All these exhibit strata of meaning that are hidden from manifest observation and that are also frequently different from what they were purported to be. It is, therefore, information that teachers need to know in establishing the conditions for their work, and in understanding the prosecution of their tasks. This is not to deny that some teachers, as natural, reflective participant observers, may anticipate many of the conclusions. This is to be expected where so much emphasis is placed upon familiar, everyday events, and inmates' perceptiveness. However, its very familiarity to teachers constitutes one of its strengths. It has been pointed out that much educational research 'has explicitly ignored the routine, the mundane and the way in which in the most ordinary and commonplace fashion, members make sense of and understand the environments in which they live' (Hitchcock, 1983, pp. 9–10). Ethnographers seek to understand why such apparent trivia to an outside observer as the loss of a free period, the positioning of a drinks machine, the allocation of duties on sports' afternoon, the colour of a pupil's socks, petty squabbles in the staffroom, can be so important within the teacher's scheme of things. Such are the stuff of the teacher's day, together with a mass of minutiae that go into the moment-to-moment action and decisions. Ethnographers and teachers are thus in league in the same terrain, with the same identifiers.

Because of this, ethnography can have considerable *practical* value for teachers. It is concerned with issues that they recognize, deals with their problems, and in their terms. Thus teachers can add to their strategical skills through the many studies of teacher-pupil interaction (e.g. Delamont, 1976). They can see how inequalities are actually worked out in the classroom, and how they themselves, unintentionally perhaps, contribute towards them (Stanworth, 1983). They can be assisted toward better diagnosis of pupil deviance. Ethnographers have considered which pupils deviate and why, tracing out how cultural forms can be exhibited in individual behaviour. They have considered the meaning of deviance from the essential 'sussing-out' of new teachers, to innocuous 'mucking-about', to symbolic rebellion, to culture clash (Willis, 1977; Woods, 1979; Beynon, 1984). They have picked up deviant behaviour that goes unremarked, and possibly unobserved by the teacher, especially in the case of conformist pupils, and of girls (Turner, 1983; Davies, 1984). Each one of these cases requires a different treatment – their identification is therefore essential.

Teachers can bring ethnographic techniques to bear on the evaluation of their work, on pupil motivation and learning, on their own careers and development. This points to another advantage of the approach. Ethnography offers researchers a large measure of *control* over the work done. The researcher *is* the chief research instrument. In a sense, the questionnaire, the experiment, the statistical tests, etc. – all the paraphernalia of other approaches – are all embodied within the person of the ethnographer. This entails difficulties, to be sure, but it also means a high degree of personal direction, and an opening of opportunities – for teachers lack the specialist knowledge to use many of the traditional research instruments. In a curious way one learns how to do ethnography as the work proceeds, making it a personal quest in method as well as substance, although all one is doing, in effect, is refining one's major research instrument. Just as one works at perfecting a questionnaire, one must work at developing personal qualities of curiosity, insight, discretion, patience, determination, stamina, memory, and the art of good listening and observing.

Of course this degree of personal involvement has disadvantages also, as we shall see, but one of the great advantages is the latitude and flexibility permitted – indeed required. One is on a personal quest in a situation that has certain unique properties. It is like a detective hunt, looking for clues, seeking to discover, analysing.

Personal resources here are everything, but so too are interests, for we are not *tabula rasa*. However much we try to neutralize our own views, opinions, knowledge and biases and open ourselves to the understanding of others, we cannot accomplish total purification. To some extent we shall be drawn where we will. The task then becomes one of trying to ensure that our methods are as rigorous as we can make them. We might then make the best of both worlds.

Ethnography thus offers teachers an engagement with research and a direction over it. Typical approaches within ethnography also offer a sense of another kind of control. For example, an interactionist orientation – the one that has been most predominant in British educational ethnography – lays emphasis on the 'self', how it is constructed, how it interacts with others and with its environment, how it is influenced by, but also influences, external forces. Interactionism recognizes an element of volition in teacher practice, without going to the extreme of believing teachers totally free from the influence of external forces – that would be as mistaken as the 'robotic' view. There are rituals; there are forces operating on schools and the people within them; but within the press of these forces, individuals possess an element of volition, and this permits us to take both an optimistic and a realistic stance. It recognizes the difficulties confronting teachers, but holds out the prospect of the self negotiating passages through them, though they may be tortuous. Thus it recognizes that teachers have their own self interests and ways of achieving them.

With the general contraction of the system, these interests are more under attack than usual at the moment. For example, many teachers are having to revise their notion of career structure. Some recent work has been investigating teachers' responses to this situation (Sikes, Measor and Woods, 1985). One might argue that this kind of ethnography has a *therapeutic* value – and indeed many people say they enjoy talking freely and frankly to researchers (see, for example, Denscombe, 1983).

This points to the essentially democratic nature of the approach through its enhanced appreciation of others' points of view. With regard to pupils' views, for example, activities such as 'being shown up' or 'picked on', 'having a laugh', 'dossing', 'blagging and wagging', 'bunking off' and even 'doing nothing' are discovered to be not irrational, childish or pathological, but to have deep meaning, and some considerable priority in the lives of pupils suffering or practising them.

Pollard (1985a, p. 232) sums up his personal experiences as a teacher–ethnographer thus:

> I found that the research process as a full participant was often tiring, frustrating and difficult, and yet it was also fascinating and very rewarding to identify patterns in the data and to hesitatingly, step-by-step, attempt to construct a deeper understanding of the events and social relationships in which I daily participated.

Some educational uses of ethnography

Some educational uses of ethnography will already be clear. At its grandest, it is concerned with understanding the human species, how people live, how they behave, what motivates them, how they relate together, their forms of organization, their beliefs, values, interests, the rules – largely implicit – that guide their conduct, the meanings of symbolic forms such as language, appearance, conduct. Sociological ethnographers are also particularly interested in social factors that are connected with differences among groups in all these various respects, such as social class, gender, ethnicity, generations, the environment, the media. Those working within schools have been particularly interested in examining the following.

(1) The effects on individuals and groups, teachers and pupils, of organizational structures and changes in them such as streaming, setting, mixed-ability groups, comprehensive schools.
(2) The socialization and careers of pupils and teachers, with the emphasis on their subjective experience of their careers rather than the objective indices; for example, with respect to pupils, much attention has been paid to key transitional periods such as eleven-plus or twelve-plus transfer, subject choice at thirteen-

plus, and leaving school. There has been interest in teacher biographies, the personal resources they bring to situations, and how they are formulated and developed.

(3) The cultures of particular groups, such as teacher subject sub-cultures, the culture of the staffroom, pupil groups from large (where they might be distinguished by simple divisions, such as examination/non-examination, streaming/non-streaming, boys/girls, white/black, middle/working class) to medium (such as a particular class, or a clearly demarcated group within one, or across some) to small (which may consist of merely two or three, or may be very fluctuating in their membership).

(4) What people actually *do*, the strategies they employ, and the meanings behind them. This includes teacher methods of instruction, and of control, and pupil strategies in responding to teachers or in securing their ends. It invariably depicts a dialectic between self and society, as one seeks to achieve certain ends, perhaps modifying them in some way, or seeking more conducive situations or to try to change them.

(5) The attitudes, views and beliefs of people, for example, teachers' about teaching and about pupils, pupils' about teachers, about school, learning, their colleagues, the future.

(6) How particular situations influence views and behaviour, and how they are constituted.

New ethnographic research is urgently needed in areas such as the management of schools, how decisions come to be made, inter-staff relationships, school ethos (suggested by some to be the most important factor in school academic and behavioural achievement); teacher identities, their interests and biographies, how they adapt to the role, how they achieve their ends; crisis points in teacher careers, and what kinds of assistance are of most value to them at what points; how pupil perspectives on teachers come to form, how pupils learn; and the psychic rewards of learning and teaching, as opposed to the problems, pressures and constraints. Ethnographic techniques can also be very useful in evaluations – of large-scale curriculum innovations or school re-organizations, of short-term inset courses, of particular styles of teaching, of the effects of par-ticular events, or the impact of particular policies. Arguably they can penetrate deeper, and operate from the span of a broader period than the one-off tests that are usually employed. However, while this is my own personal shopping list, there are, of course, many other areas and aspects of them that can be fruitfully inves-tigated using ethnographic techniques, and others may have other priorities. Only they will know what these priorities are. The examples I give are simply that – illustrations of 'the kind of things' ethnography might be applied to. Let me therefore take this a little further by considering some localized ethnographic studies that I might have made when I was teaching in grammar schools in the 1960s:

(1) Many examples of cultural conflict, clash or difference, that obstructed my teaching and pupils' learning. Key periods are when beginning in a school or meeting a class of pupils for the first time, and when changing from one school to another. If a teacher is having difficulty with a particular group of pupils, and especially if an antagonism is felt towards their ordinary behaviour (i.e. when not directed toward the teacher), it might be worth investigating their views on a range of things with a view to understanding their motivation. Cultural supports run deep: they are better identified than threatened.

(2) By the same token, cultural similarities or 'bridges' across basically opposing cultures. Typically, individual teachers build these instinctively, through humour, appearance, manner, language, attitude to pupils, school in general and their own role. A particularly successful teacher in this respect might agree to be observed teaching, and to discussions taking place between them, and between them and the pupils concerned.

(3) Labelling. With so many pupils with which to deal, teachers often have to take a short cut to coming to a judgment about a pupil. A pupil might thus be designated 'thick', 'troublesome', 'sly', 'lazy', 'immature'. The danger is, of course, that pupils will live up to these labels if they are directed at them with any force (for example, teachers discussing a pupil among themselves may harden that particular identity in their – and the pupil's – minds). It would be a useful experiment to set these interactions on a different basis and label somebody something completely different, and monitor what happens. The same experiment could be made with a group, or class of pupils.

(4) The analysis of 'crisis' events. In all schools from time to time crises occur which subvert the normal order. Typically, somebody is held to be responsible, there are conflicting views on whom it might be, tempers become frayed, and it is all very educationally counter-productive. But it need not be, for we can learn from these incidents. If we can manage to step back out of our teacher role for a moment, examine and analyse all the evidence, and conduct further enquiry into other people's perspectives, we may

discover that the crisis was not a matter for personal blame, but rather a structural fault, or culture clash perhaps, or a breakdown, through some unforeseen occurrence of the normal rules (largely implicit) that govern relationships. Such knowledge would be very useful in obviating a recurrence of such an incident.

(5) Any unplanned piece of interaction which one suspects may have been significant for pupil motivation, for good or ill. Occasionally, something – an aspect of a subject, or instructive change of teacher style, a comment, a conjunction of circumstances, a chance rearrangement of the environment or class or lesson structure – may have important educational results. Indeed, it could be argued that the pedagogical knowledge derived from these circumstances is potentially of more purport than that received from more formal training, because it happens in a real teaching situation and has real consequences.

(6) The study of a particular pupil, or groups of pupils. Though we cannot know all our pupils in detail, there is much to be learned about them from the few. This could be a holistic study, which aims to incorporate as much information as possible, both from within and outside school, and examines the inter-relationships among the various aspects of the pupil's life.

(7) Evaluation studies. Ethnography can help us monitor the effects of our teaching. One might argue that standard tests have only limited value. They do not demonstrate if or how pupils have incorporated a particular piece of teaching into their general personal awareness or group culture. Through observation of a colleague or colleagues, and observation of and interviews with, pupils, teachers can complement the usual tests. There are many possibilities here. One may wish to monitor the effects of an INSET course on one's own teaching, and on pupils; or of a new policy, such as a deliberate attempt to raise awareness of gender and racial issues; or of introducing mixed-ability classes instead of streaming; or of the effects of team-teaching, or of a different method; or of a particular subject, or section of syllabus. One might compare the methods and results of one's own attempts to teach reading with those of parents, and possibly develop new joint enterprises. One might consider the efficacy of homework. Of course teachers have their feedback devices built into their teaching, but occasionally they may feel the need to explore a little further, and in a different way.

(8) Language, and other symbolic means of communication. Tape-recording some lessons and examining the speech-form,

vocabulary, who speaks (and who does not), who to, for how long and what about. Close scrutiny of how one tries to get a point across might be combined with pupil evaluation of the transcript. There would thus be a three-sided enquiry:

(a) one's teaching intentions;

(b) one's actual teaching as shown by the transcript; and

(c) the evaluation of same by both teacher and pupils.

A transcript is a good blueprint of a lesson, and can help one assess general strategy.

(9) One's own career and biography. If teachers are to teach effectively, it is important that they 'feel right'. For a number of reasons, many do not do so. A study which re-assesses one's own experiences, abilities, interests, aspirations, accomplishments, and measures these against situations and opportunities may be salutary. One rarely bothers, in the ordinary course of events, to make such a systematic assessment, more typically just recalling periodically certain incidents or aspects. Thus it may reveal new lines of career, new possibilities, new sources of satisfaction, and new ways of harmonizing one's own personal resources with the elements available.

(10) For headteachers in particular, perhaps, a number of issues. How to accomplish change within a school, the management of staff relationships, and of governing bodies, relationships with parents (how, for example, do parents view parent evenings, interpret school reports, intervene in their children's education?), promotions, what factors control parental choice of school, staff turnover, the cultivation of a particular school ethos, how to promote staff efficiency, the decision-making apparatus in the school, certain aspects of school structure and their effects, the disposition of resources, the examination of one's own role.

I repeat that these are illustrations from my own experience. Other teachers would no doubt produce further possibilities from theirs. Additionally, other methods, of course, can be used to research them, and I would indeed argue that one should not be a slave to one method, but select according to the issues and problems under examination. However these are all items eminently susceptible to ethnographic techniques.

A point to bear in mind here is that, while ethnography can be an intensely personal experience, much can be gained from working with others. This can be either as co-workers investigating aspects of the same subject (for example, by monitoring different techniques and methods, observing each others' lessons, interviewing each other, joint discussion of own and others' perspectives), or by using colleagues as subjects, where they are agreeable. Also, one would hope that ultimately, while the work might certainly be personally rewarding, it would also yield results that would benefit others' pedagogical knowledge and teaching experience.

My major task in this first chapter has been to try to convey something of the character of the ethnographic approach, and to assess some of its possibilities as a research tool for teachers. In the following chapters I shall look at some of the basic techniques involved, and consider further the nature of the orientation and of the ethnographer.

Chapter 2

Beginning research

Getting in the right frame of mind

Like everything else, doing research requires an appropriate mental and psychological state. Research is an enquiry, a quest for new knowledge and new understanding. One must therefore be curious, must want to know new things, and must have something of an adventurous spirit. This involves a recognition that one's current knowledge is imperfect and incomplete. As I have said, teaching is a kind of job that requires positive decision-making and action, and, as presently organized, one that discourages reflection and the entertainment of doubt and uncertainty. A research disposition may not be easy, therefore, for teachers to achieve.

It is worth considering a little further why this is so. I have argued elsewhere (Woods, 1979) that teachers are subject to various pressures and constraints – examination-dominated curriculum, scarcity of resources, the teacher–pupil ratio, low morale, large numbers of recalcitrant clientele, growing demands for account-ability and for teacher assessment – and are unable to avoid them because of their personal commitment. They typically resolve this problem by 'strategic compromise' (Sikes, Measor and Woods, 1985), and by developing 'coping' and 'survival strategies'. The latter are strategies primarily that allow the teacher to survive in the post, and do not necessarily facilitate teaching; however, such is the need for professional self-esteem, they are often construed *as* teaching strategies. To take an extreme example, the separating-out of a group of troublemakers in the school of my research (Woods, 1979) into a special class with its own teacher, curriculum and timetable, was justified on the grounds of their 'entitlement to, and need of, preferential treatment'. The close relationship developed

16

with the teacher concerned was then held to be evidence of the success of the manoeuvre. As Becker and Geer (1960, p. 273) noted: 'An individual's statements and descriptions of events are made from the perspective that is a function of his position in the group.' My view was that this was a successful *control* manoeuvre that was, however, justified on (spurious) educational grounds. This is not meant to be a criticism of teachers. They are confronted with formidable control and organizational problems, which they must resolve in some way before teaching can begin. They must also, somehow, keep faith with what they are doing. Two comments from teachers in the school concerned on the above analysis pinpoint the dilemma. One said, 'It's cruel, but true. But what can we do?' The other said, 'We have to believe.'

What I am saying here is not that teachers should have their long-standing belief-systems undermined, but rather that they might allow for those beliefs representing a certain kind of truth within a certain kind of situation and for particular purposes – in other words, for their constituting an *'open* certainty' – rather like the two teachers above.

It should be said that researchers should be equally open. It is quite possible that their analyses of what teachers do is misguided, as has, on occasion, been demonstrated (D. Hargreaves, 1978). Wax and Wax (1971, p. 9), for example cite a case where the researchers hypothesized that the 'progressive "withdrawal" characteristic of American Indian pupils in schools is the outcome of a psychic inadequacy related to their upbringing'. They comment:

Were these investigations to perform some elementary ethnography, inquiring as to how the Indians perceive their community situation and the role of the schools, and if they were then to observe classroom interactions, their comprehension of what they presume to be a psychic inadequacy might be thoroughly transformed. But for this to occur, they would have to be prepared to examine the school as a real institution affecting a real interethnic community of Indians and Whites instead of reducing the school to an educational function and dissolving the Sioux child out of his community and his lower-caste situation.

The same point is made by Bartholomew. He took sociologists to task for making 'unwarranted models of the school' and for assuming that inmates operate under the auspices of that model. Thus the sociologist 'creates anomalies of his own devising and at the same time obviates the possibility for asking questions about the situated rationalities in terms of which his teachers are in fact operating' (1974, pp. 16-17). In fact, 'pupils and teachers operate the most complex strategies whose rationalities parallel any that can be imputed to the scientists' (*ibid.*, p. 17).

In other words, we should not assume that teachers are teaching and pupils are learning 'to some degree or other'. We might start by asking 'What is going on here?' or 'What are people doing to each other?' and proceed by integrating members' accounts into the interpretation. It is necessary to be able to stand outside one-self, to cultivate role distance, to see self, role, institution, and others in it as an analysable system, in which one's motives and interests can be identified as part of the system, and not guiding the analysis of it. Many teachers, of course, are quite able to separate person and role in this way: others find it more difficult.

I have to confess that I found it difficult when I was teaching. I can remember certain instances where I was sure at the time I was right, and equally certain, now, that I was wrong. On one occasion I was passing judgment on a pupil as 'sly and untrustworthy', and was (rightly) upbraided by the head for passing such a judgment. I was quite sure on the evidence I had that I was right, and that his theoretical knowledge was of little use to me in the situations with which I had to deal. Had I taken his advice, I might have transformed my relationship with that pupil. On another occasion, I argued with him over the interpretation of the deviant behaviour of a group of fifth-year boys. Basically, I thought the boys were responsible; he thought that teachers were. My view, of course, was the one that was strongly upheld in the staffroom. The head received support from nobody. Now, I recognize that as a case, not so much of his being wrong as we teachers needing to believe that he was wrong.

If this kind of problem arises from the strategic necessities imposed by the difficulties of teaching, there are even more deep-rooted ones that are a product of a life-time's socialization. For example, some argue that most teachers' understanding of their craft derives from their perceptions and experiences of teachers when they were pupils, and that it is impervious to later training (for example, Lortie, 1973). They might claim, genuinely, to have been impressed and indeed changed by the latter, but invariably revert to the old tried and trusted procedures. Pedagogical know-ledge is thus difficult to change. It may be that this is because it is dependent on the educational system, but there is a difference between recognizing this as an adaptation to the system and regarding it as best practice in its own right.

Even deeper run the imprints of earlier socialization, for example into gender roles. It is one thing to recognize sexism (and racism, and other -isms) in textbooks, the distribution of resources, school and curriculum organization, and pupils' own attitudes and behaviour; it is quite another to see it in one's own practice and perspectives. Not only our teaching career, but our whole life, our whole way of relating to people including those closest to us, and our grandest and proudest moments, might have been founded on certain assumptions that come under challenge as new intellectual movements take hold. The natural reaction is to resist them; however the teacher-researcher must engage with them openly.

This, then, is all to do with opening up the mind, inducing a mood of reflection, questioning the bases of one's beliefs, accomplishing role distance, identifying prejudices. Many teachers will be experts at this already. Others may feel the need to work at it a little. How might they do this? Apart from one's own reflections, it may help to discuss matters with colleagues. However, at times, as we have noted, this may only reinforce one's own prejudices! So it is better still, perhaps, to discuss matters with people with no personal stake in your own situation – teachers from elsewhere, inspectors, academics. This can be done by proxy through literature. The questioning spirit can be induced through novels like D. H. Lawrence's *The Rainbow*, autobiographies like Edward Blishen's various books (especially *Roaring Boys*, 1966), plays and documentaries about schools or education that appear occasionally on television (such as the 'Kingsbridge' series), or on film or stage (for example 'Educating Rita'). There are also some very readable ethnographies that I consider particularly useful in suggesting alternative realities. I would especially recommend Willard Waller's (1932) classic text on *The Sociology of Teaching*, now becoming a little dated in parts as times and customs change, but still highly relevant and thought provoking; Paul Willis' (1977) *Learning to Labour*, John Beynon's (1985) *Initial Encounters in the Secondary School*, Ronald King's (1978) *All Things Bright and Beautiful*, and Andrew Pollard's (1985b) *The Social World of the Primary School* (the last two are on junior schools).

Measuring the problem and marshalling resources

First, of course, one needs to identify the problem, issue, topic to be studied. It could be from amongst those already mentioned, but one needs to consider some other factors. For example, what is the stimulus behind one's interest? Is the incentive practical, political or theoretical? Is it to solve a problem, lend weight to a cause, or increase understanding? Since so much of the ethnographer is involved within the research, it is as well to subject the person, including one's motives, to scrutiny.

Then, one needs to ponder very carefully the proposed study's researchability. Some are much easier to carry out than others. So, what actually is involved? Does it necessitate securing and examining documentation, observing and/or interviewing? How accessible are the materials and people involved? What is the nature and size of sample required? Is the work likely to cause any problems and raise opposition? If it is to be done within one's own school, a few initial feelers and enquiries will soon indicate the answers to these questions. Certainly clearance and approval will need to be secured if it is to encroach upon others' teaching or persons. Adjustments may have to be made to the enquiry, while always, of course, remaining faithful to its underlying purpose.

Against the answers to such questions, one will match one's own resources. I include in this not only personal qualities of capacity and ability, but also features of the situation, such as the subjects and classes one teaches, how many and when. Perhaps the most important factor here is time. Those who can secure some lightening of their teaching responsibilities are clearly in the best position. Some researchers who have participated in roles within institutions have recommended an ideal of a 50 per cent teaching work load, but this might be difficult for a teacher to achieve. However, there are things that can be done. The principle of 'exchange' is a familiar one within schools. Thus it might be possible in some schools to manage a redistribution of work over a period, such as to allow time at crucial points for the research to be done. In a school where that kind of activity is generally valued, that would not be difficult. One might also volunteer for particular duties if they promise to aid the research, and use those as a bargaining counter to get rid of others that are not so relevant.

However, even where nothing can be done, all is not lost. Again, the communality of identity and purpose of ethnography and teaching come to our aid. Much of a teacher's time is spent in doing ethnographic work, observing, listening, seeking to understand pupils and colleagues, and it is a small step to orient some of this activity a little more systematically toward research. For example, there are often moments before, and certainly after, lessons when some teachers chat with pupils more informally perhaps than during lessons. These could provide good opportunities for exploring pupil perspectives. One can combine 'policing' activities with research. For example, the presence of a teacher on 'playground duty' is usually sufficient to secure order. The teacher might fruitfully employ the time in observing aspects of pupil behaviour, how they group together, what they say to each other, as well as conversing with them.

All this is about making the most of scarce resources. The same applies to knowledge of the issue or area under examination. This can be broadened and sharpened in various ways before any actual empirical work begins. In these situations there is always virtue in numbers. One's colleagues may be willing to pool their knowledge, which may contain not only their own experiences but also other research studies. This may be one short cut through the literature, and practising teachers, because of the time factor, need short cuts – they cannot afford to become bogged down in others' research, which has largely been conducted for other purposes anyway, but they could do with the essence of it where it bears on the work they propose to do. There may be some key texts that are far more important than others. There are a number of secondary sources available, that summarize whole fields of work, though they can date rapidly. They can be used, however, in conjunction with abstracts, of which a number of series are now published, and which are kept very up-to-date (for example, *Sociology of Education Abstracts*). One can request a 'literature search' on specific topics (for advice on this, and other aspects of sources, see Bell and Goulding, 1984).

The teacher, too, might seek the advice of an academic or inspector. This may be someone the teacher knows in a local college, polytechnic or university, or an accepted authority in the field somewhere else. Most academics in education departments would be pleased to give advice to teachers in this way, and it could be a means not only to a short cut through existing work, but to enriching the research through continued collaboration.

There is still reading to be done, and while styles may be very individualistic, there are strategies that can be adopted to speed up coverage. I recall an undergraduate colleague of mine, who would take a book from a library shelf, thumb through it intently, pausing to give a few more seconds of consideration to certain pages, before leaving it limp and lifeless in a bedraggled heap on the desk, as if its whole essence had been extracted from it. At the time, I was reading books from page one to the end, and not very many of them (which reminds me of another colleague, who informed me

21

forty-eight hours before his finals' exam that he still had 'thirty books' to read).

I have fortunately speeded up since then, having learnt more about the art of selective reading. This involves identifying the sections of a book or article that are of most worth to me, and skimming the rest. Often it may be contained in one chapter. 'Conclusions' are very helpful, since they often contain summaries, as are indexes, where properly constructed. One can, of course, take skimming too far (and some books do have to be read in full). I have not, as yet, tried Herbert Marcuse's technique of reading only the right-hand pages of a book and guessing the left (he said he found that made most books more interesting), but one does need to develop some strategies for covering the literature.

The teacher might identify potentially particularly helpful colleagues or pupils, if this has not already been done. It helps to lend moral support if one has even a single friend who knows what is being done and why; but more than that, it can provide a life-line into the research if one has informants willing to talk in the frankest terms or open up their classrooms to your inspection from the very beginning. As I shall explain later, these are in reality co-research workers, and the best possible resource one could have in ethnographic work.

The teacher may have some trial runs before beginning the project in earnest. An interview or an observation of a lesson may point to a refinement or new leads to the issue under examination, or the need for a little more polish in one's research technique. It would be surprising if both these did not occur. The important thing in these early stages is not to give up. All ethnographers fumble around in the dark for a while – it is in the nature of the approach – but soon, one's eyes become accustomed to the dark, shadows take shape and gradually grow more distinct. So, too, with the teacher, though in many respects, as participant observers *in situ* already, they may already be well experienced in these respects. There may still be some surprises for them on the other side of their routine realities.

Negotiating access

'Getting in' is a common problem in ethnography, and there is much good advice in the literature for researchers seeking entrance to an institution, on how to dress, how to behave, what to say (see, for example, Hammersley, 1979b). Basically you have to sell yourself as a credible person doing a worthy project. Delamont describes how she tried to blend in with the scenery in all situations:

> When I saw heads I always wore a conservative outfit and real leather gloves. I had a special grey dress and coat, for days when I expected to see the head and some pupils. The coat was knee-length and very conservative-looking, while the dress was mini-length to show the pupils I knew what the fashion was. I would keep the coat on in the head's office, and take it off before I first met pupils. When observing I tried to dress like the student teachers who were common in all the schools: no trousers, unladdered tights, and no make up. (1984, p. 25)

But what is it that one is trying to get into? We have seen that the approach involves penetrating group cultures and others' perspectives and realities. However I have also argued that these realities are multi-layered, and they are not all made available simultaneously to one's perception. One may also be confronted with different realities in different situations and at different times. For example, when I went to one school for a research project, I experienced three different levels. At the beginning, I was shown the public, outer face of the school in its Sunday clothes. This was the school at its best; indeed it was literally too good to be true, with people putting on the sort of performances reserved for special occasions, like inspectors' visits or open evenings. It was a reality of a sort, of course. Had I been there but a short time, I might have been persuaded that it reflected a more permanent state, but after a while the strict control of my movements was relaxed to some degree. Teachers also could not sustain their peak performances, and the first front began to crumble. I found myself in a kind of twilight zone between the first public front and the later, deeper natural realities. In this second stage, I was allowed more freedom, having become accepted and people acted more naturally, but there were still some areas of interaction denied me – certain lessons, certain meetings, and certain more localized discussions. And while people might agree to being observed in their natural pursuits within school, and indeed interviewed, they were still guarded about confiding too many of their innermost thoughts to me. In the third stage, I felt I had penetrated to the vitals of the organization. I was allowed into some secret meetings to witness key decisions being made, and the debates leading up to them. People began to take me into their confidence more, telling me some of their own personal secrets, their hopes and fears, pleasures and anxieties. Only at this stage did I feel that I had arrived at the heart of what was going on. Of course, things were not quite as neat as this. At all times, I was at different stages with different parts of the institution – I did not advance on a broad front. In some areas, and with some people, I never arrived at stage three: in one or two cases, I arrived there very quickly.

Negotiating access, therefore, is not just about getting into an institution or group in the sense of crossing the threshold that marks it off from the outside world, but proceeding across several thresholds that mark the way to the heart of a culture. In a sense, teachers are already *in*, but they are there as teachers, and the change of role to researcher may entail going through similar stages, depending on the subject chosen for study. Again, the affinities between teaching and ethnography should make this less of a problem than with some other methods. Teachers have access to their own classroom and a view of their own self. They participate in decision-making and policy-making processes and they may be on intimate terms with some of their own colleagues and pupils, but there may be other places and situations they need to go, and other people they need to develop rapport with. In addition, they will, perhaps, wish to reflect upon where they are in their various relationships in terms of the stages of access outlined above.

One of the main difficulties for teacher–researchers with pupils is identifying and characterizing the informal culture. Some may have cultivated social distance from their pupils, in the time-honoured tradition (Waller, 1932). Some teachers, therefore, might have to do something to *themselves* to improve their chances of being admitted to pupil culture and realities. It is a question basically, again, perhaps, of stepping outside the teacher role occasionally and forming links with them in a common humanity. Pupils and teachers are equal in this – they have equal status, access to it, and what they bring to it has equal worth. Teachers need to be open-minded and flexible if they are to partake in this. They need to know something of pupils' language, beliefs, values and customs at a very early stage, to be able to communicate on equal terms. Listening and observing, and discussing with knowledgeable others, would help. I recall when I changed schools on one occasion, I thought my new pupils excessively familiar, but they were only this by the standards of the old school, not of their own. When I saw colleagues being similarly treated, and responding in kind and with considerable camaraderie, I realized that this was the particular style of the interaction in that school.

Other teachers already have strong rapport with their pupils. They may play their games with them, making jocular abuse, flirting with the girls, denigrating the boys' football teams, making joking admonishments about rule-transgressions. One teacher we encountered in one project, when challenged by the pupils to whom he was boasting about the speed of his new car, took a group of witnesses for a motorway drive to substantiate his point.

Most pupils are delighted with teachers who show this kind of expansiveness. Acceptance into their culture can lead to all manner of confidences about their innermost feelings on subjects like school, teachers, other pupils, themselves, home life, their out-of-school activities, but once in, it does not mean permanent membership. Respect has to be continually earned, and there are a number of ways in which it can easily be lost. For example too much pressure may cause offence. We all have some secret places and private thoughts that we prefer to keep to ourselves. Warning signs will appear when such pressure is felt – a frown, a silence, even a rebuke – and we must be on the look-out for such signals.

Teachers sometimes invade pupils' private areas and earn rebuke, as in this example:

Sharon: He went off his rocker at us, didn't he?
Wendy: What was it? I know, we were talking about
Christmas pudding and my mum said me Nan's knickers
caught fire (great laughter).
Sharon: I remember, Wendy...
Wendy: We were both sat on the front desk chatting away...
Sharon: He went barmy. I told him he shouldn't be really
listening (general laughter). (Woods, 1979, p. 117)

One may try too hard to establish rapport, to be funny, to join in their games, use their language, be like them. Caution is necessary for pupils hate nothing more than insincerity and ingratiation. Entering a strange culture is best done by melting the ice, rather than breaking it with a sledgehammer.

Pupils may try to throw the researcher off the trail. They are not beyond trying something on, exaggerating, telling intentional lies, just for the sheer fun of it, or to test the teacher out. One defence is the teacher's own existing knowledge. I recall some boys volunteering some information to me on the worst gang of deviants in the school. It included the names of some of the most conformist girls! Fortunately I knew them. When it was clear to them that I recognized the attempted put-on, we shared the joke and got down to some productive discussion.

There are, happily, other defences. One cultivates an ability to spot a put-on. There might be a slight implausibility in the account, a look, a crinkled smile perhaps, or twinkling eye, a tone of voice that fails to ring true. A cautious scepticism will guard against unspotted corruptions, to be exposed or corroborated later with further evidence – the ultimate defence. It suffices at this stage not to be taken in.

Another problem is 'reversion'. However hard one tries, there are almost inevitably times in talking to pupils when one reverts to the role of teacher, adult or parent. There are times, for example, when there may be a strong desire to instruct, educate, correct, pass judgment. Unless this is done, and is recognized by all to be done, in the role of the teacher, then it is best suppressed. These teacherly tendencies are more easily resisted perhaps than the occasional instinctive reaction. I recall an incident with one particularly troublesome (to the school) boy where my carefully nurtured entrée into his confidence, of which I was extremely proud, was destroyed by one momentary lapse. I was scribbling a note. He came beside me and said, in friendly enough fashion, 'What are you writing?' I turned the paper so he could not see it, and said in a tone I thought humorous, 'Mind your own business.' That was a mistake. Even though that would have been a legitimate response in their own culture, it was one that was very much the property of teachers and the whole adult world, and that was how it was interpreted there when an adult used it. From that moment I was regarded as a 'creep' – like all the teachers – by this boy and months of careful and delicate work had been destroyed by one careless remark. My later overtures were invariably met with this sort of response:

Me: Leeds will finish above Spurs.
Boy: They might creep up the table a bit.

Such is the thin edge that ethnographers occasionally set themselves to walk along.

As far as colleagues or other teachers are concerned, one may have personal relationships with some that are particularly helpful to the research proposed. With others, it may be more difficult to achieve full cooperation. There may be a number of reasons for this. Basically, as noted earlier, teachers may fear disturbance of their own delicately-balanced survival equilibrium. Outsiders can only be perceived as a threat to this. Despite the researcher's assurances, they may feel, too, that they are being personally evaluated. They may suspect, in consequence, an undermining of their professional position in the school. If to all this is added the customary suspicion of educational research, and possibly of the researcher's motives, and a feeling that a different, unsympathetic set of frameworks might be brought to bear, yielding misunderstanding and misrepresentation, active opposition to the proposed study might result. At the beginning of Hammersley's research, for example, 'The teachers were reluctant and clearly wanted me out as soon as possible' (1984, p. 48). Beynon came across one teacher who warned him: 'I'm not interested in any tomfool research. It's completely unimportant! Anything to do with Education is completely unimportant. I want to put it on record that if it was up to me you'd not be allowed near the place. You come into my lessons on sufferance!' (1983, p. 50).

How, then, are we not only to obviate this, but to recruit support? Certainly there should be discussion, at least, with those involved. There have been instances when heads have let researchers into their schools without adequately warning their teachers (D. Hargreaves, 1967; Llewellyn, 1980; Atkinson, 1984; Burgess, 1985a). One possibility is to involve them in the research. If they can be enlisted as co-research workers rather than as guinea-pig subjects, being asked to give purely for somebody else's benefit, then many of the above fears will be removed, for they will have some say in the direction of the research and the analysis and presentation of results.

Otherwise, there may be a *quid pro quo* one can offer – perhaps support for some of their projects, or assistance with some aspect of their work. There are, too, traditional safeguards one can offer: assurances of confidentiality; a guarantee of anonymity in any eventual report; a depersonalizing of the work by showing that one's interests are on strategies, methods, cultures or whatever, and not on individuals. Above all, perhaps, is the actual pedagogical worth of the study. If it can be clearly demonstrated that it promises to benefit teaching in some way, few teachers would refuse to cooperate. On the other hand, some projects can cause a revolt. I recall one well-intentioned, but misguided headmaster, who, with the assistance of his head of religious education, conducted an enquiry among the pupils as to what they considered constituted a good and popular teacher. When they heard of it, the whole staff, popular and unpopular, went on strike. Such a project is not without educational interest and pedagogical relevance. It can be done by outside researchers giving the guarantees above, or even, discreetly, by individual teachers with their own pupils if they concentrate on categories and dimensions, and not people. However in the one that caused the strike, teachers saw themselves seriously threatened in a situation where the main gatekeeper to their various prospective career paths was conducting research which was clearly likely to reflect on their qualifications to make progress along those paths. It offends all the principles outlined above. Had the headmaster taken his staff into his confidence, together they might have worked out a way of doing it that preserved its educational value and protected teachers' statuses and identities.

It has to be said that on some staffs there are one or two intransigent anti-researchers (like Beynon's teacher above), and there may be some who are difficult in other ways. If the principles discussed above have been observed, and they make no difference, intentional spoiling tactics must be resisted. There are also conflicts and divisions among staffs, along, perhaps, subject or generation or ideological lines. The closer one is to a colleague on these various interests, the more likely the chance of cooperation, but an alliance on one of the lines may be sufficient to overcome differences on others. One might ring the changes on these alliances to ensure possibly a cross-section of staff, if that indeed is what is required.

As for the methods to employ in the early stages, these should match the level of access negotiated. Thus, if only at the 'public front' stage with a person, it might be inappropriate to start trying to delve too deeply into their views, or to request access into their secret places. It might be inadvisable to take any notes, let alone tape-record, the early conversations. The major task here is to establish rapport and generate trust, and note-taking might get in the way of that, for it might be interpreted as an indication that the research outside the immediate conversation and relationship is the more important matter. Another one of my own tragic errors was to take a tape-recorder along to a first talk with a teacher, who had said 'he had plenty to tell me'. I mistook this for indicating possible stage three access, but, as yet, I had established no personal bonds with this particular teacher. Of course, I always intended to ask if he minded our conversation being recorded – it was so much easier to think about it afterwards, valuable points might be lost, and so on – which I duly did. As it happened, he did mind, and the reason was that the tape would constitute recorded evidence that might be held against him in the future in some way; whereas if I were to relate his comments to others, he could deny them. This clearly illustrates the dangers of mismatch of method and stage of access. My error was not that I taped the conversation, but that I should consider doing so. The question, the sight of the machine, the rehearsal of the reasons for not using it – all these, I felt, took the sparkle out of the ensuing conversation.

Clearly it is most important to build up trust in these early stages, to show that you are a person of some worth and integrity. The pathways to information are opened up by trust, and the uses the researcher makes of it are safeguarded by that quality. If people are not happy that the information would be put to good use, confidences observed, and their own interests and identities safeguarded, they will block access to it. The trusted researcher knows instinctively what is repeatable and what is not. Often the most fascinating findings are not reported, because the researcher judges it a potential violation of that trust.

By far the best way to develop trust is to have an honest project; that is, one designed for the purposes of the advancement of knowledge that might improve one's own teaching and/or that of others, or the conditions of others, and not one, say, directed toward vainglorious self-seeking or some worthless, or completely idiosyncratic, aim. Then, you need to show that you are a person of discretion, who appreciates others' points of view and who can discriminate between admissible and inadmissible evidence. There may be opportunities to demonstrate this, for example when discussing some other research work or book that has perhaps 'failed' to take account of teacher views, or misrepresented them in some way, or otherwise offended against the code of ethics. Or there may be opportunities to show your ability to depersonalize events, or abstract principles from them, so that individual identification is not an issue. You may have shown yourself an honest person already over the years with some colleagues who are old friends, but you may form new allies by seeking out and establishing communality of interest with others on some subject; this may not be connected with school at all, but may be through some hobby or pursuit, such as gardening, wine-making, sport, dress-making. It all helps to show that you are a real human being, with real human sensitivities, and not a remote scientific boffin likely to trample all over them, whether by design or accident.

The question is raised, what do we do about what we know to be bad teaching, or some other pursuit that is harmful in its outcomes to others? Is this not to be exposed, and thereby eradicated? In such cases, are we not justified in keeping our objectives to ourselves and using 'covert research' to find out more about it? There are some areas where this has been done, but clearly, apart from it being ethically suspect, from the headteacher's unpopular/ popular teacher study mentioned above as only one example, it is likely to backfire on the researcher when discovered. Not only is that particular study then lost, but one's whole credibility as a worthy colleague is destroyed.

29

The guiding principle here, I would suggest, where injustice or incompetence are encountered, is to treat it as one would in the role of teacher. This calls for judgment and discretion as to the best course of action – advice to a colleague, discreetly making available alternative ways of doing or seeing things, a word to another in a position to influence the situation favourably, and so on. At no time, in my view, does it warrant deliberate and avoidable deception about what you are doing as a researcher, and rarely, I suspect, would complete exposure at a local level be the best way of treating it.

The kind of 'deception' that, perhaps, is permissible in the early stages is to keep some of the details of one's interests back until the rapport of the third stage has been achieved. This is not really deception as much as sound tactics. Sufficient preparation is made for each stage. It is not necessary to put *all* your cards on the table at the beginning, so long as you do not intend to mislead or deceive later. Your aims at the beginning are perfectly noble ones – to gain entry, to whet the appetite of others for the study, to allay their apprehensions, to display yourself as a competent and trustworthy researcher. Clearly, if you are hoping to dig up controversial material, your credentials have to be established first. Raising the possibility of controversy at too early a stage may awaken fears and close off avenues of access. If delayed, by the time you are arriving at such mysteries at the third stage, people will be feeling that they can rely on you to do the right thing in all circumstances. Otherwise, you would not have arrived there!

John Beynon (1983) gives an account of these processes in practice. He describes how he 'eased' himself into the school of his research through 'the use of "neutral topics"'; 'my knowledge of both the locality and of the routines of secondary schools'; and the keeping (in the early weeks) of a 'low profile'. He 'stumbled' upon topics of mutual interest and the ensuing 'small talk' was in fact critical in breaking down barriers. He made use of his previous teaching experience, as did D. Hargreaves (1967), to show that he knew about schools and teaching; and he 'laid low' during the first few weeks, adopting a 'non-argumentative' stance. Hammersley (1979b) actually went further than this, 'adopting a "sympathetic" attitude towards the teachers' opinions and practices' and sometimes adding 'supporting anecdotes, even though these opinions were diametrically opposed to my own views at the time of the research' (p. 116). Clearly there are ethical issues here, but as D. Hargreaves (1967, p. 199) points out, a certain amount of deception is inevitable. Having developed good relationships with some of the teachers, he found that it was when he behaved 'naturally' with them that some of the most significant things were said. However he could not suddenly point out that what they had just said was sociologically important, 'for this would seriously inhibit future relations'. Again the issue resides in a basic trust in the relationship that any material ensuing from it will be used wisely.

With such techniques, Beynon (1983) discovered after a while that the staff were only too ready 'to move beyond these neutral topics and, without prompting, spill the beans and reveal institutional secrets. They assumed that such revelations couldn't possibly be the subject of "proper research"' (p. 42). Once in, he had to 'stay in' by 'proving himself' in the eyes of the staff, by showing himself a credible person and his project a worthy one (unlike a previous researcher, who just 'dumped the questionnaires on us and collected them' – they 'told him straight that what he was doing wasn't worth doing'), and that he was not 'another bloke getting a degree on our backs' (p. 47), or as Ball (1983, p. 85) suggests 'a spy sent in by the headmaster to report on staffroom gossip and the quality of teaching' (see also D. Hargreaves, 1967). Beynon also had to negotiate 'hotspots' – moments of deep embarrassment when a member of staff disclaimed his research and another took strong exception to a particular aspect of it, when he appeared to 'be going behind their backs' and committing unprofessional conduct. Discretion, patience, and some considerable negotiating skills appear to have won the day.

Beginning ethnographic research is one of the most difficult stages, for all the reasons outlined above, but also because so much is open and exploratory. Some avenues may be closed, others present difficulties, and the way ahead may appear hazy. It is also difficult, often, to make much sense of what data is coming in during these early stages.

Hammersley (1984, p. 44) vividly describes his early problems as a young novitiate research worker entering a tough secondary modern school.

I was never at ease with the teachers, or pupils. Indeed I spent most break times alone, hanging around the hall or yard, and I went home for lunch to ease the strain. I feared that going into the staffroom would be regarded as threatening by the teachers, and would endanger my continued presence in the school! Differences in age, in political opinions, and a sense of outrage at the way pupils were treated led to great discomfort, and the feeling that it was 'clearly necessary to conceal my purposes and views from the teachers', which was 'a source of strain and guilt'. Finally, 'as a result of inadequate preparation before entering the field, I found it difficult to see what analytic payoff I was going to be able to derive from the data I was collecting ... with a rapidly mounting sense of my own incompetence and increasing doubts about the value of my work, I abandoned the fieldwork after only five days. If that seems a very short period, I can only say that at the time it seemed very much longer!'

The human spirit conquers all, with a bit of good fortune, and Hammersley soon got going again, sent by the chief education officer to the same school, where the teachers were 'reluctant and clearly wanted me out as soon as possible'. However, this time his relative youth and inexperience seemed to aid him in that it reduced the threat he posed to teachers, and he was helped by the presence of some students on teaching practice, among whose number he was counted, and upon which he played. Above all, he struck a chord with some of the teachers when he mentioned a particular interest that they recognized. '... *now* we know what he wants' (p. 49).

It is very easy to become discouraged and conclude that research is not for you. However, this is one of those points where you might treat yourself to a psychological booster. When I was sent off on my first teaching practice to the 'toughest school in Sheffield', I was told by my supervisor 'regard it as a challenge – splendid practice!' Each day as I was submerged beneath rebellious youths, I kept telling myself what 'splendid practice' it was, and how I must rise to the 'challenge'. Usually, however, the more difficult the problem, the greater the challenge, then ultimately the stronger the sense of achievement if it is met. Research is by its very nature problematic. It is like exploring unknown territories. There may be false trails, states of being becalmed, shipwrecked, attacked by lions, attempted seduction by native tribes (of which more later). What keeps one going through all this is the basic curiosity to want to know more. Without that, it is better never to start.

Chapter 3

Observation

Participant observation

The chief method of ethnography is participant observation, which in practice tends to be a combination of methods, or rather a style of research. It is a feature of this orientation to research, unlike surveys for example, that many of the techniques of actually doing the job are implicit in the initial ethnographic commitment. As Ball (1984, p. 71) has noted, it is rather like 'riding a bicycle: no matter how much theoretical preparation you do there is no real substitute for actually getting on and doing it'. What to do should almost be a matter of instinct, and this is just as well, since the participant observer comes to face many *ad hoc* problems. Even so, the experiences of others can provide reassurance and guidance, and give an idea of the possibilities and perils.

Why participate?

The central idea of participation is to penetrate the experiences of others within a group or institution. How better to do this than by assuming a real role within the group or institution, and contributing towards its interests or function, and *personally* experiencing these things in conjunction with others? Access to all group activities is assumed, and one can observe from the closest range, including monitoring one's own experiences and thought processes. Again, teachers are ideally placed for this, for they already occupy a role within their own institution. But there are dangers in this, as well as advantages. The outstanding initial danger, as discussed in the previous chapter, is that the interpretative frameworks developed over the years as a teacher might dictate the way in which we see others' experiences, instead of themselves becoming material for appraisal. There is, then, a certain 'washing clean' required of one's own thought processes, coupled with the need to make the group or school 'anthropologically strange'. We may then become more open to others' views. Participation then aids appreciation. In time, the researcher becomes a member, and can proceed by reflection and analogy, analysing own reactions, intentions and motives, as and when they occur during the process of which one is a part.

By participating, one both acts on, and is acted upon by the environment. But one must try to combine deep personal involvement and a measure of detachment. Without the latter, one runs the risk of 'going native'; that is, identifying so strongly with members that defending their values comes to take precedence over actually studying them. Diligently keeping 'field notes' (about which more later), and a generally reflective attitude which should alert one to shifts in one's own views, guard against this. The extent of the commitment, the observer's reactions and changes, all become part of the account. Redfield urged his anthropologist colleagues not to hide behind a 'mask of neutrality' (1953, p. 156). Robinson advises the researcher to 'enter a public debate with himself in an attempt to elicit the basis of his own perception' (1974, p. 251).

Sharing in life activities necessarily involves learning the language, rules and mode of behaviour, and role requisites, assuming the same dress and appearance, tasks and responsibilities, and becoming subject to the same pressures and constraints.

The nature and degree of the participation might vary according to the aims of the research, the researcher, and the culture concerned. In schools, for example, some have taken on a teaching load of half a timetable (D. Hargreaves, 1967; Lacey, 1970). A full load would militate against that required element of detachment. Some sub-cultural studies, on the other hand, have required almost complete immersion (Whyte, 1955; Yablonsky, 1968; Patrick, 1973; Parker, 1974; Willis, 1977). Whyte joined a Chicago gang; Yablonsky became a hippie.

> At a certain point in the research I decided it was of vital importance for me to *personally experience* some core hippie behaviour patterns in order to truly tune-in to what was happening. When the opportunity emerged in the flow of my trip, I decided it was crucial to my research to enter into

several acts that conflicted with the primary life-style values of a generally law-abiding middle-class professor. (Yablonsky, 1968, p. xiii)

Parker had a marginal position with his 'catseye kings'.

My position in relation to theft was well established. I would receive 'knock off' and 'say nothing'. If necessary I would 'keep dixy', but I would not actually get my hands dirty. This stance was regarded as normal and surprised nobody; it coincided with the view of most adults in the neighbourhood.

Parker aimed:

to become an insignificant variable. That is whilst one can watch and/or take part in normal group activities and so contribute to the dialogue, one must not alter the group's processual direction. One may occasionally alter content, but never form.

His liaison with them worked, but might not have done if he had not been 'young, hairy, boozy, etc., etc., willing to keep long hours and accept "permissive" standards' (Parker, 1974, pp. 219, 223).

In relation to his research in Lumley Secondary Modern School, D. Hargreaves summed up the advantages of participation thus.

In theory (it) permits an easy entrance into the social situation by reducing the resistance of the group members; decreases the extent to which the investigator disturbs the 'natural' situation; and permits the investigator to experience and observe the group's norms, values, conflicts and pressures, which (over a long period) cannot be hidden from someone playing an in-group role. (1967, p. 193)

Lacey (1976, p. 60) also 'had to teach in order to appreciate the strains that on occasion turned reasonable, kindly men into bellowing, spiteful adversaries'. Burgess (1983, p. 4) too, during a sixteen-month period 'taught a Newsam group on a regular basis for four periods a week and also took many substitution lessons in other departments in the school', and was 'a member of a house and a department'.

Though participant observers make an intensive study of one group, their findings will have relevance for other groups, not necessarily within the same kind of institution. Studies of hospitals, prisons, asylums, schools, etc., inform each other – they have certain institutional processes in common. However the research can have relevance beyond institutional life. Sub-cultural studies like those of Patrick (1973), Parker (1974) and Willis (1977) are valuable commentaries on society at large. Interactional studies of schools can tell as much about the inter-relationship between the economic, political and educational systems, as they can about social interaction in general. We can find out, for example, how far pupils are instrumentally or expressively orientated and the bases of their orientations, and this will relate to stratification and economic systems; or we might find that certain strategies and techniques of social behaviour are part of one's general social equipment, so that studies, say, of embarrassment, domination, aggression, humour and so forth in schools (or anywhere else) have wider validity. Bruyn concludes that:

> If the researcher is aware of the hazards and the rules of the method of participant observation, then he should be able accurately to find the cultural meanings contained in any group he studies – some meanings of which may lie at the root of man's existence in society. (1966, p. 21)

In the same vein, Wolcott has observed that:

> The ethnographer's compelling interest is his continuing enquiry into human social life and to the ways that human beings confront their humanness. (1975, p. 125)

Non-participant observation

Despite participant observation being the purest method in ethnography, *non*-participant observation has come to be the more commonly used in British educational research. Here, the researcher has only the role of researcher, and observes situations of interest in that capacity; for example a lesson from the back of a classroom, a school assembly from the back of the hall, a staff meeting or a playground from behind the sidelines. The researcher is, ideally, not part of these proceedings, and adopts 'fly on the wall' techniques to observe things as they happen, naturally, as undisturbed by his/her presence as possible.

It is not difficult to see why some prefer this mode. Ethnography is a complicated research approach, making great demands on the researcher's energies and time, and frequently presents a great mass of confusing and intricate data which the researcher has to make some kind of sense of. Whatever advantages participating brings, it adds to those demands. In the first place, it takes up valuable *time*. Secondly, it adds to one's responsibilities. One must meet the requirements of the role, and must meet them regularly, on the prescribed terms and at stipulated times. Thirdly, it increases the possibilities of role conflict. Objectives as teacher and as researcher may occasionally clash. As an example of the many, almost daily, ethical problems that arise from this conflict, I can cite one from my own research. I was interested in pupil–teacher interaction, and participated occasionally as teacher. However I was also concerned to discover pupils' views, and encouraged them to talk freely. I found this rewarding, but there were problems. In a sense, talk is legitimation, confirmed by 'listening without comment' on the part of an authority figure. Smoking, fornication, teacher-baiting and other activities that are deemed deviant within the school's framework of rules, all figure prominently within many pupils' lives, and hence I needed to know about them. This has to take place under terms of complete amnesty, otherwise the pupils would never have confided in me, but it meant problems for me:

(1) as an occasional teacher – should I not take steps while in this role to counter any deviance that I knew about? and
(2) as a guest in the school, I had some pangs of conscience, since I was operating under the auspices, enjoying the hospitality of, and making friendships with those who were trying to eliminate these activities.

I shall consider approaches to resolving ethical problems such as this shortly, but obviously one way to cut down on them is to avoid conflicting roles.

D. Hargreaves (1967) found he had to give up a large part of his 'carefully nurtured teacher-role' through a different result of role conflict; for, while participation aided his relationships with the teachers, and his appreciation of their concerns, it affected his rapport with some of the pupils, which it was necessary in his project for him to have. So he stopped teaching them, and 'from that point my relations with the boys improved to a remarkable extent'. Some tested him out with cheekiness he would 'immediately have crushed as a teacher', but when he 'failed to respond as they expected, these attempts at provocation ceased'. It was replaced, gradually, by a form of collusion. 'When they discovered I would not report them for offences against the school rules which I had observed, the teacher-role began to diminish, and was replaced by a new form of respect and trust.' How did Hargreaves handle the role-infractions he observed or was made privy to? 'A convenient attack of blindness or deafness proved to be invaluable in resolving such problems' (pp. 203-4).

Lacey also moved from a teacher role to a 'freer, research role', and found that this brought 'an increase, gradual at first, and then steep, in the amount of information received about pupils' (Lacey, 1976, p. 58). Clearly, participating as a teacher may be counterproductive to an investigation into pupils. Participation as a *pupil* would appear to be ideally indicated here, but is not a practical proposition for most weathered ethnographers. As one researcher notes:

> Another important personal failure which changes the research techniques a lot is the fact that I am 6 feet 4 inches tall and that most fourteen year olds in Sunderland are considerably smaller than that. This means that the sort of unobtrusive participant observation by hanging around on a corner with them was simply impossible. Rather it would have consisted of a totally different situation where (they) had suddenly picked up this large ally to use in street fights: the existence of this large ally would have grossly changed their actions. (Corrigan, 1979, p. 14)

Some, though, have managed to do it to advantage (Llewellyn, 1980), and some have been awarded a status of 'honorary pupil' (Fuller, 1984). More usually one has to manufacture a special role. Thus, Lacey became a sort of informal counsellor, entered into conversations with boys at all times of the day, visited their homes, invited them to his home, ran a school cricket team, and intended to meet them in their out-of-school activities, though this latter was never actually achieved. In other words, he 'participated' as well as he could, making a role for himself that was most productive in the terms sought for.

Refraining from fully participant observation is also a defence against 'going native', an over-identification with people's views such that one's researcher-perspective, is submerged beneath them. In ethnographic work, strong ties are made with the subjects of study. Indeed it is an indispensable requirement, as we have seen, if we are to understand their ways of life in any depth. It is necessary, too, to empathize with people's views, to see and feel things as they do. The danger is clear. The empathy may take over, and we may find ourselves according primacy to the views of a particular group, interpreting all other material through those views, and romanticizing the activities and beliefs of the privileged group. This is less likely to happen with non-participant observation. Not only does it keep the researcher from real involvement in a role, but by the same token it encourages the cultivation of a detachment necessary for the fair and scientific appraisal of material discovered and presented. This is one of the abiding dilemmas of the approach – to become involved to the extent of being able to appreciate life as a native, yet to be able to become detached at will in order to be able to represent that life properly contextualized. An awareness of the problem aids its resolution, but, again, non-participant observation is a precaution for those who find their sympathies easily aroused to the extent where it colours their judgment.

Non-participation does not completely avoid these problems, of course; and it lacks the benefits of aiding ease of access, penetrating to the heart of the group, the satisfaction of contributing toward the function of the group or institution, and its use as a bargaining counter enjoyed by participation. Whichever one adopts depends entirely on the kind of project, and the character and personal disposition of the researcher.

However, there is a sense, as we have seen, in which one is always participating. In the first place, it is difficult *not* to have an effect on the situation under observation, particularly in sensitive areas such as classrooms. David Hargreaves (1967), for example, describes how, as soon as he began classroom observation, the teachers' perceptions of his role changed, and hence their behaviour. He was no longer seen as a teacher, but more an inspector. One teacher 'made the boys work quietly out of text books, talked in a whisper to boys at his desk ...' Another 'usually set the form some written work and then joined me at the back of the room, where he chatted with me or told me jokes' (p. 196). After one lesson, one commented, 'They've got a bit noisy, haven't they? I think I'll cane a few when you've gone' (p. 197). However much one tries to reduce this effect and to gain 'stage three access', there is almost bound to be some influence, which then has to be taken into consideration. The non-participating observer, though not sharing in any of the roles under observation, is nonetheless part of the scene.

Secondly, in any long-term research, it is difficult to avoid becoming involved in some way in the life of the group or institution. My own experiences, for example, have led me to think of the 'involved observer' (Woods, 1979: see also Porter, 1984; Hammersley, 1984; Rudduck, 1984; Pollard, 1985a). I did not take on an accepted role in the institution, though, like Lacey, I occasionally helped out with supervisions, took part in activities such as playing chess, umpiring cricket matches, accompanying pupils on community service to hospitals, town halls, old people's homes and, above all, shared in staffroom life with the teachers. The involvement was in the relationship entered into with staff and pupils, an identification with the educative process, and a willingness to go along with their perceptions of my role. These perceptions incorporated me into the framework of the school. For example, I was seen, variously, as, among others:

(1) a relief agency, or counsellor, by both pupils and some staff – someone people enjoyed talking to to 'get things off their chest';
(2) a secret agent – for example, by the headmaster, who thought I might act as a force for order, report on deviant activities, and so on;
(3) a factor to be used in power struggles; for example, appealing to knowledge I might possess to support a political (as opposed to educational) case;
(4) a substitute member of staff, available for use, possibly in times of emergency; and
(5) a fellow human, who shared in the company of both teachers and pupils.

In all these various respects, I felt quite deeply involved in the life of the school, though I had no formal role within it. These were circumstances where I, and those with whom I had to deal, *made* a role which had connotations functional for the purposes of the people within the school.

Techniques of observation and field notes

One must give some thought, firstly, to one's own observability. It is necessary, as far as possible, to 'blend in with the scenery' and to disturb the action within it by one's presence as little as possible. One's appearance and situation should be inconspicuous – in a classroom, usually in a corner at the back. King (1984) actually managed to make himself invisible by observing an infant class from the Wendy House. Otherwise, the accepted mode, like Delamont (1984, p. 27) is to 'lurk and watch'.

The main requirements for observation, unsurprisingly, are a sharp eye, a keen ear and a sound memory. Film, photographs and tape recordings are sometimes used to assist the latter, and are indispensable in some projects (see Walker and Adelman, 1972). One use of film has been demonstrated by Silvers (1977). He was seeking a way of 'gaining access to the child's understanding and organizational practices of the school', so he adopted a procedure of video recording and playback. He would video a class in its ordinary activity, and play this back to the children. During the playback, he would discuss with the children what was going on. This activity was then again recorded on a 'second-generation' tape. The advantages according to Silvers, were that the children could assign their own 'key labels and main interpretations to the immediacy of the video material' instead of the researcher 'initiating' them (pp. 130-1). The second-generation video existed as a check as to how far the researcher had influenced the children in the discussion.

In the same way, photographs 'can speed rapport, involve people in the research and release anecdotes and recollections, so accelerating the sometimes lengthy process of building fieldwork relationships and locating reliable informants' (Walker and Wiedel, 1985, p. 213). Of course, photographs do not in themselves narrate, but they contribute to 'a living memory' (*ibid.*, p. 215; see also Bogdan and Biklen, 1982).

However, the most widely used mechanical aid in ethnographic educational research in Britain is the tape recorder. On occasions the most important primary material is what is actually said in a lesson by the teacher – not just snatches of it, nor approximations to it, but all of it, and as it was said, not as remembered. Much of Hammersley's work (for example 1977b) is concerned with analysing teacher talk in question-and-answer sessions, and uses lengthy sections of transcript. It could not have been noted down in any other form with the same degree of precision (see also Barnes, 1976; MacLure and French, 1980; Edwards and Furlong, 1978).

A. Hargreaves illustrates some of the benefits of tape-recording. He was studying teacher decision-making and attended a number of weekly discussion meetings.

> The transcripts provide a fascinating documentation of the complexities of the curriculum decision-making process – of the strategies employed by the headteacher to secure staff agreement on curriculum policy; of the sorts of accounts which teachers routinely provided to support their arguments; of the levels of involvement of senior staff as against probationers and so on. (1981, p. 308)

One of the strategies used was that of 'contrastive rhetoric', a device to marshal support for a view or policy by vilifying an alternative. The tactic shows up well in the transcript of the discussion on Countesthorpe.

> *Mr Pool* (deputy head):   But apart from that, there was no ...
> no compulsion to go. In fact, stay in the home base all day and
> read ... just read comics until they get so bored with it, in
> theory, that they wanted to do something else. And if you
> walked around the school, you could see kids eating crisps and
> sitting around, you know. But that's, that's right at the far end
> of what we're talking about.
> *Mr Stones*:   A long way (muttered)
> (Concurring laughter)
> *Miss Home*:   A very long way
> (More laughter)
> 'Cos I can see the kids that once they get bored sitting around
> and eating crisps and reading comics, will just go out of the
> school and find something more ... more exciting. (A.
> Hargreaves, 1981, p. 310)

However, these aids can be costly, intrusive, and time-absorbing
(I discuss the problem of transcribing tapes in the following chapter), and in most studies, the person of the researcher will still be
the main piece of equipment. It is a far more flexible instrument,
being able, in theory, to merge into the scene, to discriminate
among material, to exercise decisions and choices, to move around,
to interpret. Films and tapes are only aids to recall primary source
material that may need much 'filling-in' on the part of the observer.
There is no real substitute for what the researcher sees, hears and
experiences in person. Everything, too, that is presented to one's
gaze or ear is of potential relevance. This includes much of what
one might otherwise judge to be trivia - one person's trivia may be
another person's height of significance.

Having said that, however, one cannot physically observe and
record everything, so certain decisions have to be made about 'sampling'. These will depend on the kind of project. It may be that one
wishes to focus on a piece of mainstream teaching and reactions to
it, or even aspects of that teaching, such as how it is directed
towards boys and girls, or one may concentrate on one particular
group or person. In my research at Lowfield (Woods, 1979), where
I was interested in teacher and pupil interaction, I chose to focus
mainly on two fourth and fifth years, observing them across a
range of activities and paying particular attention to:

(1) uncommon occurrences, conflicts, breakdowns of order - as a
sociologist I am interested in these because frequently norms and
rules and the values and beliefs behind them only become visible
when they are transgressed;

(2) things that are clearly of importance to participants – that a pupil may be wearing the wrong coloured socks, or eating a sweet in a lesson may seem trivial events to an outsider, but if they warrant stricture from a member of staff, particularly (as I have often witnessed!) in strong terms, then that is a matter of interest, something demanding to be understood; similarly, much pupil behaviour, particularly deviant, might seem aimless and irrational – this to me is a warning light indicating something that is in particular need of explanation.

Even so, one needs to pay particular attention to possible sources of sampling bias (see Burgess, 1982a). Some ethnographers, looking back on their work, have indicated some sampling biases which may have affected their results. Ball (1984), for example, describes how he concentrated upon the academic teaching in the school, and saw little of the 'non-academic' curriculum, gave little attention to pastoral work or extra-curricular activities, observed those lessons to which he could gain access, and that his 'account of the school is as a result profoundly distorted' (p. 77). Hammersley (1984) also reflects on how, in his research, he made *ad hoc* decisions about which lessons to record, concentrated on oral aspects of classroom work, made irregular visits to the staffroom, indulged in uneven interaction with teachers – all of which raises questions about 'the representativeness of my data to which the lack of systematic sampling gave rise' (p. 51). I would have to confess to similar kinds of bias in my work; for example, I did not converse equally with all members of staff, nor did I manage to observe all types of lessons.

In general, it is necessary to aim for 'intentional, systematic and theoretically guided' sampling (*ibid.*, p. 53). However, that cannot always be fully achieved in ethnographic work, because of:

(1) its unsystematic, exploratory nature;
(2) problems of access; and
(3) data gathering and processing problems through one set of ears and eyes.

For these reasons, some of the problems mentioned by Ball and Hammersley are almost inevitable. In that case, as they argue, we should recognize the biases and not allow the study to appear fully representative.

Field notes

Many observations may have to be made across a range of situations before analysis can begin. In the meantime, one's observations need to be recorded. This is done by making field notes. Typically, these consist of jottings during the day sufficient to jog the memory on what one has seen and wishes to record, and more extensive notes written up later, when there is more time to do it. Ethnographers have their own tricks of making occasional jottings. Of course, it will frequently be quite proper to make notes straightforwardly, as a journalist would. Even here, however, skills of shorthand and quick summarizing come in useful. Ethnographers cultivate their own personal shorthands – word abbreviations (t for 'teacher', yr for 'your', w for 'with', ut for 'in order to'), symbols (? for 'question', 0 for 'nothing', ∴ for 'therefore', ∵ for 'because', → for 'goes to'), diagrams to explain a scene or piece of action, to portray relationships or to summarize an event. They may have a dictaphone on which they may be able to record comments from time to time. It may take some time to develop a fluent notation. Ball (1984, p. 73) remarks that his initial notetaking was poor.

> I had yet to develop that fluency of virtually indecipherable notetaking which would allow me later to record whole sections of conversation verbatim, or describe classroom and staffroom incidents in elaborate detail.

However, it may not be convenient or desirable to take notes openly. Especially if a participant, there may be no time, and it may actually interfere with the interaction. At other times, one may feel it puts others off to see someone making notes on what they do. It may make them feel they are being spied on, or evaluated in some way. Then, there may be completely unplanned occasions when something of great importance for one's research occurs, or something critical is said. Ethnographers always have scraps of paper about the person, and are quick to seize opportunities to scribble down key words, names, apt phrases to prompt the memory later. Hammersley (1984, p. 53) found himself jotting down notes in the staffroom on the newspaper he was reading. They may have recourse occasionally to certain private areas, where they can make a fuller note. Thus ethnographers may be noted to be frequenters of the lavatory for an uncommon number of sojourns in the course of the day.

There may not even be opportunity to jot the merest note. At times, then, one must rely solely on memory, though this does carry dangers, and if at all suspect, should be discounted. However, as actors learn their scripts, solo musicians their scores, and novelists and playwrights develop an ear for dialogue, so ethnographers develop a facility for recalling scenes and speech. It may depend on the same promptings – some key words, names, phrases committed to memory – but more especially here cultivating an ability to re-create scenes in one's mind and recapture dialogue, so that, in a sense, the piece of relevant action is re-lived.

The importance of making up notes in full the same evening will be seen, for the next day's events will soon be crowding in on those memories, promoting confusion and possible loss of important data. In the peace and quiet in front of the evening fireside (this situation is important – it should be favourable to recall and reflection, making no new demands on one's sensitivities), one can fill out the detail around the indicators. This is still not easy, for accuracy is essential and much concentration required. These are, indeed, tiring times for the ethnographer, but there are no short cuts.

How one records these notes is a matter of personal taste. I use a large stiff-backed exercise book, with 'field notes' on one side of the page, and 'reflections' and extra information on the other. Full analysis will come later, but there is an overlap between these stages, and some thoughts arise as I am writing up the notes. These, then, will serve as initial indicators for the analysis. There may also be, on this opposite page, references to related data. The main aim, however, must always be to record as full and faithful an account of the day's observations as possible, for the whole research depends upon the strength and accuracy of this material.

Others prefer to use loose leaves collected in a folder. These have the advantage of being easily extractable and photocopyable, and one can also add to them tidily. There may be occasions, too, when it is physically impossible to record in full all one's notes. All one can do here is to enter one's rough jottings. It makes for some ease, then, if these are all done on the same size of paper, and can be entered neatly in the file in sequence. One might then, for example, be able to divide one's notes into separate files according to the themes or objectives of the research, duplicating notes that have a multiple function. Thus Griffin (1985, p. 104):

kept several 'Fieldnotes' files: notes from my visits to schools, work-places, and a 'family life and leisure' file; a 'method' file, including my own reactions and developing ideas on research methodology, participants' views of me and of the project; and a 'Theory' file, containing notes towards a theoretical framework, and points about relevant texts.

Data collecting can be exciting and rewarding, but it can also be boring and frustrating. Many lessons, for example, are not of great interest to an adult observer, and much of what one observes in school is likely to be commonplace. However, this in itself may be conveying a message. Beynon (1983, p. 48), for example, found frequent references to boredom in his field notes, but gradually came to appreciate this, not as an adult sitting through hours of commonplace activity, but as the *pupils* that he was studying did.

> At first I dismissed their playing-up as annoying and bloody-minded, but later came to interpret it as a genuine and brave attempt to keep something of themselves alive and kicking during the long onslaught of the school day upon both their minds and bodies.

If the ethnographer is truly empathizing with his subjects, then, even 'being bored' is interesting.

There is a well-known feeling among ethnographers, the 'else-where' syndrome – that the really important action is occurring elsewhere – yet however much the researcher's programme is changed to try to detect it, it always, tantalizingly, appears to move on. These fears are compounded by a failure to catch what one does witness, through such accidents as loss of notes, failures of memory, inability to understand one's notes, mechanical failure such as a tape-recorder not recording, or sheer fatigue. The golden rule is not to invent a fiction. If in doubt, forget it. The situation may be repeated, and there may be something you can do to ensure that it is. Also, one needs to bear in mind that the limits in this kind of research are dictated not by the data, which is almost infinite, but by one's personal capacities. These have to be put to the test, therefore. It is, however, important not to confuse disorder, incomprehensibility, and variance in the data with personal failure. It is customary for ethnographers to 'flounder around' in the data for a while and there are frequent references to 'muddling through'. Life *is* like that – full of ambiguities, inconsistencies, illogicalities, general messiness. The patterns we hope to discover, and explanations we hope to introduce will not come until we have enveloped ourselves in slices of real life.

Sometimes researchers try to meet these problems at source with more systematic collection of data. At the extreme is the Flanders Interaction Analysis Category System (FIAC), adaptations of which have been used by Delamont (1976) and in the Oracle studies by Galton *et al.* (Galton and Simon, 1980; Galton *et al.*, 1980; Galton and Willcocks, 1983; Simon and Willcocks, 1981). It consists of the observer ticking off appropriate pre-defined items on a prepared coded sheet at regular intervals. Thus the observation categories of the pupil record in the Oracle studies began as follows.

Coding the pupil–adult categories

Category	Item	Brief Definition of Item
1 Target's role	INIT	Target attempts to become focus of attention (not focus at previous signal)
	STAR	Target is focus of attention
	PART	Target in audience (no child is focus)
	LSWT	Target in audience (another child is focus)

(Galton and Simon, 1980, p. 12)

The target pupil's behaviour was then coded at regular twenty-five-second intervals.

Delamont (1984) devised her own observational categories of pupil talk as one of a number of methods. It began like this:

Code	Explanation
VR	A correct, or at least acceptable answer, produced by a volunteer
VW	An incorrect, or unacceptable answer, produced by a volunteer
VT	A volunteered translation
AR	A correct answer produced on demand

(p. 35)

'Interaction analysis', as this is called, has provided useful information. For example, such systems can tell us, very reliably, for what proportion of the time the teacher talks, and what proportion of that is 'lecturing', 'asking questions', or what proportion is student talk, and whether that is 'response' or 'initiation', and so on (Flanders, 1970). It clearly has considerable use in areas like teaching styles, as Galton *et al.* have demonstrated.

However, while a well-constructed systematic instrument can ease many of the problems of more open observation, it does so at a price. The data is more limited since the observer has to ignore much of the action, as well as the general cultural milieu of the situation. Pre-defining categories also offends one of the basic ethnographic principles of allowing them to emerge from the data, and the meanings behind the observed actions may easily be misinterpreted or inadequately represented. For example, if a pupil raises a hand to answer a teacher's question, one might interpret this as 'volunteering', but it is not known how genuine the 'volunteering' is, or for what reasons it is being made. As Delamont and Hamilton (1984, p. 11) observe about the Oracle study:

> They move on to separate six teaching styles which are the main topic of the project. Again the tantalizing question is *why* the teachers chose to act as they did. The Oracle data cannot inform us about that.

For these reasons most ethnographers would not go to such extremes, or like Delamont, and Fuller (1984), they would use such instruments for limited purposes. Most prefer to 'wallow' in the data, however uncomfortable it may feel, until categories emerge and themselves direct any systematization. There is no avoiding the fact, therefore, that most ethnographic data collecting is rather frenetic. On full-scale ethnographies, it is an everyday, all-day job, requiring unrelaxed concentration, undivided energies and the forgoing of other pleasures and activities while the writing-up of field notes proceeds. However, it will pay off, because the later analysis and presentation can be done at more leisure. Their quality, however, will always depend on the data.

Questions of validity

Accounts emerging from participant observation work are often accused of being impressionistic, subjective, biased and idiosyncratic. Interestingly, from the interactionist point of view, much so-called 'hard' data is suspect in that often statistical accounts have been accepted as data without seeking to uncover the criteria and processes involved in their compilation (Cicourel, 1968; Douglas, 1970).

First, we should note that we are not dealing with absolutes – absolutely objective or subjective knowledge. As Bruyn has noted 'all social knowledge, in fact all human communication, has both an objective and a subjective dimension to it' (1966, p. 164). Then we might be guided by Schutz.

It is the essence of science to be objective, valid not only for
me, or for me and you and a few others, but for everyone, and
that scientific propositions do not refer to my private world but
to the one and unitary life-world common to us all. (1962,
p. 205)

As scientific researchers this is what interests us, and is one of the
ways in which we differ from novelists and journalists. The work
of, for example, Henry (1963), Smith and Geoffrey (1968) and
Mead (1934), show this interest in generalizable patterns of behaviour. Their relationship with the individual's 'personal', as
opposed to his 'social', properties is expressed by Jackson: 'Each
major adaptive strategy is subtly transformed and given unique
expression as a result of idiosyncratic characteristics of the student
employing it' (1968, p. 15). The researcher must seek the common
properties of the strategies before or through the veil put up by
their transformation.

This raises two important questions – how can we be sure:

(1) of generalizability (external validity); and
(2) that what we 'discover' is the genuine product, and not
tainted by our presence or instrumentation (internal validity)?

How applicable might these findings be to other schools? There are
two different approaches to ethnography. There are those who see
it as exclusively idiographic, that is to say descriptive of particular
situations; these emphasize the holistic nature of ethnography and
the distinctive nature of information discovered, which consequently is not covered by the assumptions of statistical assessment.
It does not, in itself, therefore, permit generalization, though it
might serve as a basis. As we have seen earlier, the situation is
fluid, emergent, consisting of multiple realities which are in constant negotiation. There are no 'truths' to be discovered, or 'proofs'
to be made; rather the aim is greater understanding of the social
action in the situation under study. One's descriptions might be full
of details of content, meanings, style and pattern, features which
are not easily quantifiable.

On the other hand, there are those who prefer to see it as nomothetic, that is to say, generalizing, comparative, theoretical. There
are a number of ways we can generalize through ethnography. We
can, for example, take an area of special interest, say a curriculum
innovation, and carry out intensive studies of it within several
schools; then, as the study reveals certain particular aspects of
interest concerning the innovation, widen the sample of schools.

Because the focus is narrower, the base of operations can be wider. Then we could accumulate case studies of particular features, aspects or areas, such as the classroom, the 'express stream', school assemblies. Or one can move from the study of small-scale items to larger-scale in a logical and interlocking sequence, for example from a school class to a year group or sub-culture, to a school, to a community. Occasionally, participant observations have been quantified, though more usually by 'quasi-statistics' (Becker, 1970). For instance, observations may frequently be implicitly numerical, without lending themselves to actual counting. One might observe that in one lesson, most of the class pay attention for most of the time, while in another they do not, or one might discover, by talking to people that a few, some or many of them hold certain views or have certain concerns. This all involves frequency and distribution.

My own view is that 'idiographic' and 'nomothetic' approaches are not mutually exclusive, and that we can have both rich and intensive description *and* generalizability. As far as schools are concerned, one can work from the other way round; that is to say, select a 'typical' school, class or group, using such indices as numbers, type of school, curriculum, area, neighbourhood, sex, age, social mix and so on. The more 'representative' the school, the greater the chances of the external validity of the results. Generalizability is strengthened as the theory is strengthened, and this might be done in a number of ways – by more case-studies of schools, by other forms of empirical evidence which bear on the theory, or parts of it, by improving the internal logic of the theory, or increasing the explanatory power of its parts, and, not least, in the readers' heads as they deploy their own knowledge and experience of such institutions.

On the second question of internal validity, the participant observer claims to score highly, for a battery of methods is used both to reveal and explore and to cross-check accounts. Some of these might be 'unobtrusive measures' (Webb *et al.*, 1966). Some methods imply 'reaction'; that is the subjects are required to 'react' to a stimulus, be it a questionnaire, an interview or, if the researcher is observing, his mere presence may affect behaviour (as, for example, when observing a teacher in the classroom). Unobtrusive measures are non-reactive. They include studying reports and records, children's schoolwork, assuming a disguised participant role, and observation. Clearly, some are ethically suspect, and no-one would dream of using one of the most powerful unobtrusive devices – bugging – since that would prejudice the whole outcome. It is more in the spirit of the enterprise to work oneself into acceptance as a member of a group, in the ways discussed earlier, so that one's presence is 'obtrusive' only as a member of the group. There, one is bound by the general norms and rules of social conduct, and is less likely to end up being sent to Coventry (as has happened to several), or to prison, or perhaps being tarred and feathered!

Some examples

What do these 'slices of real life' look like when we have noted them down? I give below some examples from my own researches. Of course, I have selected these as the kinds of incidents that I found interesting and demanding of explanation. My files, however, are full of material that I have made no use of, mainly because I could not see how it contributed towards the emerging themes of the study. I shall say more about these 'emerging themes' in chapter 6. For the moment, we might note that, gradually, particular items of interest begin to occur, or regularities appear that then come to act as a prime agency of selection in what to observe, and what to record of what one observes. This important process has come to be called 'progressive focusing'. It is the first step towards making sense of the 'mess' one first observes. These examples, therefore, form a bridge. They were part of the initial data collection, but constitute some of the data that led to 'progressive focusing', which we shall take up again in chapter 6.

Example 1   Extracts from field notes compiled on school's games field during trials for the school sports

I accompanied one teacher, Mr Brown, who had the task of organizing the senior girls' (14-16 yrs) entrants from his house.

9.30   Girls lead off from house assembly. E. and I. ask Mrs T. if they can be excused. She says 'Try a jump, or something'. E. looks aghast ...

10.05   *Mr B.* cajoling A. into high jump, L. into 100, hurdles, and l.j. and Chris into shot putt. They all bombard him with excuses. 'I've hurt my arm skiing', 'I've a sore ankle', 'I'm no good at that anymore'. 'It doesn't matter where you come' says Mr. B. 'We get a point just for entering'. 'You're a shot putter, aren't you

Chris?' ('No!') 'Yes you are' ('No, I'm not!') 'Yes, you
are now! Who are discus throwers?' ('Sharon! Angela!')
'Right, you can both do it' ('Javelin she's good at'.
'No, I'm not, Angela does javelin').
(*Chris* (aside):   It makes you sick this.) 'So you're in
shot and high jump, Barbara.' ('No, I'm not! Honestly,
I haven't done h.j. for 3 yrs'.)
(*Barbara* (aside):   What I want to do is discus and long
jump and he won't let me do either of the bleeders!...)

10.45   Mr B. on long jump. Angela trots up to the running
board and steps off it very ladylike, not even reaching
the pit. 'And again!' orders Mr B. She repeats the
performance 'And again!' he says wearily.
Finally – 'Angela, you're in!'
'I'm not! Shut up!' ...

11.40   'Come on, we'll all have a go at the 100. Come on,
Sharon, you've done nothing yet.'
('No! I show myself up!'). 'Come on!' (Laughing,
cajoling). He comes over and jollies her.
'Come on, get up. Everybody else is doing it!'
Sharon gets up, does it, and in some distress comes
last ...

This example says a great deal about gender socialization, girls'
development, bureaucracy, teaching methods and teacher–pupil relationships. However what chiefly interested me at the time (in a
study of pupil-teacher interaction), because it was a thread that
ran not only through this incident but also through many others in
the school, was the girls' fear of being 'shown up'. It is Sharon who
uses this term towards the end of the example (and who in fact
illustrated it perfectly), but the matter of personal presentation
seems to be behind the attitude of several of the girls. Curiously,
this teacher, who otherwise had excellent relationships with them,
seemed oblivious to this, or rated it of little concern beside the task
set and 'the honour' of the house. 'Showing up', both intentional
and unintentional, was indeed a major cause of conflict between
teachers and pupils.

Example 2   Art, 4th years, periods 1 and 2

Carol, Jamie, Susan lost for anything to do. 'Have you any
jobs, sir!' They shimmy over idly to t's desk. 'How am I going

to find jobs for you 3 for all of next term?' He sets them
arranging magazines in a file. C. has a hangdog look. 4
bracelets, boys' names. S. is v. proud of her snap photos, she
and Maisie and her and someone else's boy friend, 20p colour,
20p black & white. She was showing them to others earlier '...
  Julia and Alan in conversation – blank pieces of paper – O
done by break. Talk about such domestic things as how old
their grandads were ... Roger is copying lion and Bugs Bunny
from front of comic ... 10.30 a.m. N. still a blank sheet of
paper ... Mark is drawing motor cars. Steve goes 'brumm,
brumm!' as he goes past. Three of these were 'lobbed out' of
'O' level Art because they were making no progress.

Re-reading these notes for me re-creates the massive boredom en-
dured by the older non-examination pupils in the school, which I
felt was a major key to some of their deviant activities. There are
also interesting commentaries on timetabling and curriculum. Here,
art has a value solely for the social relations it permits, and hence
fulfils a valuable control function.

Example 3   4th year English literature, periods 1 and 2

'I'm not feeling so tough this morning, so don't expect a
scintillating performance.' 'Oh, Good!'
'Hello, Sir, got a hangover!' Girls chat to D.R. very sociably.
  9.20 Bell. D.R. – 'Is that the end or the beginning of the
lesson?'
  'Ladies, gentlemen and Kerry! I warn you I might dodge off
in the middle (Oh, Great!). Please, Laura, don't squirt hair
spray'. 'It's not, it's deodorant. My auntie gave it me – she's
dead now, her! her!' (laughs) 'What an advertisement!' ...
  After more chivying of the girls, D.R. starts on Chapter 25,
giving a character description of Troy.
  'Cheerful, and not downhearted – like our staff
                                  – like our pupils
                                  – like our m. c-p.s at the
                                      back! ...
  'A plausible rogue, and he could get away w. womanizing. It
was perfectly legitimate for the upright, even the downright,
archetypal Victorian father to have a bit on the side – a dual
standard, disapproved of in public ...' (Julie: 'I should think
so!') 'What I mean is, Troy could indulge his peccadilloes'

(Much laughter) 'In your vernacular, his "little bit on the side".
'Disapproval of his morals had often been tempered with a
smile . . . Troy was full of activity (I think he had to be – much
laughter). He took what opportunities – what women – came
his way . . . Treat them fairly, and you're a lost man – how
about that for a philosophy? But remember you women libbers,
Troy was a product of his age . . .

    9.55   Now get on with your notes, or read for the last 10
minutes.' In fact, a general chat ensues, while D.R. talks to me.
'It was all ad libbing that, you know – Ladies! ladies! That's
not the way a liberated group behaves. In other words "Belt
Up!"''

This is, again, merely a fragment of this particular lesson. I have
to confess that this is one that probably would have been better
tape-recorded, as everything depended on what was said – though
there is no guarantee that the lesson would then have been the
same! I find the lesson interesting as a typical accommodation by
a teacher in a situation of largely adverse circumstances which is
more a performance, an entertainment, than a lesson. He goes
through the subject matter, but instead of the humour assisting
transmission, it dominates it. Now, why should this be so? I would
need to consider other material to answer this, and I do this in
chapter 6.

Example 4   Staff conflict

A clash today between AR, BJ. AR learnt from the kids (once
again) that 2 House cricket matches were planned for the
morrow. (Staff meeting planned for same time.) This arose ˙.˙
the st meeting was supposed to take place this evening but the
Head hadn't a 'hope' of getting back here before 9 p.m. Staff
were given option of tomorrow a.m. or Friday before the
beginning of next term. They chose the former! (Mrs T.
speaking up. But Head thought the latter would have to come
soon like other schools.) There were some not immed.
concerned who could supervise the rest of the school on field
between them – AR, G.C., B.A., J.L., Miss Student. B.A.
spoke up and volunteered his (& AR's) agreement. (Later A.R.
went back on this to me, told me the others had agreed first &
˙.˙ cut the ground from under his feet.) When head asked him,
left with little option.

Now A.R. learnt from kids that House matches being played
pds 3 & 4. Consuming 3 staff/5 leaving A.R. & J.L. to control
500 minus 44 kids. B.J. said he'd been to higher authority, but
A.R. knew the old man - B.J. wd mumble sthing, and Head
wd mumble 'Yes' sthing back, without realizing what going on.
It was B.J.'s direct responsibility and he had betrayed an 'I'm
all right Jack' attitude i.e. get his cricket in, get his umpires -
while he himself was secure in staff meeting. (Was not the itch
why was *he* not consulted - and he has a point ·. · A.R. was
directly concerned.) B.J. flounced out in disgust, while A.R.
tiraded to all and sundry, repeating the tale to all who came in.
He was going to swot up his cricket rules so he cd umpire. He
was going to see Head 1st thing in morning. He was not going
to do it. He buttonholed I.W. - I.W. promised to intercede.
B.J. had told me earlier, a few individuals were aligned v P.E.
They resented e.g. his intervention (as Head of P.E.) in Heads
of Depmt. meetings in academic affairs, & as for A.R. - 'his
bloody arrogance'.

There were several such incidents of staff conflict, which all had
serious repercussions for the functioning of the school. It is possible
to see three problems here:

(1) inter-departmental rivalry;
(2) bureaucratic failure; and possibly
(3) some personal animosity.

Something could at least be done about (2) to head off or lighten
such conflicts. In all such instances, though strongly personalized
by the people concerned, there were detectable signs of system
failure.

Example 5   Pupil groups

In our study of pupil transfer, Lynda Measor and I were concerned
to show how pupil friendships developed. There was a stage when
the boundaries of friendship groups hardened, integrating within,
and differentiating from, other groups. Intruders were resisted. The
following extract from Lynda's field notes illustrates this.

The pupils are told to 'Get into a group of four'. Phillip,
Stewart, Giles and Erik are in their customary group. Geoffrey
attaches himself to them. The teacher says it has to be four
people. Phillip and Stewart say 'We are four, I don't know

what Geoffrey is doing here'. They are very clear as to the boundary of their group and certain who is the intruder. It is Geoffrey who leaves. Pete and Jim move right across to the opposite side of the room to work with Keith and Andrew. They make no offer to join Dominic and Mark or Matthew although they are at the next table. Geoffrey, when he leaves Phillip's group, moves to Pete's table. He is again decisively rejected, Roy telling him to 'Get out of here'. The teacher's attention is attracted by this loud display of aggression and she insists that he is allowed to stay, but it is under sufferance. (Measor and Woods, 1984, p. 92)

The psychology and ethics of observation

Ethnography can be an intensely lonely experience, particularly if a *non*-participant observer. One is marginal, an outsider looking in, and all such positions are fraught with feelings of anxiety and alienation, of being betwixt and between, neither here nor there. The life of the school goes on, people hustle and bustle about their business, and in this activity, you are of no consequence. In fact, they would probably be better off without you. While this can in fact feel quite refreshing and enjoyable for a time, particularly if liberated from an onerous post, strains will almost inevitably begin to tell. These may be compounded by genuine ethical difficulties connected with the approach. In part, these derive from the point made above – that you are totally dependent on them for what you are doing, and they are totally independent of you. In such a circumstance, as guest, visitor, supplicant, one must behave with tact, discretion and decorum, and flawless recognition of proprieties at all times. Consider these examples from my field notes:

(1) (One week into the research, an ethnography of a school) A depressing day, almost confined to staffroom, few opportunities to get out, and there the contradiction in status and duties between me and overworked staff losing all their frees and possibly viewing me as a fifth columnist. The latter might be removed by assumption of teaching role, which might give access to more teacher confidences instead of the (possibly unintended) flannel that wafts nebulously and only occasionally across my nose at the moment ... Depression was completed when discovered had left behind document with my notes on

4th year reports – where? – on floor of staffroom? Apart from: 2/3rds of day's work, how much incriminating evidence (e.g. of me as a spy) did it contain, or that might be read into it? What if AR (a particularly aggressive member of staff much opposed to my research) should discover it? I see him now, reading out extracts to his agog comrades.

(2) (2 weeks into research)

A day preceded by depression. A feeling of not knowing where going, indeed not knowing where to start and how to proceed. How to get in on the action? Offer staff the status of 'research associates'? A share of my royalties? ... But why should *they* be at all enthusiastic about *my* project? I am there on sufferance ... With this sitting on me, oversleeping after a bad night, and a horrible morning of weather, a poor day seemed in prospect. But as so often happened in my schoolteaching days, my spirits were raised by the people in the place. I had uplifting discussions with T.H., I.W., J.D., M.S., M.T. The pupils too were cooperative, and I rounded off the day with two games of chess in final period with some 4th yr. boys.

(3) (The following day)

On the whole, a good day. The data is beginning to come, people are opening up, I'm paying the school something back.

(4) (3 months into the research)

Have reached a hiatus. Have peeled off 2 layers of what's happening in the school, now a big effort is needed to strip off another. But am feeling a little bored with the operation at the moment. I have to *make* my day, and while I don't complain about the planning, it's the admin., and especially the risk of unpleasantness (why do you want to do that? Go there? See those people? How can attending *that* meeting possibly help you?). On a day like today when I am very very tired in the head (I have been all week), I wonder whether it is all worth it ... (extensive notes on day's events follow, then) ... An enormous feeling today of having saturated one type of data, and a vacuous feeling developing. But tonight, a new thought is crystallizing ... In short, it will involve re-interviewing S.J., aiming to spotlight the key features of their sub-cultures already revealed in initial trawl. How coherent are they? How many? Chief Features in Relation to School Culture? Strengths of commitment to them? etc.

(5) (10 months into research)

I had in mind beginning the second round of interviews with the 4ths. During the morning, however, a great feeling of déja

vu and boredom. Somehow it didn't seem the same place
anymore.
(6) (11 months into research)
This a day when all plans do not come off. C.S. takes his lot
off suddenly, periods 3 and 4, and Head wants them p.6. And
p.1 severely curtailed by long assembly.
(7) (11 months)
Very difficult to concentrate on writing these notes (K keeps
chatting about this and that).

These extracts give an idea of some of the psychological and physical problems of doing ethnographic work. The requirement to
observe things 'as they happen' and to be 'unobtrusive' particularly
if associated with problems of negotiating access, can mean long
periods of boredom, occasional scepticism about what the research
is yielding, and pangs of conscience about the worth and propriety
of what one is doing. Of course there may be occasions when bad
health, domestic upset, or some other factor unconnected with the
research affects it. At others, low points occur as consequences of
the research.

The first step towards a solution is to regard these problems as
part of the research, and to document and analyse them (perhaps
in a research diary - see chapter 5). This increases the chances of
staying on top of them, rather than being submerged beneath them.
There will no doubt be points when you have to call on your
equivalent psychological boosters to my teacher training 'challenge'. Otherwise, difficulties may be due to a personal fault - a
mistake or omission or misunderstanding - or the result of an
accident - which can be quickly rectified. They may be a consequence of bad planning, or lack of planning, poor progress in
negotiating access, a failure to take up opportunities, or to explore
the full range of them. It is necessary to keep the mind active, and,
within the limits of 'unobtrusiveness', experiment with ways ahead,
with gaining access to new places or new forms of interaction.
There are times when further requests have to be made, when one
is unsure of the response, but risks have to be taken to preserve
the momentum of the research. In this way, perhaps, one can *make*
something happen - or, more accurately, gain access to places
where things are happening. It is important to consider, first, however, whether the problem in the first place is not a product of the
'elsewhere syndrome'.

The other antidote is to take steps to neutralize one's isolation
by forming liaisons. These might be of several kinds. Strangers to

an institution might request a liaison person, someone within who is given responsibility for seeing if and how the researcher's requirements can be met. In time, however, the researcher may well come to form quite strong affective relationships, with some genuine friendships, as previously noted. In example (2) above, I am rescued from my troughs of despair by friendly conversations with various members of staff. Finally, the researcher may have the good fortune to discover a 'key informant', someone who is prepared to divulge a great deal of information, and who thus more than compensates for slack progress in other areas. I discuss these more fully in the following chapter, merely noting here their importance for morale.

Ethnographers continually agonize over the ethics of observation. My own conscience about certain aspects of the matter are reflected in entries (1) and (2) above. These show two basic problems.

(1) The morality of doing educational research in under-resourced areas, where one's presence might, perhaps, be more fruitfully employed.
(2) The ethics of covert, as opposed to overt, observation.

Particularly in a climate of scepticism among teachers about the value of educational research, it is right that we should continually consider carefully the worth and relevance of what we are doing. But the doubts expressed in example (1) are mainly a product of the very early stages of the research, when nothing much seems to be happening, few meaningful accesses have yet been negotiated, and I am strange both to the research and to the people in the school. It is one of the most vulnerable stages of ethnographic work, where one might persuade oneself, for all sorts of reasons, that 'it is not worth it'. It would be a pity if that were a rationalization as a way out of difficulties, rather than genuine conviction.

I have commented earlier on covert research (see also Bulmer, 1982; Hammersley, 1984; Burgess, 1984c, 1985a). My concern in example (1) seems to be that I have been engaging in some covert research and may be found out – and drummed out! In such intimate and detailed work, one is bound to observe, to hear and to record things potentially damaging to individuals. For example, in observing an undisciplined lesson, one will note deviant activities and the vain attempts of the teacher to suppress them. One may overhear critical comments from pupils on teachers, or teachers on colleagues, that seem germane to the research and which you feel you need to record, perhaps on one of those slips of paper carried about the person. The ultimate ethical test here is the use you make of such material, but there is an onus on the researcher to keep this material very safe indeed, against the use that *others* might make of it. I have broken this rule in example (1), but the example also illustrates the grey area between overt and covert work mentioned in chapter 2, for while the general parameters of the research were known to the whole staff, not all of its particulars were. It is almost impossible for this to be so in a large school. This may carry no wilful intent to deceive, but that may be how it is interpreted if discovered in disadvantageous circumstances.

Another aspect of this grey area is when one finds oneself unwittingly, and indeed unwillingly, engaged in covert research, such as, for example, in the following incident from my field notes of the Lowfield research.

> Sitting in flat, overheard G.B. giving some child a verbal flogging. By God, it was evil! Do you want me to take you in there and dust you up! ... threats, assaults, questions sustained, child reduced to tears. Together with the *appeal*; 'Why go on? Where's it going to end?' A vicious onslaught which confirmed all what kids had said (observation confirming interviews).

As I re-read this now, some ten years later, I can still sense the almost criminal vindictiveness of this teacher's offensive, and I can still feel the chill as I froze in my chair in the next small room. My presence was obviously unsuspected there, otherwise the teacher might have taken the precaution of closing the connecting door.

Where do the ethics of such a case lie? Had I been there with the intent of witnessing the incident, I could rightly have been accused of spying, in circumstances where the teacher clearly had particularly wished for privacy. I think that would have been unforgivable. I could not escape, for he would have heard me move, and after the very first sentence, I judged that he would have been deeply embarrassed to discover that he had been overheard. But I was in my room quite legitimately (I was conducting interviews in there, a fact which was well known to the staff, though at that moment there was a gap between interviews). The teacher, in fact, made a similar error to mine when I mislaid the 'reports' comments, in not himself ensuring his privacy. Even so, I did not feel that I could use the incident in any publication connected with the research (and I only do so now because it is so long distant that all concerned will have forgotten about it). On the other hand, it cast quite a dramatic light on teacher-pupil relationships, and was therefore noted, and taken into account in the analysis.

Another helpful guide to, and guarantee of, the proprieties of what one is doing is the opportunity and ability to confide in at least some members of staff as to the full purport of it. They can, for example, be very helpful in giving advice as to whether a paper should be circulated to a whole staff, certain material should be used or suppressed, or included in what publication.

Chapter 4

Interviews

Though observation lies at the heart of pure ethnography, most recent ethnographic work in educational research in Britain has relied heavily on interviews. Often it is the only way of finding out what the perspectives of people are, and collecting information on certain issues or events, but it is also a means of 'making things happen' and stimulating the flow of data. I shall argue, however, that interviews need to be used in conjunction with other methods, and that ethnographic interviews, in themselves, are of a rather special character, somewhat akin to participant observation. As with that method, before any consideration of form and technique, we need to consider the person and disposition of the ethnographer, for the key to successful interviewing lies here. Studying how others do it will refine one's method, but it will not supply the basic orientation from which many of them develop naturally.

The ethnographer and interviews

The same major attributes, revolving around trust, curiosity and unaffectedness, are required in interviewing as in other aspects of the research. People will not just talk to anyone. As with observation, therefore, there are questions of access involved, of earning respect for the project one is engaged on and of gaining confidence in one's powers to carry it through, but above all, there is once more a need to establish a feeling of trust and rapport. A good test as to what is involved in these qualities is to consider the sort of person you would be prepared to confide some of your own innermost secrets in. For me, this would have to be an understanding person, who I knew would be interested in me for myself (and not just a research project), and who would listen to and appreciate my points of view in a non-judgmental way, however weird, wicked, unreasonable, or badly expressed they may seem. If I were a teacher I would expect the interviewer to be able to appreciate the difficulties teachers have to work under, including those of recalcitrant pupils. If I were a pupil, I would expect a sympathetic hearing, including for what I honestly might feel about teachers. At the same time, I would expect the interviewer to be aware, knowledgeable and fair, and not easily taken in by any distortions of the truth I might try on.

There would have to be a relationship between us that transcended the research, that promoted a bond of friendship, a feeling of togetherness and joint pursuit of a common mission rising above personal egos. I would get a sense of this through what the interviewer said and how it was said, by how much he or she put into the discussion, by what I got out of it, by what interests we had in common, by how she or he looked at me, answered my questions, listened to me. I would definitely not have a feeling that I was being 'researched' by a superior agency, who ultimately would put all these little cogs together into a grand machine that would be for the use of others. I would want to feel that I could talk freely, and that if I said 'I tell you this in strict confidence', that that would be respected; or even if I did not say that, that none of the information I imparted would be used to my discredit, or otherwise misused. It may be that I would need to meet such a person several times over a period before I felt such a relationship had been established, but in some cases it can happen earlier with a quick identification of similar interests, thought processes, views and values, and in the various ways that people form connections.

Pat Sikes gives these examples.

Sharing Experiences: Give personal details to solicit personal details, e.g. I mentioned to Helen that I was an only child and that this placed constraints upon one. She then talked about her experiences, as an only child. We understood one another!

Setting Tests: On occasion, I've been able to 'set tests' which I feel may give me some indication of how the relationship is progressing. For example, I knew that Jim grew orchids. I also knew that he was very reluctant to talk about or show them to other people ... I thought that I'd let him be first to mention them. In another way it could have seemed as if I'd been secretly checking up on him if I started talking about a relatively private area of his life, this probably wouldn't be conducive to our relationship. In the event he introduced the topic after about an hour, and talked for something like thirty minutes about orchids and after this continually made reference to them. Without placing too much significance on this, I think it does indicate that he's prepared to share some confidences with me. I've found my knowledge of art similarly so ... Being a sporting type of person also helps ... You do have to possess, and possibly even make an effort to acquire certain basic background knowledge ... so that, where appropriate, the other person can share at a level which is satisfactory (i.e. they don't have to explain the rudiments) certain significant aspects of their lives and the things in them they value and which give them pleasure. Take Jim and his orchids, I knew very little about them, but I do have a little knowledge ... I know something about propagation and growth and can extrapolate some of that. Thus we can have an intelligent discussion during which I can learn a lot - and I've made an effort to have a look at books about orchids - they are fascinating! (Personal communications)

So far, so good. But people also have values as well as interests, and sometimes the interviewer might be strongly opposed to them. In essence, the difficulty is how to appear a fully-fledged human being, which includes having a number of interests and dispositions (political views, social attitudes, intellectual tastes) that some people might feel opposed to, and another orientation that is acceptable to all, or at least to the group in which one is interested. Fulminating about the government in power will not endear one to its supporters. Flaunting a copy of *The Times*, and doing the crossword in five minutes, might raise a few eyebrows, and suspicions of one being a 'clever dick'. Lynda Measor (1985, p. 24) describes how it came to be known, from a chance remark that she let slip, that she was a feminist, how this led to a certain amount of constant ribbing from senior male teachers, and closed off for her certain avenues of investigation. Of course one's own affiliations and values can be a valuable resource with like-minded individuals. With others, a discreet neutrality is the only option, while cultivating the things held in common.

The second attribute, and indeed a requirement of all researchers, as mentioned previously, is curiosity - a desire to want to know, in this case to learn people's views and perceptions of the facts, to hear their stories, discover their feelings. This is the motive force, and it has to be a burning one, that drives researchers to tackle and overcome the many difficulties involved in setting up and conducting successful interviews (and, indeed, going through with the rest of the research).

Sometimes informants' thoughts cannot be 'discovered' because they are ill-formulated in the interviewee's mind, and have to be explored together in a mutual quest. Sometimes they may be only partially presented in a 'stage one' or 'stage two' manner, and the researcher must call on tact and discretion to decide when to press for further elaboration and when to pass on. But one must know, or at least have a strong suspicion, that there is more. Quite often one will be presented with a rather bland, seamless account in an early interview. It may not necessarily be wrong, but it may only be a public front, purged of the more important and interesting private details. Like the explorers of old, we must search for what 'lies over the hill'. The climbing might be tough, and then it may only be desert, bog, or even another, bigger, hill, but it may also be rich pasture. The advance may not be a broad, frontal one, but a series of probes in certain areas to find a productive line. In other words, rather as one does in observation, one listens for key words or phrases, which may just as well be casual, let-fall comments not intended for the record; or looks for indicators that a matter is of importance to an interviewee; or is quick to pick up any peculiarities or anomalies. All this is powered by the desire to know more, an interest in others and to reach the most thoroughgoing understanding possible.

The third element is naturalness. As with observation one endeavours to be unobtrusive in order to witness events as they are, untainted by one's presence and actions, so in interviews the aim is to secure what is within the minds of the interviewees, uncoloured and unaffected by the interviewer. Interviews, therefore, are unstructured, designed to facilitate the expression of personal views and facts sincerely and accurately. The interviewee provides the structure, and the interviewer's quest is to help discover what it is. Care is needed, therefore, to avoid 'leading' or 'suggesting' or otherwise spoiling the outcome, and skill in discovering and extracting what is in the interviewee's mind. It follows that the more 'natural' the interviewer is, the more chances of success there will be in this task. 'Being natural' means just that – one does not adopt a special pose as 'researcher', 'expert', 'bureaucrat', but relates to people on a person-to-person basis. This is easier for teachers to do, perhaps, among their colleagues than with pupils. One does not use specialist language, wear conspicuous clothes, or otherwise cultivate a strange appearance (de Waele and Harré, 1979; see also

65

Delamont (1976) in chapter 2). Non-teacher ethnographers who go to work in schools make a point of dressing as the teachers would, with not too deviant hair-styles or make-up, again in the interests of blending in with the scenery and appearing as a credible person to whom they could relate. If there is too much variation from the norm, one runs the risk of being defined out of the culture, people reinforcing their own identity by the contrast. This often happens to student-teachers, for example.

> I had this chap in my department, I was glad when he went. He was the bees knees, God's gift to the art world. He came to school the first morning in a policeman's cape and wellingtons, bearded too, and when he walked into the staffroom everybody said 'Good God!' And they used to pull his leg. Do you have to wear a beard to kid yourself you're an art teacher? He wore corduroys and sandals without socks on. They used to rib him unmercifully. (Quoted in Sikes, Measor and Woods, 1985)

Occasionally, accidents may happen, as for instance, when Lynda Measor (1985), dressed 'sensibly', went to interview a woman teacher in her own home, and was met by her fitted out with 'peroxided hair, pink sox and a leopard skin coat' (p. 5). The woman was a 'little cool and challenging at first'. Lynda made sure, of course, on her next visit, that she went in informal apparel.

Lynda further illustrates the point with the retired teachers she interviewed in this study (Sikes, Measor and Woods, 1985).

> I ... always dressed very conservatively, never wore jeans, or even trousers, always had my shoes polished, wore neat little blouses. I feel that my intuitive reaction was right, because of data I received. Older teachers with only one exception made a point of their strenuous objection to the appearance of young people in general and young teachers in particular. They considered the young to be scruffy and messy, and in the case of young teachers, they felt their appearance demeaned their whole professional ethos. (Measor, 1985, p. 5)

Pat Sikes, in the same project, illustrates another aspect of this generation gap.

> I've only seen one retired lady teacher so far but I have to report that I experienced the 'naughty fourthformer' syndrome ... I felt rather incompetent, untidy (I wasn't), irresponsible and generally rather as if I'd been hauled up before the senior mistress for some minor misdemeanour.

There is a 'credibility gap' here, which can only be worked out by both parties over a number of meetings. It does indicate, though, that one interview on its own in itself is almost worthless, apart from breaking the ice, for people will define the situation by standard indicators in ways to which they are accustomed.

It is difficult to appear natural if one's presence is peripheral to the concerns of the school. Unless working in one's own school, one is likely to be asked, quite persistently, 'What are you doing here?' Teachers will more readily comprehend research objectives than pupils (though they will do this better the more educationally relevant and of general benefit they are). Pupils may require more explanation and reassurance. Some researchers have told them they are seeking to understand their points of view better, so that things might be improved not only for them but for others, and that ultimately they might write a book about it. This 'media-person' image is one pupils generally seem to accept. If it is giving them a platform, a voice, the opportunity is something to be grasped. If, on the contrary, there appears a risk that the exercise will be turned against them, and, for example, presented to the staff of a school as a resource to be used in conflict struggles against them, then that is an indication to keep quiet, or even perhaps to try to turn the occasion into a resource for oneself in such battles by 'shooting a line'.

The form and the character of interviews

Consequently, where the interview takes place, how it is set up, the relationships between the people concerned, the whole form that it takes – all are critical issues.

In the first place, we might note that 'interview' is rather an inappropriate term, implying a formality the ethnographer seeks to avoid. I prefer to regard them as conversations or discussions, which indicate more of an open, democratic, two-way, informal, free-flowing process, and wherein people can be 'themselves' and not feel bound by roles. They can, therefore, both represent the role and be reflective about it, and be less concerned to present impenetrable 'fronts', behind which the 'real them' lurks, private and inaccessible. However, it is easier for us to represent our ethnographic interviews in this way than to accomplish them. As Ball (1983, pp. 93–5) notes:

> The social production of an interview involves the establishment of an asymmetrical relationship between interviewer and

interviewee through the use of language as a form of communication ... The interviewee is asked to elaborate, illustrate, reiterate, define, summarize, exemplify, and confirm matters in his talk in ways that would be unacceptable in other talk situations. The interviewer controls the specification of topics and maintains a verbal monitoring of the speech situation ... The rules of conversational discourse are flagrantly disregarded in the name of social science ... The interviewer comes to 'know' his subjects without ever necessarily having to engage in a reciprocal process of personal 'social striptease'.

However, whether this is necessarily so is a matter of debate. Davies (1985, p. 83) argues that this may be a consequence of masculinist research, and quotes from Oakley (1981) who:

Convincingly argues against the notion that interviewing can be a one-way procedure, with the interviewer withholding her own views and resisting friendship or involvement. In her discussion of the sorts of questions women 'asked back', and of the quality of the research which emerged from the reciprocity and intimacy of her own research relationships, Oakley strongly resists the attitude which relegates interviewees to a narrow objectified function as 'data'.

Again, therefore, it may be a question of basic orientation, but what does this mean in practice? Consider the terms on which the interview is arranged and conducted. The more an element of volition, and the less a press-ganged determination or tolerant sufferance there is about participation, the more chance there is of achieving this naturalistic and reciprocating state. This is more important the more extensive a contribution from them is required. For example, in ethnographic work, interviews – or conversations – may take place any time, anywhere, over a fairly long period. They range from chats in the staffroom or local pub to *ad hoc* discussions about immediate events (such as a lesson that has just passed, or a new policy initiative, or some pupil disruption) to exchanges with pupils in the playground or dinner queue, to interviews that have been set up more formally. It is difficult in practice to do without such formal interviews, but they should be set up and held within the general ethnographic spirit.

As we have noted, this stems from naturalness, sampling things as they are, not as they are made to be. Much credit is therefore attached to such conversations that take place in the ordinary course of events. Then, one might win recruits to the cause, by advertising the aims of the research, the principles of the method, the possible outcomes for education, and for teachers personally perhaps. As Stenhouse (1975, p. 144) argues, 'The outstanding characteristic of the extended professional is a capacity for autonomous professional self-development through systematic self-study.' There may be some of these around. There may also be others naturally well disposed towards the research, through private as well as professional interest. Some of these might be located through informal channels. Enquiries might be made through friends or other contacts where personal knowledge, informality and trust have already been achieved, and these then recommend teacher and researcher to each other. One or two such contacts would usually ensure a snowballing effect. At the same time as one is recruiting aids to the research, it is also politic to identify any opposition, and take steps to avoid, or otherwise neutralize, them. It is necessary, for example, as a basic position, to have all the required permissions to undertake the lines of enquiry involved – this establishes one's legal and moral rights.

In a way, what one is seeking, ideally, is volunteers. Busy teachers do not actually queue up to assist educational researchers, even when it is one of their own number, but some are inevitably more drawn towards, and less opposed to, some projects than others. In their prospective cooperation might lie an element of negotiation. Guarantees of protection of identity are standard, but further than this, interviewees may have some things they wish to say which you consider irrelevant to the research, but which it is almost incumbent on you to hear out. They may express a wish for certain things to get reported, which you may promise to do if it proves possible. Stenhouse (1984, p. 222), for example, says it is:

Part of my job to give people the feeling not merely that they
have my ear, my mind and my thoughts concentrated on them
but that they want to give an account of themselves because
they see the interview as in some way an opportunity: an
opportunity of telling someone how they see the world.

He hopes, therefore, that 'the occasion is slightly flattering to the person being interviewed'.

This all indicates the potential therapeutic element in this kind of encounter. It provides a platform for people to speak their minds in a way, and in such detail that rarely occurs to the ordinary person. This can relieve stress, and provide the satisfaction of passing on knowledge and perhaps of helping to improve the world. It can also be a cataclysmic 'critical' event for the interviewee, bring-

69

ing about a redefinition of personal identity and aims. The conversations, and the thought processes set up between them, provide a kind of social psychotherapy. Pat Sikes gives the following example.

> After talking to me twice, I went for my third meeting with
> Sally to be greeted with the news that she'd got up an
> exhibition in the poshest cafe in [town] and on the strength of
> it had got some commissions for work. She hadn't done this
> for over ten years. She said she'd been pushed into thinking
> about herself and had seen that she was still very much an
> artist rather than a teacher. In having this exhibition, it seems
> as if she was making a public statement about her identity.
> (Personal communication)

Interviewees may request some other kind of 'contract'. For example, they may agree to a conversation being tape-recorded if they are given control of the tape and the right to amend the transcript. If this is a pathway to valuable information, then such a contract is worth making, though there are invariably ways in which one can continue to negotiate to secure the optimum results for the research. Negotiation allows the interviewee a sense of some power and personal investment in the research.

When interviews are 'arranged', interviewees, where possible, should be given choice of time and place. For teachers, this may be in their own classrooms, in their own homes, or even, perhaps, the local pub. This is not only a matter of convenience and availability, but again may give them a sense of control and confidence. Equally, positions within the interview situation need to be considered. The less formal, the more relaxed, the less confrontational, the more promoting a sense of togetherness, the better. I prefer to 'interview' teachers in the armchair comfort of a staffroom; if in a classroom, I try to adopt a relaxed, informal position, perhaps standing with a teacher as he prepares some apparatus, or sitting beside him at his desk. Ball (1984, p. 83) held conversations with teachers 'in the staffroom, in classrooms and corridors, on the playing fields, in the pub, teachers' homes, on school trips, in the car to and from school, and at casual meetings in the town'. Stenhouse (1984, p. 222) liked to sit side by side with or angled towards the interviewee, explaining to them that he liked to 'look out at the world with them, sharing their view'. Some have found it helpful to interview more than one at a time. Ginsburg *et al.* (1980), for example, discovered that that was useful in promoting discussion. The converse practice – employing more than one interviewer – has also been tried, and its advantages (ability to follow up points, not missing anything, triangulating responses) acclaimed by its supporters, though it would appear to be opposed to some of the principles we have discussed, and is potentially threatening and exhausting for the interviewee.

It may seem more difficult to achieve a naturalistic, relatively democratic relationship with pupils, who, so often in research studies, are a captive audience, and with whom some have difficulty in communicating. Logan (1984, p. 18) quotes a researcher.

> I never know how to ask children questions that don't seem to
> be terribly leading questions. It's hard to engage in
> conversation with a child and I just feel that they must see
> through me, see what I'm up to. It's so contrived. Course, I'm
> not an adult who normally talks to children. You know you
> don't just show up for one day and say 'this is so and so, who
> would like to talk to you'.

But even here, where the more formal interviews are scheduled, situations can be contrived to give pupils some power in the relationships. It is necessary to say something about the research in not too technical or patronizing way, and to give the usual assurances of confidentiality and anonymity. Also, you would need to explain that for the purposes of the research, you are stepping outside the teacher role, and that you may both be examining it. This may be difficult to get across, particularly in situations where there is a large gulf between teachers and pupils.

But there are other things that one can do. We have noted in some schools where there is such a potential gulf, that it has been bridged by what we term a 'middle-ground culture' (Measor and Woods, 1984). In this, pupils and teachers come to terms in order for the school to function. It was characterized on the teachers' part by allowing some latitude in appearances, both their own and pupils', by adopting some of the pupils' language forms, by incorporating elements of teenage and admass culture into their teaching, by humour, and by distancing oneself occasionally from the teacher role. We might add, too, some general latitude in the interpretation of rules, such as Reynolds (1976) discovered was such an aid to good order in his South Wales schools. The middle-ground culture is marked by its openness and flexibility, by equality of treatment, by sincerity, and by friendliness. It has its limits, and there are points beyond which teachers and pupils may not venture further into each other's cultures without penalty. For example, Lynda Measor was permitted to go along with a group of girls to one particular pop concert, but not another. The former was given by a group that had an inter-generational fan club; the latter was run by a group that was more peculiarly 'theirs', and the researcher would have been seen as intruding in a private area. One girl told me in my research, 'There are things we don't even tell you', which I took to be both a compliment and a warning. To my eternal shame, I can remember a very early piece of research I was doing for a diploma dissertation, when I 'blew' an interview with a girl with whom I was getting on very well. She was a very reticent girl, with some psychological problems, and at some stage had been in trouble for shoplifting. So well was the 'conversation' going with her, that I felt I might raise this matter with her to help find out what really motivated her. As soon as she realized I knew about that, she coloured deeply, and retired into her shell. I had failed the interview, and failed her, for having successfully established a 'middle ground', I had knocked it away from under both of us by venturing too far into private territory. That kind of thing, I now feel, should only be raised by the pupil. There may be ways of providing them with opportunities to do so, and therein lies the interviewer's skill and brief – in creating an appropriate relationship, situation and atmosphere.

The 'middle ground' offers one useful way of doing this. Another is to contrive to give pupils more power in the interview than they might have in more formal research. This might be done, again, by choosing the place of interview with care – somewhere they do not feel threatened within, and with which they may feel some personal identification. At Lowfield (Woods, 1979) I was lucky in having the services of the 'flat' – the room where older pupils practised housecraft and occasionally entertained guests. It invariably contained some of their personal belongings and decorations, and they felt free to disport themselves in it when talking to me as they would wish. It was still school property, but certainly different from a classroom or staffroom, or teacher's office. It was also different from the pupils' own private places – the loos, behind the cycle sheds, and so on – where my entry might have risked any feeling of trust that might have developed between us.

One of the pupils' defences in the school, where the power bases are loaded against them, is in their numbers. Another is in the strength of their friendships. These can be useful resources to the ethnographic interviewer. For example, I found it useful to hold conversations with pupils in friendship groups (Woods, 1979). I would go to a class at the beginning of a day, with the permission of the teacher concerned of course, and arrange a timetable for the day, seeing groups of about four pupils in double-period slots. Pupils were invariably split up into groups when I entered. If they were large groups, I asked them to split themselves up. Pairs of pupils I asked to invite another pair along. This technique, I believe, had several advantages. The company of like-minded fellows helped to put them at their ease. The bond between them and the way it was allowed to surface shifted the power balance in the discussion in their direction. As long as my interventions were not too intrusive, it might facilitate the establishment of their norms, and I might become privy to their culture, albeit in rather a rigged way. Other advantages were that they acted as checks, balances and prompts to each other. Inaccuracies were corrected, incidents and reactions recalled and analysed. From these talks I was cued into the pupil experiences that I shall discuss later – being 'shown-up', being 'bored', 'having a laugh', 'working', and so on.

These group discussions provided me with information I do not think I would have obtained by any other method. At times, pupils prompted each other – 'Go on, tell him', 'What about when you ...' They volunteered information in the company of their friends, and often to them rather than to me in the context of ongoing exchanges with them, that I would not otherwise have been privy to. I doubt, for example, if I would have received this information in a one-to-one interview.

> *Christine* I was sitting next to Kevin, and he'd got this cartridge in his pen and he was going like that (*she indicates an obscene gesture*), and I just pushed him away, and the teacher was writing on the board and he must have eyes in the back of his head ... and he says ... he turns round with a fuming face and he says 'Will you two stop fiddling with each other!' I never went so bright red in all my life, and he pushed me over one side and him on the other ... and everybody turned round, didn't they? ... In front of all my friends! You know ... he made such a ... mockery ... can't stand him! Everybody was scared stiff in that class, everyone just sits there, all quiet.
> (Woods, 1979, p. 31)

It is possible, of course, that one might take this too far, and construct such a natural and relaxed atmosphere that pupils start to hand the cigarettes around, or otherwise transgress the school rules. One can have recourse to the 'middle ground' here, gently discouraging such activities and making it clear why. It is not that you are passing judgment on the activity, but that there is a rule, and there will be sanctions on all of you if discovered. Again, some pupils use fairly lurid language among themselves, and may employ this in the interview (see, for example, Willis, 1977). They also have a sense of humour, which, at times, delightful, at others in its sexism, racism, and sheer crudity, is difficult to stomach. Some of this at times may be a 'try on'. It may be a genuine celebration of their culture in your honour. It may be necessary to give the correct meaning and emphasis to what they are saying, their use of it indicating their acceptance of and confidence in the interviewer (Logan, 1984). Other observations and talks will help indicate which it is. The more immediate problem of how to react to such strong expressions is again 'middle ground' – neither encouraging nor discouraging, approving or disapproving, but noting, and continuing to try to facilitate the flow of talk, and maintaining a sensible, discreet, broadminded but not foolish, disposition. A 'try on' will only succeed if the interviewer betrays astonishment, shock or confusion or is 'taken in'.

There are other costs in the group interview. Certain individuals may come to dominate them, as noted here.

> Talk with Julie, Linda, Carol and Tracey. These are certainly a
> solid foursome, who reinforce their anti-school tendencies
> together. Tracey and Carol the most outspoken ones, Linda
> inclined to be giggly. Tracey's influence weighed on Linda, for
> example, when pressed for her reaction to school and said 'It's
> all right', in a non-committal way. Tracey gently leered in
> mock disbelief. What is the truth? Was Linda saying that
> because a) it was a compromise, perceived as the required sort
> of answer, b) that was how she really felt, or c) she really felt
> nothing at all and that was what the answer meant? (Woods,
> 1979)

I shall say more about 'how do we know they are telling the truth' shortly, but the immediate reaction to the situation above is to make a note of it. In interpretative work there are no absolute meanings detached from any social context, so we need to know something about that context to make sense of the meanings expressed in them. We also need to see and speak to people in a range of contexts if we wish to discover their views in their full roundness as human beings. Thus, in the case above, I would make a point of talking to Linda again some time without Tracey being in attendance.

Pollard (1985a, p. 227) carried this group technique a stage further, employing some of his junior school pupils to collect data on other pupils. Certain children who were:

Amenable to participation in the study, ... reflected the range
of types and groups (and who) were fairly popular within those
groups (were) invited to form a dinner-time interviewing team
to help me, as I put it, 'find out what all the children think
about school.' The 'Moorside Investigation Department'
interviewed fellow-pupils with considerable enthusiasm,
projected a sense of secrecy and played up the principles of
confidentiality and immunity. (p. 228)

Apart from material they collected, they were very informative
themselves, now, of course, being co-research workers. Eventually,
Pollard felt able to join these interviews at a suitable point after
the 'MID' had established stage three access. By this technique, he
felt he managed to play down the symbolic significance of his
teacher role and establish trust and a feeling of security.

It is possible to ring the changes on 'group' techniques. Delamont (1984, p. 27), for example, invited groups of girls back to her
flat during the holidays, where they 'sat reading magazines while I
interviewed them one at a time in a separate room'. This gave her
'an unobtrusive measure of their sociometric structure', and presumably helped put them at their ease.

With this requirement – the need to develop relationships and
trust, and to penetrate several layers of access – there is obviously
a need to conceive of interviews taking place continually over a
lengthy period of time. And, rather like the interest rates in some
savings' accounts, the initial investment may not make an early
high yield but more (and better quality) data will come in the later
stages if the market runs its normal course. By this stage, one may
not be asking questions at all, data coming through normal interaction. In fact, Ball (1984) prefers to regard this not simply as
'interviewing' but as 'interactive research'.

Some indication of this is given in the following example.

When I worked on the pupil research I was married, but had
no children, and I had kept my own maiden name. After a
year's quiet questioning the pupils finally established all of this.
Knowing the full picture, and knowing me, provoked an
outburst of real anger from many of the girls. The ferocity of
their outburst shocked me at the time and I still remember it
very clearly. They accused me of being very selfish,
unreasonably self-centred and uncaring, and somehow wrong
not to have a child. Children it seemed were for them a dream,
a symbol of what they wanted out of life. One of the themes I
was interested in was gender codes, and the ways they are laid

down at this age and stage. This all represented very useful
data, about what they considered 'properly feminine' behaviour
to be. I would suggest that I could not have got such data so
easily by questioning. (Measor, 1985, p. 25)

At this stage of the research, the encounter is itself part of the
research – an incident to be embodied within the data rather than
an instrument designed to discover it. It thus becomes 'participant
observation', and the researcher can derive all the benefits, including affective reactions, that go with that. I was able to appreciate
pupils' contrasting experiences of fun and boredom in this way.
Once I had realized that 'having a laugh' was so important to them,
and came to focus on it more in a particular series of interviews,
some of our discussions took on a life of their own. They became
'laughs' in their own right, possibly more than the original incident
generated.

> *Tracy:* Dianne fell off a chair first and as she went to get up,
> she got 'old of me skirt, she was 'aving a muck about, and
> there was I in me petticoat, me skirt came down round my
> ankles and Mr Bridge came in (*great screams of laughter from
> girls*). He'd been standing outside the door.
> *Kate:* 'E told her she'd get suspended.
> *Tracy:* He 'ad me mum up the school, telling her what a
> horrible child I was.
> *Kate:* 'Nobody will marry you,' said Miss Judge.
> *Tracy:* 'Oh yeah, Miss Judge sits there, 'n, nobody will want
> to marry *you*, Jones,' she said. I said, 'Well you ain't married,
> anyway.' (*Shrieks of laughter from girls.*)
>
> (Woods, 1979, p. 103)

Interviewing techniques

What one actually *does* during interviews follows from the principles discussed above. At the beginning, as we have seen, it is necessary to establish rapport and put people at their ease. This means
starting off gently, and not asking intimate or intimidating questions. There may be a lot of civil pleasantries, and an extra agreeable presentation of self. Lynda finds herself smiling a lot in these
early stages. Bill Greer (1983) does an 'incompetent' routine, drop-
ping pen and papers, not being able to find his glasses, at the same
time as he is being expansive and understanding. This at least
shows that he is human, and not some coldly scientific bureaucrat.

It is important to note that they *find* themselves behaving like this – it is a logical consequence of the approach. Too studied a presentation can lead to suspicions that one is a fake – the exact obverse of what one is aiming for (Miller, 1952).

However, in some ways one has to cultivate attitudes and dispositions one does not normally possess, for one needs to empathize with the interviewee, and this means, for the moment at least, speaking their language, appreciating their arguments and appearing to take their side. This, however, is done in a certain way that stops a long way short of full identification. As one interviewer notes:

> To establish this sort of neutrality calls for rigorous intellectual discipline. I had to put myself into a frame of mind where I felt as my informants might; I practised getting indignant, for instance, at the 'callousness' of a friend in the State Department who did not seem to care about the coal miners thrown out of work by Venezuelan oil ... Then I could use terms like 'cheap labor', 'Buy American', etc. meaningfully and sincerely, having some idea of what they meant emotionally to those being interviewed. In the same way, actors have to 'throw themselves into' a part; it is not sufficient merely to repeat lines. (Dexter, 1956, pp. 156-7)

This is not to say, of course, that one should 'go native', but rather, for the purpose of high-quality data collection and ultimate better understanding, one should momentarily participate in whatever role the interviewee had in normal life. This empathy can be shown in many ways – appropriate nods, shakes of the head, smiles, gasps of astonishment, grimaces, encouraging or knowing grunts, interjectory expressions. It also involves not being offended or appearing to make a moral judgment or giving advice (Whyte, 1982). To do all this requires a considerable knowledge and understanding of the interviewee's social world before the interview (Porter, 1984).

There may be a problem where there are conflicting groups within the same institution, with all of whom you need to empathize. One's credibility as a bona fide human being may really be put to the test. However, of course one does not actually take part in any of the action, or contribute towards the thinking behind it, that results in conflict, and if put on the spot by direct questioning as to 'Whose side are you on?', the answer can only be, from the point of view of the research, 'Everybody's.'

Though these interviews are often termed 'unstructured', they are not completely so. There will be themes in and aspects of the subject of the research that are self-evident, and that you will wish to cover. The interviewee also is going to need *some* guidance as to what to talk about. I find it useful, therefore, to have a 'prompt' card, to ensure that I cover all these aspects (see also Burgess, 1984c). For example, if I were interviewing a teacher about a particular teaching method, I would want to know why it had been adopted, the teacher's account of how it was practised (to be supported by observation), and of its strengths and weaknesses, how it compared with other methods, how others' views on it were perceived, and what were the results. If I were interviewing following observation, there would no doubt be points of detail to be put ('Why did you do that?' 'What did you think when that pupil?' 'What would you have done if . . .?'). The latter type of questioning is seeking clarification and extension. The former is more of an 'enabling framework', loose, open-ended, and flexible. Alternative frameworks may occur as the interview proceeds, suggested by responses. The original is not lost, but aspects that are important to the interviewee only become apparent when they speak, and they may, in fact, absorb the original check-list. Thus, a teacher speaking about teaching methods may refer immediately to the requirements of examinations, parental pressure and resources. This would prompt in my mind a wish to know what difference a change in these areas would make, and this would account for 'Why the teacher used that method in that particular way', and 'What were the perceived alternatives?' In this way, the interviewees, ideally, come to provide the structure in their own terms, in their own order, and in their own time. One's own prompt card then represents a check, and a fall-back position.

At times, however, being too non-directive can cause anxieties (Whyte, 1982), and it may be necessary to provide some guidance. Some interviewees may not be very articulate, others may be too voluble. Again, where one has succeeded in establishing strong rapport, the interviewee may be very concerned to know if the researcher is getting what is needed, punctuating comments with 'I'm not sure if this is what you want', 'I don't know if this is any use to you.' Guidance should relate to the framework of the interview rather than to the content. It may be that one part of one's 'frame' that comes later on the card sparks off a rich chain of thought, where the others failed to do so. The elaboration may then take in the earlier areas in this new light. It is sometimes difficult to distinguish between the two, and some 'pilot' practice, and listening to oneself on tape, may be necessary to identify the 'leading question', which at all times one tries to avoid.

Interviewers try to cultivate the art of listening. This is not just a matter of hearing and recording. It involves 'looking as if you are listening', with slightly exaggerated body language and attention to eye contact. It was said of James Cameron that he was a good listener, and 'could project an almost tangible aura of interest, approval and affirmation as he listened, and this was the case even when he disagreed' (*Guardian*, 1985). There is a way of being 'interestedly quiet', with a smile, an understanding shake or nod of the head, a slight look of astonishment, a 'tut, tut', a 'What can you do about it' look, or 'Isn't that always the way?' (see Measor, 1985; Burgess, 1982b). Sometimes extra help, understanding and encouragement may have to be given during interviews that informants, for one reason or another, find difficult, as, for example, with some of our teachers describing critical incidents in their careers:

Mr Tucks: I hesitate to repeat it, I can't, I don't know what . . . you know . . . it's difficult to repeat it . . . don't like it . . .

Here, Lynda, by *gentle* pressure ('Do you want to talk about it or not?', filling in hesitations by a sentence in an understanding tone – 'That was in your first term?', aligning sympathies with the informant – 'He just came in and interrupted your lesson?', and generally supportive 'Umms' and 'Ahs') secured the tale (Sikes, Measor and Woods, 1985). Imagine the converse – if somebody yawns, and directs their gaze elsewhere while you are speaking to them. The compassionate, understanding, interested persona may come naturally to some. Others may have to work at it. It contrasts strongly with the forthright, abrasive, aggressive stance taken by many political journalists – but, again, that kind of persona is formed to match that particular arena.

Interviews also involve observation – chiefly, looking for signs for development, for cues as to scales of priority in the interviewee's perspective, and for anything that appears 'strange' – the same kinds of things one looks for during other types of observation. These will be indicators for what to focus upon in later interviews.

There are ways of assisting the interviewee once a discussion has begun, mainly in the interests of accuracy and completeness. Here are some of them.

(1) Check on apparent contradictions, *non sequiturs*, imbalance, implausibility, exaggerations, or inconsistencies ('Yes, but didn't you say a moment ago . . .?' 'How can that be so if . . .' 'Is it *really*?' 'Does it necessarily follow that . . .?' 'Why?' 'Why not?' 'What was the point of that?').

79

(2) Search for opinions ('What do you think of that?' 'Do you believe that?').

(3) Ask for clarification ('What do you mean by ...?' 'Can you say a little more about ...?' 'In what sort of way?' 'Can you give me some examples?').

(4) Ask for explanations, pose alternatives ('Couldn't one also say ...?').

(5) Seek a comparison, in the interests of finer understanding ('How does that relate to the policy, argument, description, etc., of ...?' 'Some others have said that ...').

(6) Pursue the logic of an argument ('Does it follow, then, that ...?' 'Presumably ...?').

(7) Ask for further information where there appear to be holes in the account ('What about ...?' 'Does that apply to ...?').

(8) Aim for comprehensiveness ('Have you any other ...?' 'Do you all feel like that ...?' 'Have you anything more to say on that?').

(9) Put things in a different way ('Would it be fair to say that ...?' 'Do you mean ...?' 'In other words ...?').

(10) Express incredulity or astonishment ('In the *fourth* year?' 'And does this apply to the fifth as well?' 'Really').

(11) Summarize occasionally, and ask for corroboration ('So, ...' 'What you're saying is ...?' 'Would that be correct?').

(12) Ask hypothetical questions ('Yes, but what if ...?' 'Supposing ...?').

(13) Play 'devil's advocate' ('An opposing argument might run ...' 'What would you say to the criticism that ...?').

Of course there are ways of making these comments that blend in with the spirit of the exercise, and that make them seem a natural part of the interaction. One may put up a pretence of not having heard, or not fully understood, of disbelief or surprise – the reactions of an ordinary person, rather than a calculating scientist. One may ask a question in different ways. One may wish to employ some of the interviewee's key terms and phraseology, to indicate a basic appreciation. Much, too, will depend upon the character of the person being interviewed. While in general, the polite and gentle (though not fawning and mincing) approach would seem indicated, some might welcome more aggression. This can be ascertained only after a number of meetings.

Recording interviews

As interviewing may be compared in some respects with participant observation, so making a record is rather like field notes. A tape-recorder can obviously be a great boon, but only if its use is 'unobtrusive'. There is no other way of recapturing the fullness and faithfulness of words and idiom, and it does release the interviewer from one difficult task, allowing concentration on others. So, as long as it does not threaten to impede the flow of, or distort, conversation, its use should be strongly considered. Where people are dubious about its use, some negotiation may be needed – for example, the interviewee's ownership of the data on the tapes being made clear. However, as we saw in chapter 2, care must be taken about where and when even to introduce the topic, let alone asking permission to use it.

To some extent we have been spoilt by mechanical aids, and forgotten our own tricks of memory and idiosyncratic shorthand, but these need to be cultivated, for some times the aids do not work, or cannot be used. Often, too, some key information is imparted when the recorder is switched off, in the relaxation and general chit-chat that precedes or follows sessions – golden moments for hard truths and shared confidences. Sometimes, interviewees will request that the machine be turned off, so that they can convey some confidence that they do not wish to have recorded.

While tape-recording, and sharing in the conversation, the researcher may also need to take notes. These are rather like the rough notes made during ethnographic fieldwork, when one is being assailed with a torrent of data. The cryptic jottings made at the time are sufficient to stir the memory later, when one can record the full data or impression at length. The tape-recorder may capture what is said, but it cannot capture fleeting thoughts and impressions, as something the teacher says prompts first this thought then that – the second invariably displacing the first from memory. The briefest of notes can aid recall. It is also difficult to keep in mind all the points on which you wish the informant to elaborate later – the torrent of words crowds them out. An *aide-mémoire* thus becomes indispensable.

As in observation, field notes are necessary. A log is needed of how the data was collected, and details of time and place. The researcher should record impressions of the interviewee's disposition, attitude towards the research and to the researcher generally. And, immediately after a conversation, impressions of it should be noted – doubts, evasions, sensitive areas, strong points, and so forth (Denzin, 1970). These constitute a continual form of disciplining for the researcher, as well as an essential framework for full understanding of the data.

There is one other aspect of field notes, relating to transcripts. The task of transcribing hours and hours of tape is a formidable one (unless one has the luxury of a pool of audio-typists), and almost inevitably slow. Yet the researcher needs a quick turn-round to sustain momentum. It may be necessary, therefore, to transcribe in two stages. The first stage involves listening to the tape as soon as possible after a conversation, making an index of its contents, and picking out those points for correction or guidance as mentioned above. Some particularly telling points may be transcribed then and there. The index stands as a record of the conversation and a guide to memory during the lengthy period the tape is likely to be away while being fully transcribed, or shelved, depending on the researcher doing it. During the first stage it is worth considering whether the *whole* conversation actually needs transcribing. Much time all round might be saved if some initial selecting can be done. The principles governing this will be discussed in chapter 6.

Without doubt these are best transcribed by the interviewer, however tedious a task it may seem. Audio-typists will type what they hear. The interviewer will be able to fill in tone, mood, looks, hesitations, etc., which may be essential to the understanding of the piece. For example, the style of delivery below was clearly essential to the understanding of what was being said – the description of a critical incident in the life of a teacher.

> We had some difficulty in transcribing Mr Quilley's account
> from the tape. The problem was in getting down what he had
> said. This appeared to be because he had increased the pace of
> delivery of his sentences, which were shortened and forceful,
> piling them up in a staccato fashion. This style of talking,
> which is difficult to represent in print, emphasized the drama of
> his narrative. (Sikes, Measor and Woods, 1985, p. 60)

A useful compromise would be to have tapes transcribed by a good audio-typist (a bad, or incomplete copy can be counter-productive, and a waste of resources) where possible (a question not only of resource and availability but also of the intelligibility of the tape), and for the researcher then to go through the tape, adding comments in a column alongside the transcript.

The following comment, perhaps, sums it up.

> Yesterday I came home from an initial meeting with a teacher
> to discover that I'd omitted to switch on the mike. My first

reaction was horror, then irritation, then I sat down and wrote concentratedly for ninety minutes. I'm quite pleased that I seem to have remembered everything. Admittedly this was an interview to collect career outline so I was aided by the progressive, factual nature of what had been said.

Even so I think that my attitudes have changed slightly. Before, I was totally against not using a tape-recorder; now, although I'd always use one unless absolutely impossible, I concede that judicious note taking at the time of the encounter could be sufficient. One good point is that you don't have to listen to lots of digressions – though digressions may be significant.

On the whole making a recording does obviate the panic of remembering – and we'll never really know how accurate Mayhew was anyway. (Pat Sikes, personal communication)

The validation of accounts

One major question running through all this kind of interviewing is 'How do we know the informant is telling the truth?' (Dean and Whyte, 1969). Is not this sort of material impressionistic, subjective, biased and idiosyncratic? In answer, first we might reaffirm the aim to discover people's innermost thoughts and the considerable pains taken to do this, and to try to ensure that that is what we eventually do get represented. We have given above some idea of the rigour designed to try to achieve this. In addition, the researcher will be alerted to possible influences operating on informants – ulterior motives, the desire to please, situational factors like a recent traumatic incident (for example, a disruptive incident), values, etc. – all of which may colour their judgments (Whyte, 1982); will be on the watch for signals – too emotional an account, too rosy a picture, unusual reactions; and may seek to concentrate on certain problem areas, or return to them in later interviews. Distortion may creep into accounts unconsciously through selective perception of the facts. We interpret the past through our current mental frameworks, and invariably those facts become somewhat warped. There are several checks available here. The account, itself, when obtained by the techniques above, will have a certain plausibility/implausibility. We may have some idea of the reliability of the informant, and we may know something about the mental set through which the material has been processed. However, above all, we should

83

not rely on one account, but should seek further meetings with the same person, to sample fully their views over a number of situations and at different times, and we should also seek meetings with others, where we will be able to cross-check accounts – a technique well used in law courts.

Consider the following field notes on a talk with a teacher.

Pd 1 Talk with A.H. about P.S., W.M. and H.M.

Interesting thing about this chat was how A.H. imputed his values on to H.M. e.g. 'you can never win an argument with him' (and I've noticed this about A.H., as has T.J.!) He'll never back down, whereas S.P. will, he'll think eventually, 'Oh I'm not going to win this one, it'll suit me better – make an easier passage if I give way' (N.B. a *bad* motive attributed – not *acceptance* of A.H.'s argument) – 'H.M. will never give way. He's also *gutless* – will make a great show, lot of noise and splutter but weak as dishwater inside. For example, a cricket ball came to him yesterday along the ground, and he got out of the way! Whereas a little bespectacled lad, a third of his size was busting a gut to stop it!' A.H. slippered him the other day (for someone else), and he argued, saying 'I wasn't the only one!' A.H. continued, 'I know you weren't the only one?' (H.M. was aghast at this, he expected a different retort.) A.H.'s argument was 'I didn't give him the old story about "this hurting me more than it hurts you". I said "come on, it's a fair cop (that's what he expected of H.M.) take your punishment, then it's over. I'm not going to carry on about it".' A.H. interprets H.M.'s protestations as *cowardice*. I posited an alternative explanation of his attitude reflecting the values of his culture, which regards all authority and establishment men with suspicion and requires a constantly vigilant, and aggressive attitude towards them with a touch of 'never surrender' except at the ultimate demand. But this argument was laughed out of court.

This discussion suggested more to me about the teacher than the pupil he was commenting on. It indicates his commitment and values as a teacher, and something, too, of his mental frameworks, for example, that 'You can never win an argument with him.' I was alerted to this, not only from my own experiences, but from 'T.J.', mentioned early in the example. In one of our many detailed discussions, for example, T.J. noted that A.H. was 'aggressive, and must score points to preserve his ego'. As the year tutor, T.J. had always, as a matter of policy, to let A.H. have his say and give him credit for whatever was resolved ('As you suggested ...'). Others also noted this quality about A.H.

This indicates another of the benefits of having *key* informants. As noted in chapter 3 these are people, with whom, over the course of the research, one comes to form an especially close relationship. They identify with you and the research objectives to such an extent that they almost become research assistants (Lacey, 1976). The classic example is 'Doc' in Whyte's *Street Corner Society*:

> That's right. You tell me what you want to see, and we'll arrange it. When you want some information, I'll ask for it, and you listen. When you want to find out their philosophy of life, I'll start an argument and get it for you. If there's something else you want to get, I'll stage an act for you. Not a scrap you know, but just tell me what you want, and I'll get it for you. (Whyte, 1955, p. 292)

Key informants help give perspective to the entire methodological front. They can be a source of vast amounts of information, in a sense being proxy participant observers in areas inaccessible to the researcher. They can help identify the nature of other people's talk and behaviour. One instance of this arises from the distinction between educationist and teacher talk (Keddie, 1971). It is not surprising that in some contexts there is a big difference between what teachers say they do and what they do. In a different context, they might say things that accord more with that performance. The gap will be wider if one does not progress beyond the first two levels of access, and it might be difficult to spot if there were no informants. Similarly, key informants can alert us to alternative explanations of the talk and behaviour of others that we perhaps have no other means of knowing about, so that we can get a grip on the various rhetorics presented to us, and a knowledge of how consciously and seriously they are held. On the important temporal dimension, also, informants provide a sense of history, interpreting present events as part of a long, ongoing process.

Of course there may be forms of bias within our key informants. The usual safeguards apply to them, but also it helps to have various kinds of informants. The more they constitute a cross-section of the population in question, the easier we might feel about the danger of bias. For example, in one study I was lucky in being able to forge close ties not only with an older reformist left-wing teacher and a young libertarian beginner, but also with a traditional-conservative head of department, and a traditional-liberal teacher. Their accounts agreed on some matters, disagreed

on others. Between them they enabled, I felt, fairly accurate appraisals to be made (for further discussion of key informants, see
Burgess, 1985b).

If we manage to get all this right, we may still somehow ourselves
influence the results through *our* perceptions and interpretations.
Faulty note-taking or transcription may omit some key points or
otherwise colour the data. There is much to be said here for 'respondent validation', that is, returning the processed account to
the informant for appraisal. There are two levels at which this
might prove useful. Firstly, in checking the accuracy of the data.
Have you got the report of that event straight? Are certain impressions fairly represented? Have all relevant points been taken into
account? Secondly, on any interpretation or explanation, the informant may have some useful comments to make.

I thus found it helpful to feed back papers summarizing aspects
of my research to the Lowfield staff (Woods, 1979). This proved a
useful check on the data given therein (largely corroborated), gave
rise to interesting discussions on the interpretations (not all agreed
with my views, which led me to re-examine my argument and
modify it in parts while strengthening it in others), and in some
instances led to new developments in the research.

It is not always necessary, possible, or indeed desirable to take
things this far. The points made at the beginning of chapter 2 about
'getting in the right frame of mind' for the research can hardly be
expected of one's subjects or school staffs. They will tend to interpret matters, therefore, from perspectives deeply influenced by their
positions within the school. Scarth (1985, pp. 78-9) reports a response of a 'working party' of seven of the teachers in the school
of his research to two draft chapters on timetabling and examinations.

> The first discussion which focused on timetabling was reduced
> to the Deputy Head responsible for timetabling defending the
> arrangements and trying to identify staff members from their
> reported comments. The teachers, for their part, were put in
> the position of being either 'for' the school timetable or
> 'against' it. This polarization of viewpoints was even more
> marked during the second seminar on examinations and
> discussion frequently centred on personalities rather than
> issues. As a result, I was put in the position of, on the one
> hand of being asked to name the respondents, and on the
> other, of defending staff members' criticisms of the Head and
> Deputy Head. I did not feel in a position to do either; I

couldn't reveal confidential data and I wished to avoid being personally associated with teachers' comments cited in the text. I tried to direct discussion away from simply focusing on personalities by highlighting some of the general patterns across both departments and subjects. Unfortunately the general feeling at the end of the second seminar was such that future meetings were cancelled.

Thus one may risk, on occasions, giving offence, being misinterpreted, or having one's material used for different purposes; and it would never do, of course, to betray any confidences. However some respondent validation is useful (see Ball, 1984, pp. 83-9). Again it is a matter of judgment when, how, and with whom it is used.

The major means, however, of validating accounts, and observation, and indeed anything else in ethnographic work is through 'triangulation'. Triangles possess enormous strength. Among other things, they make the basic frames of bicycles, gates, and house roofs. Triangulation enables extraordinary precision over phenomenal distances in astronomy. Similarly, in social scientific research, the use of three or more different methods or bearings to explore an issue greatly increases the chances of accuracy. For example, we might interview a head teacher with regard to policy concerning new intakes of pupils. His view of that policy would be interesting, but it would be far more interesting, and we should have a much better idea of its accuracy, comprehensiveness, strengths and weaknesses, and actual part in the process, if we had the benefit of other vantage points, for example the various meetings that are held with parents, pupils and teachers, the views of people in these groups, as well as observing aspects of the policy in action.

Another form of triangulation when one wishes to study a teacher's performance in a particular lesson would be:

(1) to discuss with the teacher, beforehand, what was planned for the lesson;
(2) to observe the lesson as it happened; and
(3) to discuss with the teacher afterwards what had happened and why, if aims had been modified and how far achieved, etc.

One form of this was practised by Hargreaves *et al.* (1975) in their study of the structure of common-sense thinking about rules in school. Since most of these are implicit, rarely articulated, or even thought about, they had to take care not to 'impose a structure that would misrepresent and distort it rather than explicate it' (p. 45). They accordingly used a variety of methods over a lengthy period of participation, including asking teachers and pupils about rules, observing lessons and asking teachers to make a commentary on events or verbal statements that had occurred during the lesson. These commentaries were then, in turn, analysed. In yet another form, Elliott and Adelman (1975) propose that role-partners, such as teachers, pupils and researchers can cross-check each others' accounts to expose discrepancies and inconsistencies. Similarly, the group of key informants mentioned above provided alternative powerful viewpoints bearing on the same incident or matter.

Lynda Measor gives another illustration.

What is happening is that I'm getting data about Teacher A from Teacher B or from other person C. This then informs my next set of questions at the next interview. For example, I interviewed D.R. Then I got information about him via the Labour Party and from another teacher. This changed my view of the man somewhat, or to be more accurate, it led me to consider another view of the man, and it led me into a different sort of question with him to get more data on those areas of his personality and attitudes. It also leads into theoretical issues, like the fact that he must have exceptional role distance qualities. The man in the interview was so very different from the man I've been told about. (Personal communication)

Undoubtedly, the strongest bond is when interviews are accompanied by observation. In chapter 3, I gave an example of observation of a games' period, where one of the main organizing principles of the pupils' experience appeared to be the fear of being 'shown up'. This was repeated (voluntarily), and explained at greater length in interviews, where we were able to explore the nature of the experience, when it occurred, whom it concerned – in other words, thoroughly 'saturating' the concept until no new information was coming in on it (Glaser and Strauss, 1967). At the same time, I was observing lessons, and other areas of the pupils' day, and made particular note of any such incidents. This put me in a stronger position, not only to delineate them accurately, but also to assess the pupils' accounts for bias, exaggeration and misrepresentation. In other words, it gave me a vantage point from which to view those accounts and to consider what they were 'doing' for the pupils – how far, for example, they were 'letting off steam' or 'getting back at the teachers', or even, perhaps, just 'playing me up' or 'trying it on'.

The two methods combined also permit a fuller participation. During pupil discussions, for example, another dominant experience I was cued in to was 'being bored'. Time and again they described their boredom, putting great feeling, at times, into their expressions. 'It's so *boring*, here!' 'Those lessons were such a drag, what a bore!' I came to realize that the term is actually onomatopoeic: 'It's so bo-or-or-ing!' delivered with all the pent-up pain and frustration accumulated over a lengthy period. Though I had less reason to hold the veracity of this part of their accounts in suspension, I still would not have fully appreciated the point without actually observing some of the circumstances particularly conducive to the experience. In these lessons, with the teacher talking for hour-long stretches in a dull monotone, with very little pupil participation, some would occasionally turn to me (sitting at the back of the class) with the same pained expression on their faces, and I knew exactly how they felt. Observation, then, grounds the experience in a real-life event.

The special character of interviews in ethnography should now be clear. Through 'interactive research' one aims to penetrate the experiences of others, empathize with others, become like them, look out at the world with them, speak and look like them, share with them. We might say that they are all the stronger as a research tool where used in conjunction with other methods, especially observation, but while this is true, the main point about ethnographic interviews is that they are themselves a form of participant observation.

Chapter 5

Written materials

Useful support to observation and interview is given through the judicious use of written or printed materials. Again, these are in the main best viewed as quasi-observational instruments, standing in for researchers in places and at times they find difficult or impossible to be present at personally, and as part of a range of methods that might be employed, as a follow-up or as a precursor to others. They can, however, at times provide the main body of data.

The most widely used of these are official documents, personal documents, and questionnaires.

Official documents

These include registers, timetables, minutes of meetings, planning papers, lesson plans and notes, confidential documents on pupils, school handbooks, newspapers and journals, school records, files and statistics, notice boards, exhibitions, official letters, textbooks, exercise books, examination papers, work cards, blackboard work, photographs. Few qualitative studies would take no account of some of these at least. However the qualitative approach to them is quite distinctive, for while they might in themselves convey useful information, they always have to be contextualized within the circumstances of their construction.

Take, for example, registers, delinquency rates and examination passes. These all provided key data in the work of Reynolds (1976). He was able to make comparisons between nine secondary schools over a seven-year period in attendance and delinquency rates (defined as 'being found guilty before a court or officially cautioned by the age of fifteen'), and academic attainment. On the basis of these he constructed an 'order of merit', and then investigated processes within the schools (such as teacher perspectives, school rules and how they were enforced, general school ethos) associated with good and bad performances on these criteria.

However, the basic data do not present an absolute truth. For example, with regard to pupil attendance, there appears to be a certain amount of 'concealed' absence, with such devices as pupils arranging for others to answer for them, attending for registration and then going missing, or taking time out for periods in the course of the day (Wright, 1977). Only observation and interviews of the type discussed in chapters 3 and 4 could establish this, but *with* them the registers make a powerful combination of methods if they accord, and point to an interesting problem that demands attention if there is a discrepancy.

Similarly, delinquency rates are notoriously unreliable. As Reynolds (1976, p. 221) recognized:

> It is easy to see how a school with a high delinquency rate may
> get a bad name with the local police, who may in turn patrol
> its catchment area more intensively and be more likely to
> 'book' offenders in that area rather than use their powers of
> discretion to warn them.

There are also, over a period of time, changes in the law, changes in society which bring about redefinitions of crimes, and possibly changes in attitude of police and public. One example in the criminal statistics is the reduction in the number of 'sex crimes' following changes in the law regarding homosexuality. Again, an apparent increase in, for example, drug-taking *may* be a consequence of increased police vigilance and rates of detection (Young, 1971).

School records on disruption are unlikely to be complete. The greatest manifestation of a teacher's competence is the ability to control (Denscombe, 1980). Individual teachers within the autonomy of their classroom do not wish to be seen as incompetent, so, for many, referral is a last resort. Similarly, headteachers do not wish their schools to be seen as particularly disruptive. Somehow, such incidents and records reflect back on the staff, so reports may be modified.

Punishment books may not reflect all the punishment that has been administered. Tweaks of the ear, slaps of the face, rulerings of the fingers, assaults with missiles (such as books or pieces of chalk), bangings of heads together and all manner of verbal and social punishment do not get recorded. Much of this is deliberately concealed. One experienced teacher told me once that 'You must hit them where they don't bruise.'

The 'how' of punishment is also usually omitted. The '3 strokes of the cane administered to Stephen Winters by Mr Gordon for persistently and deliberately refusing to bring his games' kit' omits to say that the boy had to be held down, shouting and struggling, by three other teachers while the punishment was carried out. The '6 strokes of the cane administered to Richard Garbutt for personal abuse of a teacher' does not say that this was a vicious, revenge assault by the teacher involved; nor does it give any details about the circumstances of the 'abuse'. I was a witness to both of these incidents, so that I know that behind the bald statements of fact lay considerable historical detail (as well as profound moral questions about pupils' and teachers' rights that may have altered our perception of those facts) and showed an urgent need to explain how matters had arrived at that point. The 'punishment book', therefore, stands as part of a process, rather than as a commentary upon it. It gives some of the facts – the official version – but not others.

The same has to be said for any facts, evidence and statistics that are produced. The most notorious misleading presentation is perhaps in the area of examination results. While many schools and teachers do this fairly, some have been known to represent them in a misleadingly favourable light. The most common way used to be to give them as a percentage of those entered, having made sure that those entered had a good chance of passing and having omitted borderline and other dubious candidates. Even the sacrosanct timetable hides individual teachers' adaptations, of, for example, how an arts teacher copes with a four-period block of lessons necessitated through being set against practical subjects, or how a teacher distributes commitment and energies, as well as syllabus, across a week's lessons. Official minutes of meetings may be heavily biased, depending on who wrote them and the group concerned. But all these, of course, have a value as the picture those with power in the institution choose to present.

This indicates another use for documentary materials – as providing useful ways in to more detailed qualitative work. One may wish to explore how some of the above items are constructed and interpreted. On a more limited front, notice boards give a good indication of news, forthcoming events, relationships and rules. Again, they are part of the situation. The week's duty roster and the day's substitution lessons have little meaning divorced from the intentions of the compilers (adequate coverage of lessons and duties? fairness? victimization or diminishing the status of particular people?), and their reception (acceptance? anger? anxiety? resignation?). Similarly a gradual increase in notices around a school may indicate greater efficiency, an unwarranted growth in bureaucracy, or, perhaps, a deputy head's desire to impress in the light of a forthcoming headteacher vacancy.

Is the fact that these matters are transacted by notices, rather than verbally, significant? Sometimes they are the most convenient and economical way of conveying information and instructions. Sometimes they are a useful political and bureaucratic tool. A head's letter to the parents of a troublesome child carries an authoritative weight unleavened by the sympathetic cushioning that usually goes into face-to-face encounters. Notes sent round a year's subject teachers by a head of year establish an official formality to the presentation of the task, establish a record of it, satisfy the demands of accountability, and help legitimate and institutionalize the status of the position *vis-à-vis* the recipients. The same was true, I suspect, of an attempt by some radical teachers in a traditional school of my acquaintance to establish a school council. The documentation, with formal agendas and minutes, helped to legitimate it.

Just as documents can lend weight to something, they can also be used to *appear* to give weight to something. Hunter (1980), in a study of 'participation', monitored its working over a spate of vandalism in the school. The school council, though, was 'dominated by the Head of School'. The headmaster wrote up a 'Hansard' report of the meeting and 'Notes for Form Tutors' to discuss the meeting with their groups. They were asked to report back. Hunter was allowed to see the replies and:

> Inadvertently left them in my desk and four weeks later
> returned them with profuse apologies. They had not been
> missed ... I was forced to conclude that the whole exercise was
> a tokenist form of participation, used to present to the pupils
> the views of the Headmaster and some staff, and attempting to
> isolate the 'vandals' in the school. (Hunter, 1980, p. 222)

The report, notes and comments, then, were a 'front', disguising authoritarian control.

The art teacher at Lowfield indicated another kind of 'front' (Woods, 1979). He claimed that his subject was seen by the headteacher primarily as a means of showing the school to good effect to the public. Approved pictures were hung in prominent places. Disapproved ones (such as one of a bare-chested Tarzan) were ordered removed from the walls.

All of these documents provide useful pegs on which to hang further, more detailed, work. One can check on news items with one's informants; arrange to attend meetings, or ask a key informant to monitor those you are unable or not allowed to attend; follow up untoward reactions (Why were you so surprised? angry?); fill out one's knowledge and understanding of the rules (Why are there such elaborate rules about the coffee machine and its use?); search for patterns in what is on display, and try them out on teachers and/or pupils to see if you have detected any dominant themes or ongoing trends. This last is equivalent to analysing material that is jointly available to you and others, and asking for their 'respondent validation'. Equally, they may try out their analyses on you ('Have you noticed how all the notices in this place say "Do this! Do that!" with never a hint of please?' 'All the photographs, pictures, decorations around the school must accord with the basic authoritarian–paternalistic philosophy' 'Why over a period of a month have some teachers lost twice as many free periods as others?' 'When it's something to his credit, he makes a big song and dance about it – notices everywhere. When it's a failure, you never hear about it except by accident.') So, collections of documents can hold the key to analysis of whole areas of social interaction.

Sometimes a need for documentation follows the use of some other method. Lacey (1976, p. 60) in a methodological commentary on his Hightown Grammar (1970) research said that while his core method was participant observation and observation, 'the most important breakthrough for me was the combining of methods', which included a key use of documents:

> The observation and description of classrooms led quickly to a
> need for more exact information about individuals within the
> class. I used school documents to produce a ledger of
> information on each boy, for example, address, father's
> occupation, previous school, academic record, and so on. I
> built on this record as more information became available from
> questionnaires. (See also Meyenn, 1980; Player, 1984)

Similarly, in the construction of life histories, official documents relating to certain episodes can be a useful spur to memory and an aid to validity. For accounts of meetings, though one's major interest may be how they fit into a particular individual's experience, one could do with the agreed official minutes, if only as an alternative triangulating view of the individual's account.

Documents can help reconstruct events, and give information

about social relationships. In these ways Burgess (1984c, p. 136) found official letters 'indispensable' in the course of his study. There were 'letters between the Headmaster and external groups such as the governors and local education authority officials, letters from teachers to parents and parents to teachers, together with notes that took the form of letters for internal circulation among teachers'. He gives the example of letters from the Headmaster on a boy's suspension.

> To the parents the emphasis was upon the boy's
> misdemeanours and how he was to be excluded from the school
> until they had come to discuss his future with the Head. To the
> chairman of the governors there was a formal statement
> followed by a remark that indicated that teachers had
> persevered with the boy, while to the director of education the
> same letter ended with a note saying that the boy might have
> to be permanently removed from the school at a later date
> unless further support through the social services and
> additional teaching staff was given to the school.

These indicate the different relationships involved, and, with other documents and methods, can help build up a rounded picture of the event. Burgess rightly draws attention to questions concerning one's right to use such documents, to the kinds of selection and sampling problems discussed here in chapter 3, to questions of authenticity and distortion, and to the need to view them in context, with the support of other methods.

Sometimes documents form an essential, perhaps the most important component of a school process. This is particularly the case in communications with parents, such as the letters and notices that go out when a child is about to begin at the school. These, backed by visits to the school (which not all parents attend) and the headteacher's address, give a good indication of the kind of school ethos they wish to cultivate. It all may be slightly larger than life, rather like the myths that pupils put out about going to the new school (Measor and Woods, 1984), but it may be essential to have this ideal official view as the baseline comparative element in one's research. School handbooks, for example, clearly set out a school's aims and rules, and provide a yardstick for estimating what constitutes normality, and what deviance. Davies (1984, p. 218), for example, had access to handbooks:

> Which set out on the one hand the instrumental goals –
> learning areas, extra-curricula activities, examinations taken,

95

careers opportunities – and on the other hand the facilitating goals – grouping, timetabling, pastoral care, the social order, the 'consensual and differentiating rituals' of behavioural rules and uniform. The thirty-eight-page staff handbook gave clear indications, too, as to 'expected' roles and rules for pupils and teachers, information supplemented or orchestrated by written reports of staff meetings and discussed topics, notice boards and assemblies.

Similarly, Scarth (1985) discovered a great deal about his school's ethos from its official brochure, as much from its omissions as anything else. For example, great emphasis was given to examinations and subject knowledge. Other aspects of the curriculum received much less attention, and there was no reference at all to the fact that the school was a comprehensive. The purpose of the document, Scarth argues, was to promote an image of the school as a 'little grammar school' (p. 104).

Even more important, arguably, are school reports, for they give a studied and crystallized evaluation of a pupil's progress over a period: for many parents they are the only such indication they receive. On them, subject teachers typically give a grade or mark, often in relation to the rest of the set, form or year, and add a comment. The form teacher adds a general comment, and all may be countersigned by the head.

There is more to reports, however, than evaluation. Though, as a teacher in the 1960s I had myself completed thousands of reports from that point of view, I had never come to see them from a more distanced researcher's role, as I did at Lowfield (Woods, 1979). Here, I was allowed to see current and past reports on the groups of pupils I was chiefly interested in. With the benefit of my appraisal of other aspects of pupil–teacher interaction, I came to see these largely as cultural products, frequently inaccurate in their assessment of ability (at least in the way it was presented in comments in the report), and in their depiction of attitudes and behaviours as products of personality rather than institution. If that was the case, there had to be a more important function lying behind the manifest pupil-evaluation, and I argued that it was the advancement of teacher professionalism. I shall say more about this in the following chapter. The point here is that the written reports themselves were the major source of data. Though there were other ways in which teachers presented their professionalism, none of them was nearly so integrated, coherent, detailed, available, all-embracing and clear as the batches of reports I was given.

96

It is still necessary, however, to see them as one of a number of materials bearing on the same issues. The ultimate analysis was supported by interviews with pupils (in which several displayed all the qualities of maturity, judgment, intelligence and courtesy they were accused in their reports by some teachers as lacking); with teachers (who explained how they viewed such things as 'ability', their thinking behind their comments and the problems associated with such things as shortage of time, large numbers of reports to write, etc.); and with parents (several of whom felt overawed by the teachers and unable to question their judgment).

However, the written documents of most importance in schools are, arguably, those to do with their manifest function of teaching and learning – textbooks, work cards, syllabi, blackboards, exercise books, test and examination papers, films and other visual aids. These are popular areas of enquiry. There have been several studies of children's books, for example, for signs of gender or ethnic bias. Lobban (1978), for example, among others, has shown how children's reading schemes demarcate certain jobs, activities and attitudes as feminine or masculine. Hicks (1981) similarly examined fourteen commonly-used textbooks on the British Isles and found they 'tend to convey both ethnocentric and sometimes racist images of the world' (p. 171).

There have been several studies of progressive teaching. The essential start for such projects is the official documentation. Thus Atkinson and Delamont (1977) had to examine the 'Science Teacher Education Project' and the 'Scottish Integrated Science Scheme' as the baseline against which to compare actual classroom practice, which they found followed, at heart, traditional lines. Similar appraisals have been made of the use of work-sheets (Barnes, 1976; Edwards and Furlong, 1978; Ball, 1981). By comparing the 'resources' with their observations of what occurred, all these concluded that it makes little real difference to the basic teaching model – it just helps teachers keep order, and gives pupils a semblance of autonomy. Barnes in fact noticed that the work-sheets referred mostly to course textbooks. Ball (1981, p. 201), however, noticed that in some subjects with some teachers (for example, geography) 'The introduction of the work-book allows some variation in the pacing and selection of knowledge by the pupils', and that 'much more of the learning in this context (i.e. mixed-ability) is socialized ... than was usual in banded classrooms'. There was, however, great variety of attitude towards mixed-ability classes and towards the use of work-sheets, even within the same subject. Clearly, basic attitudes both of teacher

97

and of pupil are all-important. Teachers might use work-sheets to consolidate their traditional position in new circumstances, and some pupils might regard them as a useful resource in their quest for entertainment, as in one example I saw at Lowfield (Woods, 1979) of 'The Wrong Boots'. The work-sheet depicted the story of a young man, accompanied by a woman, buying a pair of boots in a shop; finding they did not fit when he got home; returning to the shop and demanding a refund; remonstrating with the manager; and finally going to the Citizen's Advice Bureau. The pupils were asked to fill in the likely words spoken in the balloons coming out of their mouths. They had great fun in vying with each other to use the foulest and most abusive language they knew or could devise. My own knowledge of such language just about doubled in that one lesson! Work-sheets, then, can be appropriated in to the pupil culture.

However, work-sheets do have a pedagogical function, and an interesting study would be to explore which sheets are more successful in their stated aims, and on what occasions, than others. This would involve considering how they were interpreted by pupils, and what impact they made on their learning processes. I sat in on and tape-recorded one group of fourth-year deviant boys who had been given architectural plans, photographs, statistics and tenants' comments on two housing estates, and a list of questions to consider. The discussion was quite intense and productive, and when I played it back to them a few days later, one commented 'Cor! We was workin' 'ard then! That's the 'ardest I've worked all term!' This, needless to say, was a considerable feat. I would have liked to explore further the learning processes involved – clearly they were inspired, in part at least, by the materials given them in line with the manifest teaching intentions behind them.

Personal documents

Among these are diaries, creative writing exercises, pupils' 'rough' books, graffiti, personal letters and notes. Some may already exist or come into being independently of the researcher and be available as primary data. Sometimes the researcher may use them as a chosen method. Among the former, pupils' work, especially where it has a strong personal investment, can provide indications of their views and attitudes towards a range of subjects, and a great deal of information about their own backgrounds and experiences within them. They may contain much more information than can be acquired by other means. Apart from the time needed to interview large numbers of pupils, and the problems of rapport and access, some pupils may respond better to the situation where they have time to think and construct, an official allocation (homework or lesson) and an inducement (mark), and can take a pride and pleasure in what they produce.

One example of their usefulness was shown to us in the pupil transfer study, when the pupils' middle-school class teacher set them such an exercise immediately after their two 'induction' visits to the upper school. These helped us to map out their reactions and pinpoint their anxieties. They wrote about 'When i first whent to olt tow i thoth it was big, there is a lot of teachers in olt tow' (sic); and 'But, not like the bit that we have to do home woke' (Measor and Woods, 1984, p. 43). These sentiments were repeated many times in different ways across the sample of pupils, providing a quantitative, as well as qualitative, check on other material collected by observation and interview. Some studies of transfer have depended almost entirely on pupil essays, perhaps written before and after the transition. Bryan (1980), for example, did this and, while ethnographers usually would be unwilling to rely on this as a sole method, its usefulness is demonstrated by the extent of corroboration received from other studies, including our own.

I have been greatly assisted in my studies of pupil culture by pupil writings. I was interested at one time in making comparisons among forms of humour in children of different ages. I was unable to get in to many junior schools to explore them at first hand, but received many illustrations from work organized by cooperative teachers, among them the following charming examples (without, alas, their equally charming illustrations) from some seven year olds.

One day in class 1 Ivan was getting undressed from gym when Ivans niknoks came down with his shorts and everyone started laughing. Ivan notised and quickly pulled them up and the next gym day Sally Robbins took her niknoks down on purpose.

One day Paul Martin was talking to Damon Cooper when he slipped and fell in a puddle and had to go home and get changed. Ha ha.

When my brother and I were waiting outside school for Kathryn and Elaine my brother said I'm a shepherd in the maternity play and he meant to say Nativity play and I burst out laughing and when Kathryn and Elaine came I told them and they laughed too.

On Friday when we did our cooking Rachel and I did the icing on the cakes. Rachel got dirty and so did I and Laura was licking her fingers.

One day Dominic took Rachels pen and he rubberbaned it to his hand and left the pen sticking out when Rachel triyed to get it she couldn't it was very funny.

One day in the afternoon sirs coat kept falling down and he said 'Stop falling down' and then he said 'Don't answer me back' because the coat kept falling off the peg.

When Richard Major got told off and went outside Richard sang. Our teacher said 'Change channels Richard' Richard went br br br br Then the class said change to BBC1 and everyone laughed.

When Mr Jones went under the mobiles he banged his head and didn't know who had done it . . .

This morning our teacher said we are going to go in the car park to see if there are any bird droppings on my car and we all laughed.

The teacher herself made an entry in this particular series of incidents.

Class 4 were having a music and movement lesson from the radio yesterday. The children had to dance a funny dance and try to make the prince, who was Andrew Cross, laugh. The children were so funny and laughed so infectiously that I began to laugh too. I laughed and laughed all the way through.

Reading a whole folder of such incidents has the effect almost of transporting the reader into the scene. One of the distinctive features of some ethnographic presentations is their evocations of the cultures they describe. 'This is how it is experienced by the people concerned', and the reader is carried along by such descriptions such as to feel very much like a participant observer. These young children, with their simple descriptions and drawings, have that effect on me, and I can share their hilarity at someone's nik-noks coming down, a boy falling in a dirty puddle, and trying to make the grumpy old prince laugh. However they are viewed – as descriptions by proxy-ethnographer or as illustrations of cultural forms – they would be likely to form a major component of the eventual presentation.

Children's 'news' and 'story' books contain a fund of information, much of which would be difficult to obtain by other means, for, often in 'creative' exercises they will take us into secret places. This, after all, is what the ethnographer is primarily interested in – what is in people's minds – and that cannot always be readily 'observed' or obtained by interview. Through them we can discover much detail of their home life, their parents, other relatives and friends, and their relationships with them, what television programmes they watch and what they think of them, what games they play, food they eat, holidays and entertainments they have. They convey, too, a range of perceptions and feelings – hopes, fears and expectations about the future ('When I grow up ...'), views of others ('My ideal teacher', 'Our school', 'A tramp'), experiences of special events ('Our autumn fayre', 'My First Day at school'), fantasies about hypothetical situations ('If I was rich', 'If I was invisible'). Such fantasies, of course, can be good indicators of the kind of influences operating on children. Consider, for example, this ten-year-old boy's 'idea of Heaven'.

> I think Heaven is made of air all around the universe and when you die your spirit goes there. I think Heaven is really the next world with a palace made of clouds which God and Jesus live in, where they can see all over the universe. I think Heaven is really like Earth apart from the facts that you cannot see it and to go there you have to be kind, good, helpful and loving. If you are not any of these things but the complete opposite then you will go down to Hell which is where the Devil lives. Down in Hell I think there is total darkness and the Devil has a black horse on which he comes into our world catching spirits to go back with him. In Heaven I think every family has at least one angel to look after it. I think that God or Jesus do not need to catch people to go to Heaven. Their spirits just float up. In Heaven I think that there are never any rows or squabbles. The angels are the mothers of the familys and they have to do all the housework and the shopping, and the women help them. The men just laze about and don't do anything.

One might feel tempted to analyse this for what ideologies lie behind the characterization of Heaven and Hell and the personal qualifications needed to get there. The sexism at the end is yet another illustration of that tendency in children's writing noted by King (1978). He:

> Carried out a content analysis of the 'stories' books of a class of rising sevens. . . . Every girl wrote stories and drew

accompanying pictures with a domestic setting referring to home and children, and every girl wrote more of these stories than any other kind. Nine boys out of fourteen wrote such stories, but all wrote more of other kinds of story, mostly concerning rockets, ships, fighting, bombs, fires, crashes and accidents. These were the occasional themes of only eight of the thirteen girls. (p. 68.)

How teachers rate and comment on these exercises is also of interest (the one above on 'Heaven' simply had a tick, from a male teacher). All of these things may be indicative of attitudes, and can be followed up by, or added to, the products of other techniques employed.

Of course, this material would need to be interpreted with care. There may be a tendency to romance, exaggerate or falsify. Pupils are not usually instructed on the virtues of accuracy before composing these materials – that is not the aim. They are intended as creative exercises, not scientific documents. Their accuracy can be helped by other cross-validating methods (interviews with pupils and teachers, observation), but they may contain detail and shafts of insight that might not be procurable by other means. They may also capture a world and emotional state of the moment that is lost over the distance of time.

However, accuracy of detail is not the sole concern, or even at times a concern at all, for pupils' creative exercises, like their forms of play, are of interest in themselves. Why do they take the form that they do? What influences appear to be operating on them? Social class, gender and ethnicity have been important themes. Pupil creative exercises can also add a valuable commentary on personal development, as any parents will know who have kept their children's writings and drawings over the years. This becomes more apparent the more they accumulate and provide comparisons between stages.

The pupil documents discussed so far are those produced for others, and intended for public consumption. However there is a vast subterranean pupil culture where the written element is in the form of diaries, notes, letters, drawings and graffiti. Some of these are more publicly in evidence than others. That is the whole point, of course, about graffiti. Its volume has been regarded as significant by some (for example, Rutter *et al.*, 1979), as a useful indicator of behavioural standards. However, there are all sorts of graffiti, and its actual nature, as well as its quantity, repays study. We found unofficial pupil jottings quite crucial evidence in our study of pupil transfer and adaptation (Measor and Woods, 1984); for example, in initiating cross-gender interactions, great risks were involved. If a girl showed interest in a boy and was snubbed, that would involve great embarrassme' :, so a means had to be devised of conveying the message without that risk. The answer was for the girls to let it be known among themselves who they 'fancied', and then for others to write the boy's name on the girl's pencil case (later, her apron, and then exercise books). Then she could deny the truth of it if necessary. Another tactic was for girls to write 'I love –', with a blank space for the name on the front of their hands', which signalled their general interest in cross-gender involvements and did not risk any rejection. On the palm of their hands, where they could keep it well hidden, they would write the name (Measor, 1985).

Some materials illustrated pupil development. A group of twelve-year-old girls were at an 'in-between' stage, still interested in some of their old childish games (like playing with dolls) but now becoming increasingly interested in more advanced pursuits (such as boys). This entry in Sheila's autograph book sums it up:

When Sheila was a little tot
She liked to play with toys,
Now Sheila has grown up a bit
She prefers to play with boys.

(Measor and Woods, 1984, p. 99)

The 'rough book' was a special item in these teenage girls' relationships.

Girls wrote all over their rough book covers, and also inside them. Later, when the covers were entirely obliterated by graffiti, they covered the rough book with a poster of some kind, which gave it a fresh surface. This meant that the graffiti could change fairly rapidly, mirroring the shifting relationships and interests that occurred. The two most popular topics were boys' names and rock groups. . . . The possession of a decorated rough book was a signal perhaps of interest in the informal culture. Ros attempted to involve Sally in this activity, and wrote 'Sally likes?' on her rough book. Sally looked cross and rubbed it out, signalling perhaps a wish to be 'out' of such activities.

(*Ibid.*, pp. 118–19)

Later, the imprinting spread to some exercise books, and, with some pupils, to their own body. Shirley, for example, 'wrote the name of the rival comprehensive in orange felt-tip pen in large letters up her arm: M.A.Y.O.R.F.I.E.L.D.S. R.U.L.E.S. O.K.? On the bottom of her bag she had a series of moderately obscene pictures of one of the counselling staff' (*Ibid.*, p. 153).

Undoubtedly there is a great deal of exuberant fun in many of these pupil activities, but we might argue that many of them involve other purposes, conscious or unconscious. I thought that, at Low-field, for example, pupil laughter had a highly political content on occasions, especially when poking fun at the staff. An important part of this were the 'numerous jingles, poems and anecdotes which decorated the pupils' "quarters". Interestingly, sexual prowess and parts seemed to conform to the staff hierarchy' (Woods, 1979, p. 116).

If this is conflict humour, the basic point of which is to diminish the status of the opposition in their eyes, and elevate their own, there are more harmonious practices, in which pupils practise their new-found roles and identities. Sometimes the two are combined.

Things about Mr Wilson (One of their teachers)
Good
He is good-looking (slurp, slurp)
His French is coming on well
He has got nice legs
His German pronunciations are coming on
He has a sense of humour
He gives us easy work
He is our favourite teacher (slurp)

Student Wilson is always impertinent and never
does any work. I strongly recommend that
he be expelled from Harefields School.

HEAD OF FRENCH AND GERMAN: Rachel Grant.

Bad
He's got bow legs
He exposes his legs too much – longer trousers are the answer
He is a jabberknowl
He gives too much homework
He can't afford a razor
He is grizzlie
He's too good at rugby
Too much work
His feet are too big for his body

This 'school report' was presented to the teacher concerned amid much giggling. I have also come across 'proto' examination papers.

'O' level 1985
Section A
1. Who are these people?
   a) Oh my God!
   b) Urdu
   c) Choppers
   d) Niglet
2. Draw Jacky Joppers in detail, and label.
3. Explain why Mary Silvers has a big nose in not more than 30 words.

This mocking of others' irregularities or idiosyncrasies, however slight they may be, is a common feature of teenage culture. It celebrates the normal and rejoices in what they take to be their own approximation to it. A great deal of it appears in written form.

The sexual element is never far away from this kind of literature, usually very crudely expressed. Pollard (1984, p. 245) discovered the following rhyme in a top junior girl's autograph book, noting that it was typical of the 'gang' involved, but not other groups.

Eh by gum
Can your belly touch your bum,
Can your tits hang low
Can you tie 'em in a bow,
Can your balls go red,
When you rub 'em on your bed,
Eh by gum
That's it!

Sometimes, however, pupil scribblings can be quite sophisticated – and realistic – as in the following example involving two fourteen-year-old girls in a comprehensive school:

Ann, I've got a big problem but I want to trust someone. I've been a bit silly.
Oh yeah? Ann awaits your reply!
Well, you see, its not a laughing matter. Can you have a good guess what its about?
S--?
You've hit the nail on the head.
Have you missed your monthly?

Yep. It was on Monday (supposed to be) but nothing
happened.
It could be just late. Did you take any precautions?
No that's the problem, and it was on the 14th day!
How long ago?
Yes, but he's in the Army and he goes back on next Monday.
I think you ought to tell him your fears and then you can
either both go and buy an indicator test. The sooner you know
for sure the better. You might feel that you don't want to tell
him, but after all it <u>is</u> half his fault!
I know, but what's worrying are the following points
1   He's in the Army.
2   I haven't got any close friends or people to tell.
3   If I am, I can't tell my mum because she's going to hospital
    soon 'cos she's overworked.
Or, you could go to a family planning thing for a test, as they
are always saying they are 'there to help'. If you don't want to
tell R. unless you know its serious – I'll come with you,
Stevens. You know I will. Could go this Sat unless you wait to
go with R.
Trouble is there are a few minor hitches:
1   I'm not allowed out until half-term because of last Friday
    night.
2   I haven't got the foggiest where a place like that is.
3   I just feel like crying. I've got this sort of butterflies feeling
    in my stomach 'cos I'm scared.
But Stevens, you can't sit in the house not knowing. Would
you be allowed up to my house? To find out where one is I
could ring the Samaritans!

The exchanges went on like this, with one rehearsing her fears and
problems, the other giving strong moral support and very sound
guidance. To me at first reading I must say it appeared too realistic,
even to the emotions involved, to be anything other than the truth.
Such things do happen! But I eventually concluded, given other
evidence, that it was a game, a piece of theatre, in which the girls
entered the parts of people involved in very real-life drama. In fact,
one could argue this was an important aspect of their education.
Human dramas, moral problems, civil rights – how to react, how
to cope, how to treat others, what to do, where to go – all constitute an important part of the curriculum. No method a teacher
could devise would be likely to be as effective in such 'private' areas
as this kind of interaction. Certainly the kind of official 'sex edu-

cation' given in schools falls a long way short of adolescent needs (Prendergast and Prout, 1984; Measor, 1985). This is a vast, as yet almost totally unresearched, area of pupil self-education, despite the vogue of 'child-centredness' in the 1960s, and a great deal of it takes a written form.

How does one come by these documents? Some, of course, are easily available, but many of them are private communications, belong to their owners, and can only be used if they make them available and give permission, as with the examples above. However, pupils are often careless in their use of them, as when, for example, some of this activity might be going on in a formal lesson, contrary to its main purpose, and a teacher 'intercepts' a communication. One such incident in my teaching experience led to a boy being suspended from school. More usually, teachers view such activity with tolerant amusement. Some, in fact, are awarded complimentary stage three access to this area of pupil culture, and actually presented with documents, on occasions.

Some of these writings constitute a kind of diary. These are of particular interest to ethnographers, for, in a sense, they are being made privy to the participant observation of another. Diaries are an important complement to life histories, for past events may be recollected and interpreted through current mental frameworks, and quite often remembered facts may be wrong or somehow distorted. A diary can produce corroboration, or otherwise, of facts, dates, places, people, views and feelings.

Again, one has to take care. As Iris Murdoch makes one of her characters say, 'I could write all sorts of fantastic nonsense about my life in these memoirs and everybody would believe it! Such is human credulity, the power of the printed word and any well-known ... personality' (1980, p. 76). Perhaps she had Virginia Woolf in mind, for Quentin Bell, in considering the truthfulness of her diaries, says 'No unequivocal answer can be given. Virginia Woolf's reputation for truthfulness was not good. She was supposed to be malicious, a gossip, and one who allowed her imagination to run away with her' (Bell, 1977, p. xiii). But it is the ethnographer's business to be sceptical and to seek to understand the interpretative frame behind all the materials that are presented. All diaries are selective. They record what the individual concerned wishes to record. So why should somebody keep a diary? Hardly ever, I suspect, to preserve an objective view of facts. More likely it is to be for reasons like personal satisfaction in wishing to remember interesting events that have brought pleasure; or as a kind of celebration of self in annotating one's deeds, lest one forget; or

107

as an apologia; or a kind of therapy in working one's way through a series of events that have brought personal diminishment, pain or embarrassment; or with a view to later publication and public view.

So one needs to know the basis on which the diary has been compiled. Sometimes this will be realized and pointed out by the person concerned ('I was having a ding-dong row with the head-master at the time', 'I was concerned about the forthcoming appointment to deputy head in which I thought I had a good chance', 'I had domestic problems all that year, and that tended to colour my judgment'). Sometimes it can be inferred from the material itself, especially if it contrasts with other data.

One teacher diary that was made available to me was compiled, intermittently, by a man who said he simply wished to make a record of certain events, and wanted to understand them and his part in them in a kind of 'exploration of self'. The diary is full of observations of his colleagues and pupils, descriptions of their inter-relationships, especially where they occasioned conflict or hu-mour, both at work and at play, evaluations of his teaching, refer-ences to his mental and physical health during certain episodes and at key points of the term and year, and indications of how his career as a teacher fitted into his life. This, of course, would be an extremely valuable document in a life history of that person, but it could also enrich an ethnography of the school concerned with the areas, for example, of teacher and pupil culture, teacher strategies, staff management, or teacher careers. Here are some brief extracts from the diary.

May 8th, Tuesday (During his first year of teaching)
A lesson this morning reminded me of the uselessness of my job. 2F English, I had just listlessly designed comparing two poems for sound effects. I asked Miller what he thought of them. 'Daft', he said. The reason was that they were written in archaic language. Hadn't they enjoyed 'Midsummer Night's Dream' the term before? Five definitely had, five definitely hadn't, which left fifteen unimpressed either way. One cannot investigate the styles of language with thirteen year olds. Yet somehow the discussion got round to what they liked to read ... Cheveley mentioned 'Lady C.' which inaugurated a lively discussion. Yet their lighthearted, superficial gaiety, at other times so pleasing to me, struck me with despair.... Here we are, nearing the end of the year. I have introduced them to various gems of English Lit. and merely because I represent the

establishment, they have become sloughed in that artificial, pedantic aura which they rightly find so nauseous. I thought I had a flair for overcoming this, but what has happened to me over this past year has almost extinguished it. I have aligned myself less with them, become more of the schoolmaster, and somehow my elevated self finds this just as revolting as they do. One needs their confidence, not mere tokens, lip-service to power and adulthood. Have I the courage to reassert my individuality – or am I to be content with these mechanics?

May 10th, Thursday
Storm brewing with Coles and 4D. A little man inside and out, who finds strength in the authority the law has given him. His 'tea-parties' are notorious. Every evening of the week Mr. C. will be keeping some form behind for some trivial transgression. Individuals too – 'What did you do wrong?' 'Don't know.' 'Well stand there and think a little while!'

My form in uproar this p.m. What had he said? – 'Get on with something.' 'They're not getting on so I'm keeping them in.' He hesitated when he told me this as if awaiting my reactions, but I had none then. In fact it seemed a good idea for all the tribulations they've caused *me*. Later it seemed rather unjust – I could tell from the tone of the form. 'What do they expect, no teacher 'ere?' 'These language teachers are all alike – 'e's worse one in school.' 'Persecution mania.' And it was all Miss P's fault for not providing a substitute.

I tackled Mr. C. on it. He explained 'When I go into a room and give an order, I expect to be obeyed.' Good officer material, one of the lesser, peevish types. Sure, sure, but don't order them to jump out of the windows. Fancy telling 4D to 'get on with something' with no teacher present. 'I think you are being unjust, C., and thought I'd let you know where my sympathies lie.' 'Very well, let a delegation present themselves to me during break. I am never unjust.'

I explain to 4D at p.m. registration, but for various reasons they shirk the task, especially Major, who showed his true colours. I therefore express the hope that 'Mr. C. will keep them in all weekend, and I shall tell him so. You complain to me, then back out of the real job!' This rouses them. They see Mr. C. – a group of nice girls, and impress him with their 'reason' as he called it. He does not keep them in.

March 23rd, Wednesday (Two years later)
Surprisingly enjoyable lesson with 5S and a much better

discussion with 6B on an even more boring subject – Sweden, though had to censure Angela Best and Margaret Crawthorne for wittering.... Rugby with 1sts, I in my berserk mood, whipping up enthusiasm with tongue, 'Charge!' 'Stop him!' 'Pull him down!' I demonstrate a tackle on some poor lad. 'Don't embrace him like this! Put him on the deck like this! ... Sorry! Are you all right!' 'Yah! Butterfingers!' 'Don't sit down, wretch!' ... H.M. drifted into my last lesson with 5A. I'd just won the battle of Waterloo. 'Have you got over your climax?'

These extracts give perhaps an inkling of their nature, potential and dangers. There is an almost inevitable self-indulgence, which may or may not reflect the circumstances of the case (some teachers *are* self-indulgent). Objective analysis may become obscured by celebration of the self, the diary having, perhaps, mainly therapeutic and entertainment functions. There are dangers, too, perhaps in looking at parts of the diary in isolation from others. The first entry, for example, contrasts strongly with the third, reflecting a typical contrast not only in a teacher's life, but also a week, even a day. One might expect that a regular diarist would aim for a certain roundedness over a period, given that it takes a long time to think and to write things down. So now one selects this activity, this mood or line of thought, now that ... (see Fothergill, 1974). This certainly helps to assess the accuracy of a diary like Virginia Woolf's, for 'she is true only to her mood at the moment of writing, and when the mood changes she often contradicts herself, so that when she writes a great deal about one person we frequently end with a judgment balanced between extremes' (Bell, 1977, p. xiv).

With these cautions in mind, such diaries can be immensely useful to the researcher. They represent the experiences, observations and studied reflections of a participant, totally unobtrusive and unsolicited. There are 'no holds barred' in a personal diary of this nature. The writer is frank and open, lets us into confidences, is direct about others, provides a commentary on the undercurrents of school life which govern its movement but are never visible. There *is* analysis, as the second extract makes clear, immediate and *post hoc*, invaluable for the teacher in the task of managing relationships within the complexities of school life.

However, few people, I suspect, keep diaries. Their more customary use in ethnography, therefore, is when the researcher requests them to be made for particular purposes. This may lose something on unobtrusiveness (they will be writing diaries 'for the researcher'), but might gain in other respects; for example, by indicating what is needed, the events, reactions, views, the *researcher* is interested in, one may exert some control over selectivity. Some have taken these directions quite a long way. Zimmerman and Wieder (1977), in their study of the Californian counter-culture, paid subjects to keep a diary for a week, advising them to record activities according to the formula: 'Who? What? When? Where? How?' Diaries can also be structured chronologically, and by activity. One technique used by Davies (1984, p. 213), for example, in her study of girls' deviance, was to ask pupils 'anonymously, to log their own behaviour against a list of conduct rules or conduct infractions'. Such structuring is in accordance with the principles associated with the ethnographic interview – what structure there is being facilitating, not directive, aimed at framework, not content.

As they are made during the time-span of the research, checks for typicality, clarity, lacunae, validity, etc., can more easily be made by use of other methods. Among these the interview is most useful, wherein people are invited to comment on their diary entries in what has become known as the 'diary-interview' (Zimmerman and Wieder, 1977; Plummer, 1983; Burgess, 1984b, and 1984c, pp. 128–35). Here one may check up on facts, seek clarification and exemplification.

I have found diaries particularly useful in studying pupil cultures, and, if they are interested, pupils are well prepared to cooperate. I would hesitate about asking busy teachers to keep diaries unless I could offer something in return, such as relief from some of their lessons. Pupils are good for short bursts, but find it difficult to sustain interest over a period of more than a few days. Thus I try to capture a brief cross-section of activity, or some particularly interesting event or series. The entry may be little more than an *aide-mémoire*, to be followed up in interview later. Thus, I have been particularly interested in forms of pupil humour. A group of boys were going on a rugby tour in France, and I asked one of them to keep a diary for me. I wanted examples of humour, and some indication of how they rated them, so I asked him to give the examples a rating of A for extremely funny, B for moderately funny and C for quite funny. Here is an extract from the diary.

Rugby Tour
24.10.81
During a massive meal I cracked up. This was because we had millions of rolls and spilt noodles all over the table. B. Just now Fitz has got the table stuck on its side and everyone is

bursting with laughter. A. I was putting my pyjamas on when Bugsy walked in. A. Bugsy had his wallet down his jumper and was very worried cause he thought he'd lost it. B. We cracked up. We was having pillow fights in the dark. Then Bugsy walked in while Fitz was putting his pyjamas on. A.

25.10.81
Tonight we had a mass pillow scrap. A.A.A. On the bus back from a rugby match we had a mass sing song. A.A. We raided peoples rooms knicking sweets. A. On the bus we was having a good old sex talk. A. At breakfast I thought the woman said 'have you had enough?' She did say 'any more?' in French of course. I said, 'Oui' so she brought another jug of chocolate. A.

26.10.81
Biffo (Mr Smith) laughed and everyone impersonated it. A. We saw a photo of Lobby asleep. C. We went to the Chateaux today and Biff pretended to understand the guide who was gabbling on in French. C. Fitz was singing a sex song. A. Fitz put the wastepaper basket over his head and pretended to be a dalek. B. In the bus we was singing 'Go home you bums, go home you bums go home. A. Andy Stevens sat on the fence by the football pitch and it snapped. Later on Lobby lent against it and fell on the floor. This was because Anus (Andy Stevens) had tied the fence up with string. A.

Clearly I could not have obtained this information in any other way, and though some of it might have been recovered by interview after the tour, I suspect it would not have been so complete and systematically evaluated. Other pupils (both boys and girls) of different ages were also making diaries on this theme and, together, they helped give me a great amount of detail to complement my observations on different forms of pupil humour in different groups and at different ages. They provided me with access to places I could not attend and events I could not witness, and acted as fellow participant observers.

We also used diaries in the 'pupil transfer' study, and these helped to confirm, for example, one set of differences between the girls involved. 'The conformist girls spent the majority of their leisure time with their families. The deviants' activities centred around their peer group' (Measor and Woods, 1984, pp. 143–4). Ball (1981, p. 100) also found them useful in his Beachside study where he found that:

> Material from diaries kept by some of the pupils . . .
> demonstrated both a lack of subtlety in the sociometric
> instruments and the degree to which the collection of
> sociometric data could be socially constrained.

The diaries 'filled in' much qualitative material necessary to understand the bare bones of sociometric questionnaires (wherein pupils were asked to say who their friends were), indicated the casual friendships that existed outside school, and the cross-sex friendships that were just beginning with these pupils; and showed an increase in the number of unsupervised social activities.

There are, then, particular purposes for which diaries may be especially useful. These include the monitoring of special events or critical periods (such as a teaching practice, beginning teaching, or a new job or responsibility, undertaking a difficult task, experimenting with a new project), or, more simply, when one wishes to account for, or reflect on, the ordinary course of events in order to represent how one occupies the day or how 'insiders' see the ordinary course of events.

Another important kind of diary is the researcher's own. This is different from the 'field notes' of observation and the records of interviews in that it monitors the researcher's own involvement in the research, quite honestly, 'warts and all' and without thought of ultimate presentation to others. Thus it might include details about how the research was initially conceived; how, perhaps it related to one's own personal development; attempts to get the research launched; the problems involved in negotiating access; failures and blunders, as well as triumphs; changes of mind, doubts, fears and worries; how the research relates to the rest of one's life and so on. Primarily such detail is necessary to help both oneself and others to evaluate the results of the work, for research is, in a sense, a kind of personal quest. Ethnography, too, with its emphasis on participation, involves the researcher as a person rather more than some other research styles. Research diaries, then, have a validating function, in that they help to identify these personal elements. Davies (1982, p. 5), for example, found some biographical detail essential for the understanding of this kind of work.

> In reading similar research, but without personal knowledge of
> the author, I have sometimes been bothered by lack of such
> knowledge and found myself turning continually to the dust
> jacket and the front pages of the book hoping to pick up some
> glimmer of information about the person writing.

Research diaries take us behind the scenes of data collection, sampling, analysing, theorizing, and each one has certain unique properties. As Hammersley (1984, p. 61) tells us of his research, 'it was a voyage of discovery and much of the time was spent at sea'. And Ball (1984, p. 71), in the same volume, declares that fieldwork:

> Involves a personal confrontation with the unknown and requires that the aspirant come to grips with the use of theory and method in the context of a confused, murky, contradictory and emergent reality. That is light years removed from the systematic theories and pristine research reports.

We need to know something, therefore, of how those neat accounts were arrived at, something of the journey, of the time spent at sea, how the storms, icebergs and monsters were negotiated, means of navigation devised, changes of course mapped out. Research diaries are ideal for this, and they not only help to contextualize the research, to give it 'body', but they also may make a very useful contribution to the methodological literature (for example, Burgess, 1984a).

They have yet another use. Ethnography can be a lonely pursuit, as I have remarked before. Indeed, the natives may also be hostile. At times, the ethnographer may yearn for the company and confidence of a like-minded person who has some knowledge and appreciation of the problems being experienced, but meetings with these may be far apart. During these lonely periods, the diary becomes the confidant. There is a therapy in committing thoughts to paper, that enables an unburdening of self and often sets up a dialogue, possibly creating new thoughts which point to solutions, improvements, or alternatives. Where these are not immediately achieved, the record stands to service the memory later when the account is presented to others.

Questionnaires

Questionnaires tend not to be popular with ethnographers. Indeed, some rule out their use altogether, arguing that they belong to a style of research with basic assumptions diametrically opposed to ethnography. One of these is the belief that social facts can be measured in the same way as natural facts – hence the employment of objective and quantifiable measures such as questionnaires, attitude scales, controlled clinical experiments, and statistical tests of distribution, correlation and significance. Recently, however, there has been a softening of this position, so that a growing number of researchers are ceasing to regard this as a dichotomy of different paradigms, and rather as a dimension with different poles (see, for example, Hammersley, 1984). By this argument, the ethnographer's choice of methods is basically governed by two sets of criteria:

(1) fitness for purpose; and
(2) the various interpretative requirements that have been continually emphasized in earlier chapters.

These include the establishing of rapport, unobtrusiveness, naturalness, and the need for cross-checking. These rule out some methods, such as controlled experiments, but some others - questionnaires among them - have their uses (see, for example, D. Hargreaves, 1967; Lacey, 1970; Delamont, 1973; Fuller, 1978; Ball, 1981; Player, 1984; Davies, 1984). These are primarily:

(1) as a means of collecting information, especially as a convenient means of collecting data from a wider sample than can be reached by personal interview;
(2) as a starter to the use of more qualitative methods; and
(3) in respondent validation.

In all these instances, questionnaires are just one method in a package. In none of them do the data they contain stand alone. In the first use, for example, a form of triangulation might be employed. Initial ethnographic work might indicate a range of categories, perspectives and reactions that may lend themselves to representation in a questionnaire, that is then sent out to a wider sample. So far, this is a fairly basic model of traditional research; but whereas this would see the survey as the major instrument, ethnographers would view the questionnaire as subservient to interpretative techniques. Their use would therefore require further qualitative work after the questionnaire to check that respondents were interpreting the items in the same way. This would go somewhat further than the reliability checks traditionally used.

The 'harder' one can make such items in this kind of use, the greater the validity of the instrument. Such items require responses that remain the same in all situations - personal details, known facts - though even these are subject to the same requirements of access and rapport as are interviews (otherwise the number of pupils whose fathers are 'brain surgeons' or teachers who are misplaced 'teaboys to a steeplejack', or 'Irish peat-cutters' mates' grows alarmingly!). There is a great deal of good advice available on the

actual construction of questionnaires, so I shall not go into that
here (see, for example, Youngman, 1984).

That questionnaires cannot embrace the sense of process, flux,
inconsistency, contradiction, which is at the heart of ethnographic
work, can be turned to advantage, for they can help cut through
the swathe of social life and assist the perception of structures and
patterns. One example of this is the sociometric questionnaire,
which seeks to find out who relates to whom within a group, and
in what way. Meyenn (1980), for example, used these in his study
of how boys and girls in one cohort (four classes) organized their
social life in a middle school. He asked them (at three different
points over a two-year period):

(1) Who do you play with after school (evenings and weekends)? ·
(2) Who would you most like to be friends with at school?
(3) Who would you least like to be friends with at school?
(4) Who do you usually play with in the playground?
(5) Who do you usually work with in class?

(Meyenn, 1980, p. 250)

The results, illustrated in the form of a sociogram, showed quite
vividly the differences between boys and girls, the latter forming
'tight cliques which in many ways were quite separate from each
other' while the boys formed 'one largely undifferentiated class
group which did contain some much more loosely formed smaller
groups' (*ibid.*). The 'character and culture' of these peer networks
were then studied over a period through observation and interview.

Sociomatrices formed an important part of the study by Lacey
(1970). Changes in friendship patterns thus revealed were then 'related to academic performance, "behaviour" and social class in
order to show how these factors influence the "face to face" interaction of the pupils'. Another sociomatrix was used 'in developing
quantitative indicators of the process of "polarization" in the
friendship pattern' (*ibid.*, p. 96). (Lacey argued that pupils at 'Hightown Grammar' were 'differentiated' into two groups, good and
bad; that these were then faced with different problems – of success
and of failure – and that the resolution of these problems led to
'polarization'.) In his methodological commentary on this work,
Lacey (1976, p. 60) says:

> The analysis of the sociometric data was a completely new
> experience. I can still remember the excitement as one after the
> other of my ideas about the patterns of relationships held up
> during the analysis. The conceptualization of the processes of

116

differentiation and polarization grew out of this interplay between observation and analysis of sociometric data.

Ball (1981) also used sociometric questionnaires to advantage, and also stressed the need for them to be used in conjunction with other methods, particularly observation. He thought this a powerful combination, their accuracy suggested by:

> The stability of the social structures over time. This seems to suggest that, rather than being the product of momentary whim or the variations in data-collection procedures, the choices made by the pupils in the sociometric questionnaires accurately reflect the structure of friendship relationships in the form.
> (pp. 53–4)

However, as noted earlier, Ball found that much subtle detail was omitted from these questionnaire responses, later provided by interviews.

However, questionnaire responses can sometimes convey subtle detail, for, while those discussed above are in search of hard data, in the sense of either simple, easily tabulated information or definite responses to firm categories already revealed by qualitative work, they are sometimes used to assist the production of qualitative work. This may be pursued through completely open questions or with a little gentle guidance. An example of the latter is the 'sentence-completion' item:

> 'When lessons are boring, I . . .'
> 'When teachers tell me my work is bad . . .'
> 'Teachers in this school think of me as. . .'
>
> (Ball, 1981, pp. 62–3)

These seem to have largely gone out of favour lately, but they are, after all, only providing a facilitative framework, in the same way as 'guided' unstructured interviews, and there is no reason in principle why they should not be among the ethnographer's armoury of techniques.

Sometimes, the ethnographic questionnaire serves a number of purposes. Two kinds of questionnaire I used in *The Divided School* study (Woods, 1979) illustrate this. In both instances I saw them as a strategic bridge to more qualitative data. One was sent to the parents of third-year pupils at the time they were making their subject choices. Parents are difficult for any researcher to get round to once, let alone several times, so, suspecting that this was a topic in which most parents would be very interested, I hoped that a questionnaire would provide me with some useful information, as well as an entrée into the more interested homes. In pursuit of the former aim, therefore, I wrote parents a letter stressing the importance of the subject-choice process and asking for their help. In the accompanying questionnaire I asked such things as whether their child had asked their advice, whether they attended the special parents' meeting, how suitable they thought their child for the various subject groupings on offer, what had influenced their views, and what career, if any, their child had in mind. They were asked finally if they would indicate if they were willing for me to call round and discuss the matter with them. The fact that I was working at the school and that their children's interests and futures were at stake no doubt worked in my favour, and I received replies from 73 per cent of homes. I eventually managed to visit a third of these. Both the questionnaire and follow-up interviews supported the general 'social structural model' that I was formulating to help explain the workings of the subject-choice process. The fact that they provided evidence in line with that of other methods, and the extent of their interests in the topic and commitment to their children's futures, increased, I felt, the chances of their validity, as did the fact that those who volunteered to be interviewed were very keen to cooperate and to give their views. These approaches were supported by repeated, ongoing interviews with pupils and teachers, and observation at special meetings and informal discussions.

The other occasion when I used a questionnaire, was to test the reactions of the staff to an early part of the research, and to test the research. I intended to hold an open meeting to discuss this paper, but judged (rightly) that only a small proportion of the staff would attend. The questionnaire, then, was a device to try to secure a more widespread response, but one, nonetheless anchored in the security of the ongoing ethnography. Further, it was offering the teachers the opportunity to view some of the results and to comment upon them, and the research in general, thus forging links, I hoped, in the relationship between researcher and teachers. I also inserted some open-ended questions on some of the issues arising ('Why do you think this is so? If "yes", please explain.' 'Any other comments?'), and thus, I hoped, would receive some pointers to further information about the teachers' views. Now, while the data received from this instrument was generally nowhere near as detailed as that from the interviews, it did come from sources in some instances not otherwise reachable (because of the time factor in getting round them all) and occasionally contained telling comments, some of which were quoted in the final report (see Woods,

1979, pp. 96-100). In fact, in some of these instances, comments were actually superior to some of those received elsewhere, in that they were better formulated, more succinct and to the point. The fact is that there are times when the written word is more useful and more powerful than the spoken. It gives time for thought, reflection, memory, and composition, and this suggests that for certain purposes and in certain instances the questionnaire is intrinsically a better instrument than interviews.

Again, these responses formed one unit in a package, and the fact that I was on site and could follow up items with the individuals concerned increased their usefulness. For example, I mentioned previously the distinction between 'educationist' and 'teacher' contexts (Keddie, 1971), wherein teacher perspectives tend to be influenced respectively, either by ideal considerations or by practical contingencies. One needs to know the context in which questionnaire answers are being given, and a general ethnographic framework aids that identification.

Questionnaires, therefore, can be useful in ethnographic work, as long as their use conforms to its principles. They need to take into consideration the question of:

(1) access (What kind of relationship does the researcher have
with the respondent? Has stage three access already been
negotiated? Is the subject matter or circumstances particularly
likely to encourage full and truthful responses? To what extent
have they volunteered to participate?);
(2) the nature of the data required:
   (a) if the purpose of the questionnaire is to find out factual
       details or to seek responses to firm categories, the 'harder'
       the data requested the better;
   (b) if the purpose is to help discover new qualitative material,
       then the more open, unobtrusive and unstructured – as
       with interviews – the better (usually one finds a mixture
       of (a) and (b) in ethnographic questionnaires);
(3) the need to identify the context in which replies are being
given; and
(4) the need for checks, balances, extensions and modifications
through the use of other methods.

Questionnaires are not likely to be a prominent feature of ethnographic work, but where they accord with these principles they have a distinct value.

Chapter 6

Analysis

There has inevitably been some discussion of analysis in previous chapters, since in ethnography it goes on simultaneously with data collection. As one observes, interviews, makes up field notes and the research diary, one does not simply 'record'. There is also reflection, which then in turn informs subsequent data collection. This interplay between techniques and stages of research applies at all levels. For example, one may have formulated a fairly sophisticated theory, but aspects of it may need some basic 'filling in' with supportive data, while all will need to be subject to testing by comparative material. Or, after some initial speculative analysis, data from a different source, and perhaps revealed by a different technique, may alter or modify that analysis and point the way both to more focused data collection, perhaps using different techniques, to substantiate and elaborate, and to more abstract concept formation.

Lacey (1976) gives one example of this in what he termed a 'spiral of understanding'. Insights were 'escalated' through 'moving backwards and forwards between observation and analysis and understanding', using now classroom observation, now school records, observation again, then sociometric or background questionnaires or diaries, and so on (p. 61). Lacey feels 'very strongly that the world under investigation seen through one method of collecting data becomes enormously distorted by the limitations of that data and the available method of analysis' (*ibid.*). The closer we can bind them together, therefore, through triangulation, escalation, interaction, or whatever, the stronger the eventual product.

With this in mind, therefore, I shall consider those aspects of analysis that seem most prominent in recent ethnographic research in education. These are:

(1) speculative analysis;
(2) classifying and categorizing;
(3) concept formation;
(4) models;
(5) typologies; and
(6) theory.

I shall consider (1)–(5) here, and theory in the following chapter.

It will be seen that these activities and constructs are on a scale of increasing abstraction and generality, though (4) and (5) are roughly equivalent. Not all ethnographies go through all these stages; they may stop at any one beyond the first, depending on resources, time, nature of study and data. They then become part of a growing 'pool' of ethnographies, available to others to be taken into consideration in the later stages of analysis of their studies. In some instances there may be such a wealth of material from several, separate ethnographies, informing activities (1)–(3), that it creates a demand for somebody to take account of them all in advancing the analysis to activities (4)–(6).

However these are by no means always discrete areas of activity. In some studies, or aspects of a study, they merge imperceptibly, or they may take a different order, an outline theory, perhaps, taking shape in the mind as the data grows, suggesting where to look for concepts and calling for some classifying in the later stages.

With these provisos in mind I keep to the more traditional pattern.

Speculative analysis

This is the tentative reflection, perhaps revealing major insights, that is done throughout data collection. It can vary in sophistication. That of Davies (1982) was perhaps more considered than most. She recorded her comments beside the transcription of her discussions with pupils, and included these in the final report. This helps to tie the discussion to the main analysis.

9 <u>Jane</u>: She might leave a letter out in a word and I'd say, 'Oh yeah, you've left out a letter in that ', and she says 'All right!' and I say 'OK I won't talk then!' Then she gets mad and then I get mad and we don't talk to each other.	9 Jane describes a pattern of criticism causing offence, then counter-offence, followed by withdrawal of friendship. This is told in a dramatic style which recreates (displays) the incident for my benefit.
10 <u>B.D.</u>: How long do you stay mad for?	
11 <u>Jane</u>: Aw, about ten minutes until we've said our pieces to each other and then we'll go back to good friends, won't we?	11 The pattern of mutual offence is typically followed by mutual reaffirmation of friendship after a period of no interaction. (Neither of them has contingency friends to withdraw to at the time of this conversation.) (Davies, 1982, p. 80)

These comments may have been polished up in the interests of presentation and integration. Initial, *ad hoc* reflection is more typically speculative and less well formed. They may include others' reflections, as in this comment in my Lowfield field notes, set against an account of a 'new style senior assembly' in which a young member of staff 'told the story of his life'.

DB says the message was to urge them to try to think for self – within, as opposed to putting all oneself into these frenzied activities. The answer is inside oneself rather than seeking it outside. The answer is not outside.

Basically different from Head's assemblies because he speaks <u>down</u> to them. DB trying to operate on one level. A whole host of political and social implications behind that.

He felt terribly exposed afterwards. No staff commented. Mrs N. he consulted beforehand, and she gave a stock response – 'It's an idea' – non-committal like. B.V. had encouraged him to do it – too old himself. (The year tutors are taking it in turns.)

Good example of DB perspective, though note contradictions in his approach.

Here we have a clarification and extension of data through a key informant, a pointer to a basic comparison, to deeper considerations behind the observed actions, and to other related (in this case, contradictory) data.

The following day there was a different kind of assembly, again recorded at length in my notes, and with this comment beside.

- punch line moral, traditional virtues
- preaching, though by example
- strong attempt to arouse empathic feeling - 'When I was young ...' Youthful pursuits etc.
- use of modern gimmicks - guitar, pop, a-v aids, sports, programmes.

But the pedagogy and content has not really changed.

- it's only a veneer. The change in essence is a generational one. C.D. talks biographically - but his background is more truly reflective of the aged, established, m/c, prosperous, settled, superior man.

Here, I am making initial judgments about the data recorded, and this points to another virtue of this practice - it helps to keep such judgments out of one's *data* records.

Thus, my field notes (written on the right-hand side of the page) are complemented by more casual comments on the left. Here we have 'a good illustration of T.M.'s individualism and "the bureaucratic personality", because here he is invading the private area of family life with the language and attitude of his role'. Elsewhere there is a reminder of Weber's definition of power; a reference to a related piece of literature; a note about a collectivizing concept (D.B. deals with minorities - gypsies, society of friends, malcontents on staff and among pupils - a marginal man - perhaps purposefully cultivated); a note about the mental framework of an interviewee ('failure to take the role of the other, complete immersion in own belief system, and *emotional* involvement'); note of a lie ('This is nonsense - a few weeks later a boy was caned in the corridor' against a claim that 'the cane was there, but never used'); a reminder to 'follow up in 5D interviews', and so on.

Interview notes contain similar comments. Below is an extract from an interview with a teacher about the members of his form. I took notes at the interview and wrote it up the same evening. A few days later, when time permitted, I reflected on his comments, and added some notes.

Teacher	*P.W.*
Tim Brown – very disappointing. I noted a decline last year and I spoke to him about it, and he's a right lout isn't he? Always shuffling around with his hands in his pockets, instead of being a nice young man, as he was, but he's far from ...	(Immediately he reveals his conception of the ideal pupil, at least the behavioural one. Note the importance of appearance, and the choice of terminology – a 'right lout' is counterposed to a 'nice young man' – and a great deal seems to be inferred from his appearance and demeanour. There is a great deal of this among the staff ... he could be subscribing to my double standard hypothesis, and assuming that kids may well be different at school from what they are at home; it is what he expects that is important, and the very fact that he sees fit to divide his comment into 'academic' and 'behaviour'. So I conclude, tentatively, that JG is subscribing to the prevailing image of the ideal pupil, and that his choice of words and unqualified use of them is an indication of his commitment to that ideal.)

These, then, are the first tentative steps in analysis. They may have a certain untidiness about them, their object being to suggest lines of analysis, to point the way to connections with other data and with the literature, to indicate the direction of future enquiries, rather than to round off in neat, considered packages.

Classifying and categorizing

However, there comes a time when the mass of data embodied in field notes, transcripts, documents, has to be ordered in some kind of systematic way, usually by classifying and categorizing. At an elementary level, this simply applies to the data one has. There may be no concept formation, importation or discovery of theory, creation of new thoughts at this stage. The object is to render one's material in a form conducive to those pursuits, and that means ordering data in some kind of integrated, complete, logical, succinct way.

The first step is to identify the major categories, which, in turn, may fall into groups. The data can then be marshalled behind these. What the categories are depends on the kind of study and one's interests. They may be to do with perspectives on a particular issue, certain activities or events, relationships between people, situations and contexts, behaviours, and so forth (see Bogdan and Biklen, 1982, pp. 145-70). At Lowfield, the first exercise I undertook was to collect the views of the whole of the fourth year on the issues that concerned them at school, while observing them in lessons and 'at play', using the methods outlined in chapters 3 and 4. These yielded four thick files of material. Subsequently, the first task was to identify what these issues were and then to identify the major components of the issues. Thus 'pupils' views of teachers' was clearly a major issue, as was 'having a laugh', 'work', and 'being shown up'. I found it convenient to label the interviews alphabetically, and to number the pages. These gave me a simple code for identifying which parts of the material were applicable to which issue, and to which aspects of the issue.

Thus the 'pupils' view of teachers' issue broke down as follows.

(1) Teaching technique
  (a) Helpful, explains
  (b) Provides variety (interesting)
  (c) Allows more freedom
  (d) Encourages
  (e) Knows subject well
  (f) Organizes lesson well

(2) Teacher disposition
  (a) Cheerful, humorous, comical
  (b) Friendly, kind, nice, understanding (treats you like people, equals)
  (c) Others

(3) Teacher control
(4) Teacher fairness

The test of the appropriateness of such a scheme is to see whether every aspect of the material can be firmly accommodated within one or other category (as far as is possible one category alone), and that the categories are at the same level of analysis, as are the sub-categories (see Atkins, 1984). The chances are, however, that they will not be completely exclusive and they will certainly be interdependent to some degree. Teacher disposition, for example, has links with 'control', and 'fairness' and may strongly influence the 'teaching techniques' adopted – a reminder that, behind such a schema, the most important factor is how its elements come together within the person of the teacher. What we have to make sure of, above all, is that we have correctly identified the relevant parts of that person in the eyes of the pupil. One usually therefore has to have several shots at this before coming to the most appropriate arrangement, reading and re-reading notes and transcripts, experimenting now with this formulation, now with that.

I found it helpful to summarize each set of interviews, and to tabulate them on a chart, according to pupils' 'favourable' and 'unfavourable' remarks:

4A   Teacher Perceptions (Interview with pupils R.S., N.R., J.N.)

	Favourable	*Unfavourable*
R.S.	treat you like people	depersonalized technique
	attitude – humane	always watching you
N.R.	dedication – number of activities	
	humour	
	individualistic	
	(flouting institution)	
	makes things interesting	
	explanation	doesn't explain
		doesn't seem bothered
		with them
	kind, understanding,	
	on *your* side	

– and so on, throughout all of the four forms.

Such a distillation helps one to encapsulate more of the material 'in a glance' – or a thought – as it were, and thus aids category formulation. The pay-off for this work is that these categories, if the interviews have been conducted according to the principles

126

discussed in chapter 4, will be *theirs*, and any ensuing theory will be thoroughly grounded in their perspectives. (For more detailed consideration of this, and similar, forms of analysis, see Spradley, 1980.)

The scheme that emerges is of interest in itself of course, but really it is a template to use for other purposes. One may wish to know in what priority these categories were ordered in the pupils' minds, which could in turn tell us a great deal about their attitudes to school. Do they judge teachers by personality or by how they teach? What aspects of teaching do they consider most important? How necessary is it for a teacher to have control to win their approval? If we attempt to answer such questions in the final report, we must be prepared to operate the categories in reverse; that is, not simply to present the scheme but also to give enough supporting material to show what pupils meant by 'control', 'explanation', 'friendly', and so on.

We might wish to investigate how the frequency and distribution of categories differed, if at all, between different categories of pupils. The example above revealed interesting differences which demanded explanation. Why were boys generally more concerned than girls about 'teaching technique'? Why were girls more concerned about 'teacher disposition'? Why were the 'non-examination' pupils so concerned about the sub-category 'friendly, kind, understanding', both in comparison with their own other mentions, and with those of 'examination' pupils? Answers to such questions depend on other material, comparing other issues and 'distillations', which takes us into theory-construction, to be discussed in the next chapter.

We should take care here, in comparing groups, to ensure not only that the validating procedures discussed in earlier chapters have been observed but also that it is either a total population or that strict sampling procedures have been undertaken, and that all have had equal opportunity to speak on the matter in similar circumstances. Additionally, one needs to ensure that it is not some other factor that is producing the difference, and that there are not other, perhaps more important, differences.

This is but one instance of a simple organizing technique that can be deployed in many different ways, according to individual preferences and the demands of the issue under examination. I began my analysis of school reports and subject choice in the same way, except that in these instances I was concerned to relate it back to the individual pupils involved. Thus, a content analysis of teacher comments about pupils on reports yielded four main categories, of 'personality', 'ability', 'behaviour', and 'work', broken down into thirteen sub-categories. These were numbered one to thirteen, and a table plotted showing the category entry for each pupil in a selected sample for each subject and for all their years in the school. Trends in comments over time and between subjects were thus more easily detectable, both for individuals and for selected groups. I could perceive, for example, the far greater incidence of comments on 'behaviour' among the lower, non-examination, forms, and on 'ability' among the higher, examination forms.

However, with pupil views of teachers one needs to know exactly what was said; with reports one needs to know the content of comments. So, as I went through the mass of material, I made a selection, using the criteria of validity (as discussed previously), typicality (the import of a comment being reflected within a majority of the group), relevance and clarity, and made a special note of these. For example, the columns belonging to individual pupils in the 'reports' analysis have a space at the bottom for sample illustrations of the categories indicated. A particularly interesting comment which did not meet the above criteria would be indicated by an asterisk or an exclamation mark. I thus obtained a qualitative summary, as well as a numerical indication of trends.

With the 'subject choice' issue I made out a ledger, with pupils and their 'chosen' subjects down the left-hand side of the left page and categories (the different kinds of motive, advice received, etc.) along the top of the book, placing ticks and comments where appropriate. It soon became clear that different kinds of pupils were making different kinds of selections for different reasons. This then helped me to formulate a model which included two group perspectives, wherein some chose with various shades of enthusiasm, others with diffidence; these were to play a key part in later analysis.

With the formulation of such notions as 'group perspectives', we are of course moving a degree of abstraction away from the substantive material. So what are the criteria by which we might measure the accuracy of such a representation? Becker (1958, p. 655), who had earlier developed the idea of 'group perspectives', argues that this will vary according to the evidence, which might take any of the following forms.

(1) Every member of the group said, *in response to a direct question*, that this was the way he looked at the matter.
(2) *Every* member of the group *volunteered* to an observer that this was how he viewed the matter.

(3) *Some given proportion* of the group's members either *answered* a direct question or *volunteered* the information ...

(4) Every member of the group was asked or volunteered information but *some given proportion said* they viewed the matter from the differing perspective ...

(5) No one was asked questions or volunteered information on the subject, but *all members were observed to engage in behaviour* or to make other statements from which the analyst *inferred* that the ... perspective was being used by them as a basic, though unstated, premise ...

(6) *Some given proportion* of the group *was observed* using the ... perspective as a basic premise in their activities, but *the rest of the group* was not ...

(7) *Some proportion* of the group *was observed* engaged in activities implying the ... perspective while *the remainder* of the group was observed engaged in activities implying the (other) perspective.

The greatest confidence would come where all the members of each group had volunteered information of each perspective, in the naturalistic circumstances discussed in chapter 4, corroborated by observation (chapter 3) and documentation (chapter 5).

It might be increased still further through the informants themselves, where appropriate, vetting the analysis. For example, in life histories, one may be confronted with anything from a hundred to five or six hundred pages of transcript for each single life history. Again, the first stage in analysis is to distil the essence of the biography into more manageable form, retaining the teacher's 'ordinary' language for the most part, but organizing the material in a sociologically meaningful way. The main principle of selectivity here would be the degree of importance attributed by the teacher to the data. One seeks to subsume a great deal of the data under general categories, and to list them in priority. The organization of the distillation may be guided by the general aims of the research, which will refer to structures or elements common to a number of life histories. Finally, the illustrations chosen are those that best seem to signal the general categories.

This distillation might then be returned to the informant for comment. It is essential to get this right, for upon this, and others like it, the ultimate theory is founded. It will be impractical to return to the baseline data where several life histories are involved, so the informant is pressed to say 'Is it correct?', 'Is it fair?', 'Is the kind of interpretation appropriate – and if not, why not?', 'Are there any "mystifying" features about it?', 'Is the ordering and prioritizing correct?'

I did this in my study with 'Tom' (Woods, 1984), and was surprised to find certain misinterpretations of data I had made, and one or two actual mistakes. I was surprised not because of a belief in my own infallibility but because, in this case, I thought the data collecting had been particularly accurate and the distance between data and analysis seemed so small. However, we need to bear in mind that informants are not always infallible either, nor, as was noted in chapter 4, is it always advisable to seek respondent validation.

Concept formation

Another aspect of ethnographic analysis which can follow on from the kind of elementary analysis discussed above, or operate independently of it, is the formulation of concepts. Sometimes these take the form of 'cultured symbols (usually encoded in native terms)' (Spradley, 1979) which are discovered in field work and decoded in analysis. Sometimes they are formulated by the researcher where it seems several different pieces of data, or issues, seem to have certain structural properties in common, but which are never actually expressed as such.

Examples of the former are 'being shown up' and 'having a laugh', the alerting to which and data collection for which I discussed earlier. Again, I was at pains in analysis to establish what kinds there were, but in these cases I went further, for I was interested in exploring what the structural properties of these concepts were, their functions, who was, and who was not, involved, and whether those groups had anything in common. Thus 'showings-up' require a public arena, make particular use of time, follow a particular progression of events, may be unexpected and their consequences infectious; they have the functions of 'socialization', 'negative sanction', 'establishing and maintaining power', 'motivation' and 'revenge', and so on. One arrives at these through intensive study of:

(1) the data, organizing it into groups accordingly and trying very hard to explain them in some other way, as a test of the comprehensiveness and exactness of the overall model; and
(2) the literature, which, in this case, on embarrassment and laughter, is scattered about over the years, mainly in sociological and psychological journals.

These may suggest properties, or aspects of properties, that you have missed, or your data may suggest the same about the literature.

It is in fact at this stage that other studies and researchers become more important. The researcher will have done some preliminary reading to gain a view of the field and the approaches that have been made, and will have considered related works along the way. However, during analysis one needs interplay not only among methods and stages of one's own research but also among the ideas provided by others'. Thus, ideally, one both borrows from, and contributes towards, knowledge in the field.

Colleagues can help in this interplay of ideas, in seminars, workshops, private informal consultations or from being invited to comment on early drafts of material. They help sharpen up concepts, spot weaknesses, suggest alternatives, provide more data. One always needs a certain amount of critical appraisal. It is especially important during analysis when one is experimenting with certain formulations – a new concept perhaps – and needs to test them out.

An example of these various processes is given in the following communication to me from Lynda Measor, in the course of the 'Teacher Careers' work (Sikes, Measor and Woods, 1985). It is presented as it was written, as an illustration of the emergence of a new theme, and carrying with it a sense of excitement at a new discovery, speculation at the possibilities, but also hesitancy in case, after further consideration, it is not such a good idea after all!

4.1.83
A new idea, and as yet not very well thought out, but here goes. Also I'm not certain if it has been used and talked about by interactionists as I'll try and indicate later. I know the 'bibliography' in other fields – mainly political theory actually.

I'm working towards a notion of 'special events' in the individual's life. This would connect into the theme B we have discussed, that of 'critical periods'.

Methodology
How did I come across the idea? As I'm building up numbers of interviews, that is I interview the same person lots of times, I've noticed that they repeat their account of certain incidents, usually fairly important ones in their lives. The other salient factor is that the account is given in the same words each time, with remarkably little variation. In addition this kind of repeating of tales is elicited most often when there has been a

gap in my interviewing of a few weeks, so the narrative has gone cold. They cannot immediately recall exactly what they told me before. Then I get the repetition of incidents, and the repetition of phrases, e.g.

1   Matt Bruce on being the leader of the invasion force into Jersey and the way that got him introduced into schools on Jersey.
2   Maggie Corbin on the picture in her portfolio of her father, he had a C.P. badge of the Soviet hammer and sickle in his lapel and as a result the headmistress of Varndean, who was interviewing her found out she was a Communist Party member herself.
3   There actually are quite a number in R. C. Clarke, and in Reeves.

Explanations and ideas

It might simply be that the repetition of incidents is due to lapses in memory, especially as people are getting older, that would not be surprising. But there is a problem there, because it fails to explain why these incidents should be repeated in exactly the same phraseology. Why doesn't the lapse of memory extend to that too? Why also is it that it is only certain things, certain incidents, that get repeated?

So maybe we can work towards a notion of 'special events' in people's lives, 'key incidents' yes, around which pivotal decisions revolve, incidents which lead to major decisions or directions being taken.

But it seems to me that there is something else of interest too, and that is what people make of these incidents. A range of devices seem to be employed to make these incidents 'special' or more accurately 'more special'. I'm afraid I delve back into folk loric stuff again, people seem to make a kind of mystique hang around these incidents and events, they make them out of the ordinary, they bestow special 'meaning' and special 'status' upon them. They seem to do this by a variety of oral devices, storytelling, ornate tale-making devices, which have the effect of drawing the listener's attention to them. Humour is used too, or more accurately 'wit', humorous short phrases surround the telling of the event, again these act as a signal flag, what Lewis called an 'alerting factor'. I'm also reminded of Sykes' material you found in the article on tale-telling in the factory, some of those devices seem to be at work.

The device seems at a theoretical level to be involved with putting meaning, organization, shape to a life, trying to understand a career? I picked up the idea of 'special event' however from political theory (again I'm afraid it's my thesis material). It comes from people like Sorel and Edelman. They discuss it in terms of the political life of a nation, and point to the way that particular events in that nation's history become special. Bastille Day to the French, and the taking of the Winter Palace to the Russians, it's a bit harder to do for England but maybe the Battle of Britain, or Dunkirk, as an example. These events do get a lot of attention anyway, they are meant to have meaning for the citizens of a nation, in that sense they are 'special'. But for political theorists it is the secondary devices which describe them which is equally significant. It is the films, a TV repetitious coverage, and the telling the tale again and again by many media means, which helps build up the mystique. Telling the tale, reciting the events, helps make the thing 'remade', 'different' and special. In fact there is more to this from classical theorists, especially those on Greece, with a whole lot of stuff about 'Kerygma', which might I suppose be relevant, it's all about events – real events, being seen as revealing underlying purposes and directions. In a people like the British, who have been very affected by Judaic–Christian and then Darwinian notions of onward progress and purpose underlying it, we might be able to see something of that socialization. Anyway that may be getting too fanciful. You may think the whole thing is too fanciful. (Measor, 1983, personal communication)

We did not consider the idea fanciful when we discussed it in the research team. In fact Pat Sikes was able to provide further substantiation from *her* data, and the theme was written up as one of the key features of a teacher's career (Sikes, Measor and Woods, 1985). Its discovery was made possible by certain clues – repetition of the incident, use of the same words. There is also something special about the words used, which put one on the alert. The same clues guided us to the significance of pupil myths in the 'transfer' study.

Pupils typically prefaced their accounts with signalling phrases such as, 'There are all these rumours that' or 'There's stories about' or 'I have heard that', which are cues indicating that a particular kind of information was about to be given. (Measor and Woods, 1984, p. 17)

133

Other clues might be irregularities that one observes, strange events, certain things that people say and the way they say them, things that get people excited, angry, surprised. And in the researcher is the recognition that 'something is up', prompting the use of a 'detective's nose' for putting the available pieces of the jigsaw together to form a larger, more meaningful picture.

I like to think this is how I came by the notion of 'survival strategy' at Lowfield. This, I argued, is something that goes on beneath the surface of teaching, and indeed often appears in its form. It may, I suggested in chapter 2, come to form part of a teacher's belief-system. I was alerted to it by a number of, what appeared to me, very strange happenings which defied explanation in any sort of normal way. For example, I observed a series of science lessons where the teacher, an experienced senior member of staff, went through all the processes of teaching a double-period practical, with apparatus, doing an experiment, drawing conclusions, demonstrating its importance in industry and relevance to the pupils' concerns – all of this taking about eighty minutes. It was a model lesson in many ways, but for one point – none of the pupils was listening, and it was clear that the teacher knew they were not listening. Normally, it seemed to me, teachers remonstrated with pupils, demanding their attention, but this one just taught on. The only time teacher and class came together was for the last ten minutes of the lesson when, by common assent, and in almost total silence, the teacher either wrote up notes on the board or dictated them and the pupils wrote in their exercise books, for the record as it were.

Other strange things happened, such as the case of 'the wrong film'. A teacher had promised a form a certain film in their next lesson, but when he came to unwrap it he found it was the wrong one, totally unrelated to the subject in question. However he showed it to them, none the less. Why did he not go on with more formal work, saving the proper film for next time? I thought that odd, as I did 'the good lesson' – a lesson I had been allowed to observe, which seemed to me utter chaos, but about which the teacher opined afterwards 'I thought that went quite well.' There were several other things – anxiety over the loss of free periods; enormous wastage of time; personality changes in teachers and pupils in the course of a day; a heavy reliance on dictation; great variety in teachers' relationships with pupils, from punitive dominance to matey fraternization; the extent of games and entertainment in the lessons I observed, and so on.

With the basic ethnographic question in mind ('What is going on here?'), it occurred to me that teachers were not teaching in many of these instances so much as 'surviving'. I think there were several factors in the gestation of this idea:

(1) an open mind that did not necessarily see what was going on as 'teaching';
(2) the atmosphere of 'struggle' that pertained within the school, with clear differences of managing or 'coping' among the staff, with some having considerable difficulties;
(3) the more obvious manifestations of how teachers managed – the use of humour in the staffroom, practising absence (days off, time out, unpunctuality), the use of therapy (giving them 'something to do');
(4) my own personal experience as a teacher, which allowed me to empathize with these teachers to some extent, and to reflect on similar instances with which I had been associated; and
(5) the literature – though there was not a great deal written on this subject, one or two key articles helped to give shape to the idea, particularly Westbury (1973) on 'coping strategies' and Webb (1962) on the reactions of staff in a beleaguered school.

Once the seed has been sown it tries to take root. Again I reviewed all my data, field notes and teacher interviews, and it seemed to me that a great deal of what I had observed in lessons could be interpreted in this way. Was not the chemistry teacher, for example, practising a kind of personal therapy, neutralizing the control problem by concentrating exclusively on the 'stimulus' aspect of teaching and totally ignoring response? Was not the 'wrong film' teacher bargaining with his class for their good order and responsiveness, perhaps, on another occasion? Is it any wonder that teachers should feel so vexed at losing free periods, when a relief from one's own survival problems is suddenly turned into having to cope with somebody else's? One goes on from here to more hidden cases, examining, for example, teachers' accounts of what they do, and why they do it; and while some come close to identifying the survival theme, others provide different rationales. Perhaps these themselves are survival aids? One therefore needs to find the major kinds of survival strategy. That still leaves the question, of course, of why teachers behaved in this way, and I shall discuss that in the next chapter.

Analysis

Models

A model is a replica of something else, which, though on a lesser scale, remains faithful to the proportions, and to the parts and their interconnections, and to the functions of that which it represents, as with the model of a ship or cathedral or steam engine. The usefulness of models in qualitative analysis should therefore be clear – they purport to represent on a smaller scale the essential components of very complicated processes, capable of being readily grasped by our limited intellects.

Constructing models is no easy task. We are not presented with kits of materials and detailed instructions on how to put them together. We have to work that out on the basis of our data. Sometimes links between parts of that are fairly obvious, sometimes well concealed (as with survival strategies above, or so it seemed to me). What we look at when we come to examine our data are partially constructed (or demolished) models, and we then have to puzzle how the rest fits together. Sometimes we do not have enough materials, so must go in search of more. Always we have to provide the mortar that fixes things together. Inevitably, physical models are less than perfect, and those of social life, with all its intricacies, inconsistencies, contradictions, are even less so. It is no rare thing, therefore, for people to propose 'alternative models' to those we might have suggested, perhaps claiming that we have missed an essential feature, without which the rest collapses (the flying buttresses perhaps), or that part of it, or indeed the whole of it, is misshapen, or that we have sand but no cement in our mortar. The more complete and strong our basic materials, the more thought we give to their assembly, the more telling the tests we employ to ascertain their strength, the more secure our models will be.

Models have been employed at all levels of educational analysis:

(1) at systems level, for example representing interconnections between political, economic and educational systems, and their sub-systems, as in Smith (1973);
(2) at institutional level, purporting to show how school processes work, for example, D. Hargreaves (1967) and Lacey (1970) on the process of 'differentiation and polarization', and Woods (1979) and Ball (1981) on the process of 'subject choice'; and
(3) at individual level, where we find models of teacher decision-making (Hammersley, 1979a; Berlak and Berlak, 1981), of the 'ideal pupil' (Becker, 1977) and 'ideal teacher' (Gannaway, 1976,

and see the classification of pupil views above), even of researchers of their particular approach, which they may or may not be conscious of (D. Hargreaves, 1977).

Given the complexities involved, it is unlikely that a complete, strong, original model will emerge from one study. Hence the custom of entitling papers 'Towards a model of ...' or even 'Towards a provisional model of ...' The hope here is that other studies will contribute, and this suggests the alternative – relating one's studies to an existing model or models.

Again, the notion of 'strategy' provides a useful illustration of this kind of cumulative work. At the same time as I was making my analysis of 'survival strategies', Lacey (1977) was developing a model of teacher 'social strategies' and A. Hargreaves (1977, 1979) one of 'coping strategies'. It is interesting that these three approaches were all made, in the first instance, independently of and unknown to the others, which is a fair indication of the general theoretical and methodological influence of symbolic interactionism and ethnography. We have seen how I categorized and documented teacher 'survival' strategies, having identified the strategical thread, stitching the various discontinuous elements together. However, though this may have represented the predominant mode of teacher adaptation in that particular school, it may not represent the generality of teachers, since it is at one end of a continuum governed by resources and policy; and, since it was mainly concerned with school and classroom interaction, it favoured the 'micro' element. Hargreaves, however, was interested in developing the theoretical base behind the notion of 'coping' as it was acted out at the intersection of micro-interaction and macro-structures, while Lacey was concerned to fill out a balanced model which allowed for consideration of personal redefinition of situations as well as situational redefinition of persons.

Lacey's model of teacher social strategies looked like this.

1   Strategic compliance, in which the individual complies with the authority figure's definition of the situation and the constraints of the situation but retains private reservations about them. He is merely seen to be good.
2   Internalized adjustment, in which the individual complies with the constraints and believes that the constraints of the situation are for the best. He really is good.
3   Strategic redefinition of the situation, which implies that change is brought about by individuals who do not possess the formal power to do so. They achieve change by causing

or enabling those with formal power to change their
interpretation of what is happening in the situation.

(Lacey, 1977, pp. 72-3)

What we had, then, were three different models which addressed
themselves to the same kind of teacher action, but along different
dimensions:

teaching ———————	survival (Woods)
micro ———————	macro (A. Hargreaves, Pollard)
self change ———————	situation change (Lacey)

Later work then considered the relationships between them, as well
as developing certain aspects of each of the models.

Lacey rooted his theoretical argument within the Chicago school
discussion of perspectives and cultures (Becker *et al.*, 1961), and it
could therefore be regarded as a refinement of some of that work.
I later drew on this when reconsidering some data I had acquired
on two teachers in a previous study (Woods, 1981). I was thus able
to provide further documentation of the model as it might apply
to more experienced teachers (Lacey was concerned with students
and noviciates), and some extension of it through the further consideration of two individuals (thus maintaining the 'grounded'
nature of the emerging theory).

A further development was then provided by Pollard (1982) who,
in considering the Hargreaves' analysis of coping, found it stronger
on the macro end of the dimension than the micro. As Lacey,
therefore, Pollard had found an *imbalance* in existing work, and
sought to strengthen the weaker area. He did this by developing
my work on teacher survival, through the notions of 'self' and
'interests-at-hand' (the latter well documented in his own ethnographic work – see Pollard, 1979 and 1980). Thus where Hargreaves tended to approach coping from the macro side, from the
point of view of what had to be coped with, Pollard concentrated
on the subjective meaning of coping and emphasized the importance of teacher biography, while attempting to pull all relevant
factors together in a theoretical model.

This now makes a useful springboard for further empirical and
theoretical work. One feature of all this work is the extent of its
grounding in the data. There has even been confirmation and extension of the 'survival strategy' data base (Stebbins, 1981), and
further modification of the Lacey model with the notion of 'strategic compromise' (Sikes, Measor and Woods, 1985). Now some
aspects of the Pollard model, derived by what we might call 'logical

integration', demand investigation. One such aspect is 'teaching biography'. We have little knowledge of how teachers' early experiences affect their careers and strategies.

In this development we can identify some distinctive guidelines for consolidating and stimulating research and the part played by models in doing it. These are, in the first instance, the initial *emergence* of the concept 'strategy', from ethnographic data, and the thorough *description* of the various types. This led to the production of the concept 'strategy' and its theoretical refinement. That this should occur contemporaneously in three independent studies was itself a *confirmation* of the significance of the concept, as well as an indication of the influence of the general approach – in this case symbolic interaction – leading people in the same direction. Also in evidence is a desire for *balance* in approaches and conclusions, and a drive for *integration* of various, and often apparently disparate, elements into a coherent framework. These last two indicate an interest in *scope* of the model or theory to cover a wide range of situations. Once the various studies begin to face each other openly, instead of going their own separate ways, then *cumulation* begins to occur. This of course is not a neat task of simply adding bits of model or theory together. Like the basic approach that guides it, the model itself that is produced is a continuous *process*. *Critical* testing goes on and further questions of balance arise continually. For example, the Pollard model may prove too complex to be of any theoretical use; we may, for instance, discover too many factors operating on teacher biography to hold all of them separate in any meaningful way. But that remains to be seen. Behind it all is the desire, eventually, to *explain* teacher behaviour and to *predict* the possibilities, given certain factors. What differential weight must we give to resources, policy, 'institutional bias', personal commitment and identity, and so on, in what teachers do? What combination of factors is likely to put teachers 'at risk' of failure (see Lacey, 1977)? To what degree can personal drive compensate for structural impediment? These are some of the questions this research may be able to offer answers to. The construction of models assists in drawing up the list of questions and in framing their nature.

Typologies

Typologies have a similar function to, and indeed the term is often used interchangeably with, 'models'. They can improve our vision

139

and sharpen our focus by drawing together a mass of detail into an organized structure wherein the major types are indicated. They can give us an idea of the range of such types. They point to relationships and interconnections (possible models?), and provide a basis for comparison and for theory-construction. Again, they can apply to different levels, from typologies 'for the classification of educational systems' (Hopper, 1971) to those of teacher commitment to teaching (Sikes, Measor and Woods, 1985).

Some of the material discussed earlier either involved typing, or led naturally on to it. For example, the next step in the survival theme was to identify the main types of survival strategy used in that school and to organize the relevant data accordingly. Such a typology is drawn up on the basis of a concept and data generated in a single study.

Another method is to formulate a typology according to certain concepts and principles, drawn from many sources. Thus Hammersley (1977a) drew up a typology of teaching styles on the basis of a number of dimensions he had abstracted from the literature (both conceptual and empirical), and his own research. He argued that typologies that divided teaching styles into two types, such as traditional–progressive or child-centred–subject-centred, one usually seen as good, the other bad, were over-simplistic. Such typologies offend the criteria mentioned earlier in formulating categories in that they:

> Often both overlap and conflict with one another as well as compounding what on analysis turn out to be distinct dimensions ... Needless to say, given this situation of descriptive inadequacy, the causes and consequences of particular forms of teaching have not in any sense yet been established. (p. 15)

Here Hammersley echoes the need for accurate description, clear organization, and discrete dimensions and categories. His categories and dimensions were:

A summary of the dimensions

1 *Definition of the teacher's role*
   (a) authoritative role ↔ no distinct role
   (b) curriculum ↔ method
   (c) narrow ↔ wide
   (d) high degree of teacher control ↔ low control
   (e) universalistic ↔ particularistic
   (f) product ↔ process

2 *Conceptualization of pupil action*
  (a) licensed child ↔ apprentice adult ↔ adult
  (b) individualistic ↔ deterministic vocabulary of motives
  (c) pessimistic ↔ optimistic theory of human nature

3 *Conceptualization of knowledge*
  (a) distinct curriculum ↔ no distinct curriculum
  (b) knowledge objective and universally valid ↔ knowledge
      personal and/or tied to particular purposes or cultures
  (c) hierarchical structure ↔ no hierarchy
  (d) discipline-bound ↔ general

4 *Conceptualization of learning*
  (a) collective ↔ individual
  (b) reproduction ↔ production
  (c) extrinsic ↔ intrinsic motivation
  (d) biological ↔ cultural learning path
  (e) diagnosis ↔ pupil intuition
  (f) learning by hearing about ↔ learning by doing

5 *Preferred or predominant techniques*
  (a) formal ↔ informal organization
  (b) supervision and intervention ↔ participation and non-
      intervention
  (c) imperative mode plus positional appeals ↔ personal
      appeals
  (d) class tests ↔ assessment compared to past performance
      ↔ no formal assessment
  (e) grouping ↔ no grouping
  (f) grouping by age and ability ↔ random, friendship or
      pupil-choice grouping.
                              (Hammersley, 1977a, p. 37)

Where, exactly, do these categories and dimensions come from? The categories are fairly standard, though traditional dichotomies tend to place more emphasis on category 5. A sociologist would obviously consider role (category 1), and developments in the sociology of knowledge in the early 1970s indicate categories 2, 3 and 4. As for the dimensions, some are fairly well known ('formal–informal classroom organization'); some utilize concepts from other areas of sociology ('vocabulary of motives'), or from other related areas ('the nature of human nature: pessimism–optimism'); some refine the notions of others who have been working in the same field ('pupils treated as "licensed children", "apprentice adults" or as "adults"' develops the 'childhood continuous–childhood unique' distinction used by Berlak and Berlak, 1981); some are inferred from existing literature ('specialized, authoritative teacher role–no distinct teacher role'); and some have such links with each other that they might be logically suggested, though they would need to have empirical support (1(b) follows on from 1(a) by asking what is the basis of the teacher's authority).

On the basis of these dimensions, Hammersley proposed a considerably more detailed and precise typology of teaching than usual ('tentative' and 'not exhaustive'), focused on four main types, which he termed:

(1) Discipline-based teaching
(2) Programmed teaching
(3) Progressive teaching
(4) Radical non-interventionism (a term borrowed from E. Schur)

Thus, discipline-based teaching involves:

> An authoritative teacher role legitimated in terms of and based on a curriculum. The teacher role is relatively narrowly defined and the orientation to pupils is characterized by universalism, a concern with product and a high degree of control of pupil action ... etc., etc. (*ibid.*, p. 38)

While Hammersley drew on a wide range of studies, I drew on a particular line in developing a typology of pupil adaptations. My aim was similar – to develop a more comprehensive schema than prevailing over-simplistic dichotomies (such as conformists–deviants, or the 'pro-school' and the 'anti–school' sub-cultures). For this, I adapted a typology of adaptations, originally formulated by Merton (1957), which employed a well-known and useful device of constructing a matrix composed of two critical elements. Those Merton identified were:

(1) the culturally defined *goals* held out as legitimate objectives for all or for diversely located members of the society;
(2) institutionally prescribed *means* of reaching these goals.

He proposed five major modes of adaptation to the social order based on combinations of acceptance and rejection of official goals and means. These ranged from conformity (acceptance of both) through innovation (acceptance of goals, rejection of means), ritualism (rejection of goals, acceptance of means), retreatism (rejection of both), to rebellion (rejection of both, but with replacement). This was applied to an English public school by Wakeford (1969), who added the important type or mode of 'colonization' (indifferent to goals, ambivalent towards means).

It seemed from my observations and discussions with pupils that the basis of this typology was sound, but needed further elaboration. For example:

> Acceptance of goals and means is too broad a category, for people can accept in different ways and to different degrees, as any ethnographer working in a school would readily observe. An absolute acceptance implies a mode that I term 'ingratiation' ('creeps', 'teachers' pets').

I therefore proposed that a strongly positive response to goals and means might be termed 'indulgence', and a more moderate one 'identification', the latter yielding a type of adaptation I called 'compliance' (see Figure 6.1).

These modes, then, themselves may have sub-types. For example, where goals are vaguely perceived but strongly identified with, we might find 'optimistic compliance'. Where the goals are identified with only so far as they advance the individual concerned's interests, we might find 'instrumental compliance'. Both of these emerged from my observations, firstly of new pupils at the school, secondly of 'examination' pupils in the fourth and fifth years.

A simpler typology employing a matrix structure is that in Figure 6.2 which characterizes teacher commitment by its nature and its degree (Sikes, Measor and Woods, 1985).

This typology draws on the results and analyses of several previous research studies (Lacey, 1977; Woods, 1979; Nias, 1981) and adds its own findings, which enabled the distinctions to be made. We hoped this would help to clarify and 'tidy up' the area, where several had made distinctive, but partial and at first sight opposing, contributions.

The commitment matrix in Figure 6.2 employs a category and a dimension. An illustration of the use of two dimensions is given in Figure 6.3, which purports to represent teachers' perceptions of subject choice. The matrix is formed by representing pupils' structural position in school (examination–non-examination) against the degree to which they are seen to have identified correctly the cues given them to make the 'right' choices (system acceptive–system disruptive). Both of these were strongly indicated by the data. The matrix, it will be noted, yielded four types of pupil in the subject choice process. Identifying the types in this way clarifies a problem for the teachers - of moving pupils along the lines indicated - and

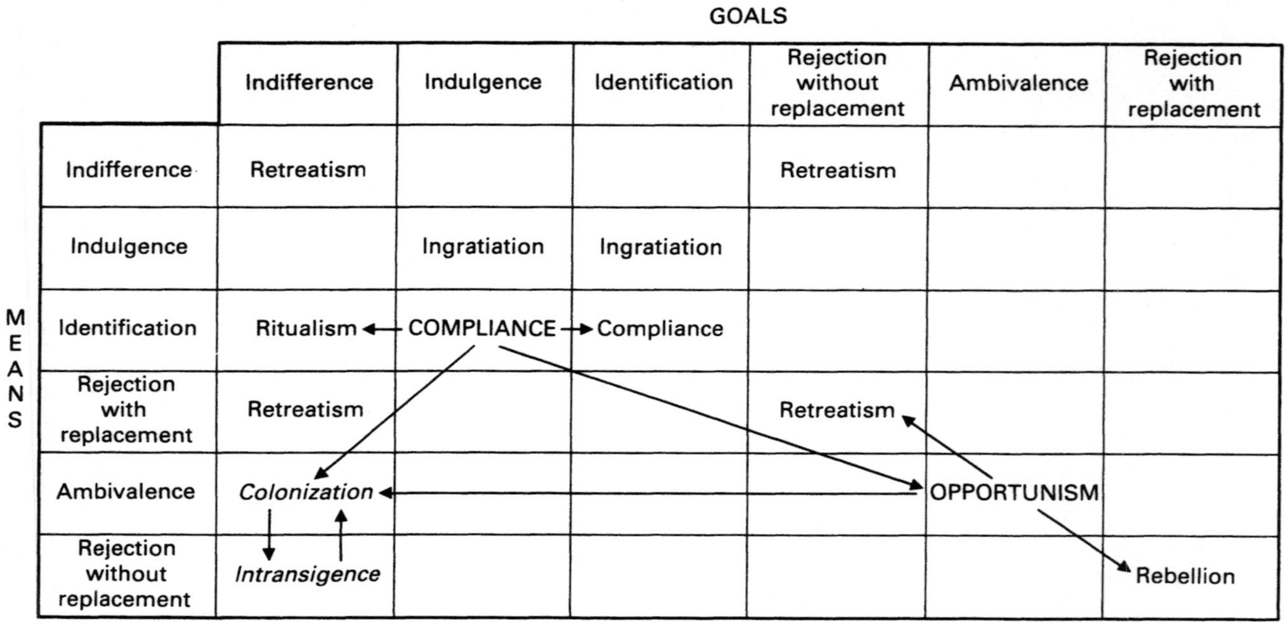

KEY

Capitals typical of earlier years
Italics typical of later years
Arrows some typical movements

Figure 6.1 Revised typology of modes of adaptation in the state secondary system

Forms of teacher commitment

	Vocational	Professional			Instrumental
	Education	Subject	Teaching	Institution	Career
Core					
Mixed					
Peripheral					

Figure 6.2

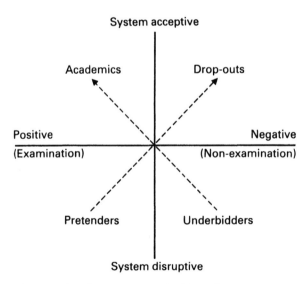

Figure 6.3   Teachers' perceptions of subject choice

raises questions about which pupils become these types and why (see Woods, 1979, pp. 52-4).

Models and typologies are primarily forms of description. In themselves they may aid our understanding of a field of social activity, for they are a special form of description, requiring distillation of large amounts of material, analysis and abstraction. No wonder they are often ends in themselves, or that a research study addresses itself to an aspect of a particular one.

However, their primary purpose in the research endeavour as a whole is to aid explanations of why things are as they are, or occur as they do – in other words, to promote theory construction. Thus Hammersley saw his typology as helping to lay the basis for a consideration of the causes and consequences of different teaching styles; Lacey devised his model of social strategies in the hope that it would promote research in neglected areas, and thus fuel a more adequate theory of teacher action; Pollard also pointed to new areas of 'coping strategies' that required investigation if we were to advance theory in the area of the relative impact on teacher action of micro and macro factors; and while I was interested to have come across 'survival strategies', I was even more interested in *why* teachers at Lowfield spent so much of their time 'surviving' rather than 'teaching'. Theory, then, is the ultimate aim, and that is the subject of the next chapter.

Chapter 7

Theory

The views of Glaser and Strauss (1967) have been very influential in the construction of ethnographic theory. The main emphasis is on discovery rather than testing of theory, but analysis is sequential – it is both guided by and guides data collection. Categories and their properties are noted and 'saturated'. Concepts emerge from the field, are checked and re-checked against further data, compared with other material, strengthened or perhaps re-formulated. Models of systems are built up in the process of research, and gradually a theory comes into being, with its distinctive characteristics of explanation and prediction linking the revealed concepts into an integrated framework, the operationalization of which has been demonstrated. Its plausibility may be strengthened by further case studies in the same area, though it may be continuously refined since it must accommodate all data and not simply answer to a 'majority of cases'. Later the level of abstraction might be raised by this 'substantive' theory becoming 'formal' theory, as case studies from other substantive areas are compared and examined for common elements.

However, though theory might be said to be well 'grounded' in the data, it does not simply 'emerge' or 'come into being', nor is it immediately *revealed*. However detailed and perspicacious the observations, at some stage there must be a 'leap of the imagination' (Ford 1975) as the researcher conceptualizes from raw field notes. This, just as much as later stages of theorizing, requires certain attitudes and qualities of creativity.

Theoretical limitations of ethnography

However, the creative powers of ethnographers working in educational research in Britain have been somewhat held in check by three factors:

(1) the nature of ethnography;
(2) trends in educational research;
(3) the desire to make ethnography a more rigorous scientific study.

It is necessary to understand why these basically beneficial elements have become obstructions.

The nature of ethnography

Ethnography by definition is descriptive. In anthropology it means, literally, 'a picture of the way of life of some interacting human group' (Wolcott, 1975, p. 112). In sociological ethnography, in particular, great attention is often devoted to the intricate detail of the picture, and the ethnographer, like the artist, works with great care at capturing both the general and essential characteristics and the myriad finer points which underpin them. The artist, however, has more freedom of interpretation. Faithfulness to a culture as it is found is one of the guiding principles of ethnography and immersion in the culture under study the general strategy towards this end. However, while it may aid descriptive finesse, it may also block theory construction. As Sjoberg and Nett (1968, p. 72) argue, 'a researcher must often be able to remove himself intellectually and emotionally from the immediate social situation, to step back and examine his activities in broader perspective'. But immersion and retraction do not go well together. A typical fear of the sceptics of ethnography, therefore, is that they 'might be left with endless description and a sequence of plausible stories' (Eldridge, 1980, p. 131). They might also be quite unrelated to each other, for it was feared that, as the common criticism of the Chicago school goes, they 'so stressed the uniqueness of their subjects' worlds, they could not articulate the linkages and interdependencies of these groups and the larger social system' (Brown, 1977, p. 63).

There is the oft-quoted Howard Becker remark to a student who asked his opinion of how to choose a theoretical framework 'What do you want to worry about that for you just go out there and do it' (Atkinson, 1977, p. 32), often taken (incorrectly) to imply a devaluing of theory. The student might also have been given Denzin's warning that 'If sociologists forget that the major goal of their discipline is the development of theory, a process of goal displacement can occur such that operational definitions and empirical observations become ends in themselves' (1970, p. 58). The problem becomes not how can we explain what is happening, but how can we describe what is happening. The researcher's inventive powers are thus directed towards representation.

Another trend which has tended to militate against theory has been the extent of concentration on the construction of meaning of interactants. It was felt that sociologists were running much too free with their second-order constructs, while the views of people in the real world on their own actions and thoughts were being disregarded. However a concomitant of 'bringing people back in', a highly laudable aim, was to crowd out analysis with a torrent of first-order constructs. As Eldridge (1980, p. 130) argues, 'Having brought people back in, perhaps the sociologist, a privileged observer, commentator *and* theorist should be brought back in as well.' Moreover it tends to become a representation of a culture as a snapshot, a picture frozen in time. This immediately compromises the main aim and offends, for interactionists, the basic principle of 'process and flux'. However conscious of past and future the ethnographer may be, consideration of those must always be of a different order to that of the present period of data collection. The fact is, however, that few ethnographic studies (my own included) have taken past and future into consideration to any extent. We have looked at situations as we have found them, and have become so 'immersed' that we have spent much of our time documenting and classifying. The problems of the moment consume much of our time, effort and ingenuity. We hear frequent references to 'muddling through' – indeed this is the preferred mode. Wolcott (1975, p. 113), for example, thinks ethnography best served when the researcher feels free to 'muddle about' in the field setting. Our attention is drawn to the precariousness of the situation, to the enormous logistic demands (rushing off to secret places to make field notes) and to severe ethical questions (Burgess, 1984c). These problems are always present for any ethnographer. The development of a more sophisticated methodology provides comfort but does little to remove them. Ethnography, too, is a highly personal affair. A community of ethnographers is a community of individuals, far more so than any other group of researchers within sociology. This is, in part, a product of the belief that all situations are unique and that, consequently, in a sense the research worker makes a unique study with individualized adaptable methodology. In part it is a product of the unavoidable conditions of research work, which involve individuals investing a great deal of time in a single organization. The ethnographer, as his/her own major research tool, emerges imprinted in part with the peculiarities of his/her own private negotiation with one particular organization.

Apart from being inherently an individualized approach, the history of the current ethnographic trend in Britain has not yet allowed for much collective appraisal. The ethnographic studies that we have, so far, have mostly been produced by individuals persuaded by the interpretive approaches that were coming back into favour in the early 1970s. There were no coordinated efforts (apart from the Manchester-based studies of the 1960s – D. Hargreaves, 1967; Lacey, 1970; Lambart, 1976). What we have, therefore, is a number of localized case studies, with their own points of reference, which here and there happen to touch on common concerns, but which for the main part are heavily introspective. This in fact is not peculiar to educational ethnography (Payne *et al.*, 1981, p. 114). Though this may have been unavoidable to date, in the long run it is not conducive to the generation of theory.

Trends in educational research

The requirements of *educational* research have also put a premium on description. Early sociologists of education in Britain in the 1950s and early 1960s showed an almost exclusive concern with input/output factors, and used quantitative survey techniques. Since the 1970s the 'black box' (Lacey, 1976) of the school has been opened up, and ethnographers have been celebrating the find ever since. There have been so many fascinating areas to investigate. Armed at last with an appropriate method, we have sailed into the innermost recesses of the school to try to uncover its secrets. We might characterize ethnographic work in schools over the last decade as a 'charting' or 'mapping' of areas of social life within the school. While this has covered wide areas, some have expressed doubts abouts its value. McNamara (1980), for example, speaking from an educational point of view, has accused ethnographers who have been working in schools of being 'arrogant outsiders', unappreciative of the problems faced by teachers in their work, while Delamont, from a sociological point of view, has argued, on the contrary, that educational ethnography has produced a picture that is 'all too familiar' (Delamont, 1981). There is a danger, therefore, that educational ethnography might fall between two stools, of practice and policy on the one hand and sociological theory on the other.

I prefer to regard what has been done so far as phase one of the overall enterprise. In a sense, the data have outrun the theory – in some cases categories have continued to be discovered and few have reached saturation point, while in others categories have 'flooded over' (as I illustrate later).

My claim, therefore, is that ethnographers have, for the most part, been riveted to a descriptive approach because, on the one hand, of their attention to fine-grained detail and, on the other, of the size and complexity of the substantive area confronting them and the pressures to 'cover' the ground of a new area. There have been easy riches for the picking, and armchair theorizing has been left to other approaches which value empirical work less highly.

Methodological rigour

Academic study always generates a methodological commentary running alongside it, and the ethnography of the last ten years has been no exception. Not surprisingly in view of the objectives rehearsed above, attention has focused largely on the primary tasks – the delicacies of gaining access, the intricacies of data collection, the niceties of the ethics involved – and the root question of validity, the essence of the ethnographic achievement. So ethnographers have addressed the question of validity with almost phobic zeal, rehearsing various forms of naturalism, techniques of observing, taking notes, employing informants, triangulating and presenting. I do not wish to disparage this work; on the contrary, I believe the methodology has been considerably refined during the ethnographic surge in recent years. My point, rather, is that it, understandably perhaps, has followed the contours of the work that has been done, and that has been data collection. The generation and formulation of theory has been a lesser concern.

Theoretical possibilities of ethnography

That is the dark side of the 'theory' picture. There is a lighter side. In the first place, there have been some notable exceptions to the general a-theoretical ethnographic trend, especially in the areas of pupil cultures (D. Hargreaves, 1967; Lacey, 1970; Ball, 1981), teacher socialization (Lacey, 1977) and teacher perspectives (D. Hargreaves *et al.*, 1975). Then, some ethnographies have made a strong commentary on some existing theories. Hammersley's teaching typology, for example, has serious implications for theories based on more simplistic typologies (for example Esland, 1971). Willis' (1977) ethnography of the 'lads' demonstrated the empirical weakness of correspondence theories, such as that of Bowles and Gintis (1976). Furlong (1976) showed that the sub-cultural formulations of D. Hargreaves (1967) and Lacey (1970) gave less credit than was deserved to pupil interests. There are several such examples, reminding us again of the interplay of stages and the part ethnography can take in that. Thus data collection leads to a particular theory being formulated, perhaps tentatively; further research casts new light on it, perhaps inspiring a more strongly constructed model or typology, which in turn prompts further research in areas previously not well covered; this might lead to modification of the theory. A particular ethnography can fit into this overall enterprise at almost any point. In itself, it may be descriptive, but it is contributing to the overall theoretical endeavour.

Further, it would be incorrect to regard many ethnographic studies in themselves as purely 'descriptive'. Lacey's (1977) and Pollard's (1982) models of teacher strategies are more like hypotheses, awaiting testing, which might demonstrate if and when the various types occur and interconnections operate. A. Hargreaves' (1981) comparison of 'contrastive rhetoric' and 'extremist talk' leads to the theoretical prediction that 'if we wish to look for sources of change in current educational practice, extremist talk would appear to be a better bet' (p. 229). Davies' (1982) discovery of the rules of friendship operating within children's culture *in themselves* help to explain a great deal about children's behaviour. My own accounts of pupils 'having a laugh' and 'being shown up' inevitably involved some consideration of *why* people behaved in those particular ways. There are many such examples.

It would be wrong, therefore, to represent ethnographic 'description' as something counter-posed to 'theory', and of inferior status. It is itself theoretically laden, and part of the general research enterprise.

Theory production

We are always seeking, in the end, to explain and to predict. If this is so, how is theory produced?

'A leap of the imagination' sounds rather grandiose. Have we got such imaginations? Can we do it? In fact, theory production is probably mostly sheer toil. One common avenue, as in other aspects of ethnographic work, is through making comparisons. There is a certain chemistry involved here. By putting two elements together, they may make a third, which, like steel, is stronger than the compound elements, and which was not there in the first place. This is how I like to think I worked towards a theory of teacher typifications. Having been through and organized my data, I re-read the related literature, which included Keddie (1971) and D. Hargreaves *et al.* (1975). This reading sparked off lines of thought, which I noted down. I give below an extract of these notes, just as I wrote them.

> p 145   Theory of Typing – speculation
> elaboration
> stabilization
> [Use my notes on teacher typifications, when discussed lists of pupils – see J. G., J. H., J. T., A. B., etc. LINK with Reports]

DHH (i.e. Hargreaves *et al.*, 1975) assumes teacher goes through all these phases or some of them – but see J. G. – some pupils he is just not interested in – girls, for example. Teachers can stabilize on extremely speculative data (of own experience at Branley – didn't like kids' look on face. Self-confidence of teacher's power position.)

p 152   Not very convincing. Do teachers do this – or more likely, the bulk of average, simply receive impressions from time to time (or not!), while others – v. good or v. bad, they might go through a more elaborate procedure.

H. (i.e. Hargreaves *et al.*) assumes a common response to all pupils. A different model needed for bulk in middle.

This theory is far too definitive.

Doesn't allow for initial viewing → compounding of prejudice → construction of type on initial insecure base.

An alternative theory puts the knowledge (pupil types) first (H. puts the pupil first – implies built up from knowledge learned over time) cf Keddie perhaps, and my unit on stereotypes. Less charitable than H.

Theory will then follow
– (knowledge of stereotype assumed)
– identification. Chance?
– accumulation (elaboration?)
  piecemeal and fortuitous
– stabilization (because teachers do arrive at firm views of
  pupils, by whatever means)
  reinforcement or alteration

Some know a great deal about pupils – family background etc. Most, however, know very little – they haven't the time.

Is the 'speculation' done for the researcher's benefit?

On its own this extract may make little sense, but it does illustrate some of the common ways of generating thought. Basically it is holding one's own data, and one's own experience, against a related theory, and trying to see which parts of it, if any, it supports, which it opposes. It makes strong use of contrasts. The main point was that the teachers in my study just did not appear to typify pupils in the same way as Hargreaves' teachers. This led me to speculate, provisionally, on an alternative theory, but within a similar framework to Hargreaves, and with some assistance from an earlier work in the area (Keddie, 1971). I then had to account for these differences. It could be a product of different methods, and I pose some questions about the Hargreaves' study, suggest its basic assumption, point to some weaknesses, and raise a query at the end about its methodology. It could be a product of different circumstances, in which case both theories could be valid. In the end I favoured the latter explanation (see Woods, 1979, pp. 173–9). The result of this was, I hope, a more comprehensive (though by no means complete) theory of teacher typing.

As one works through data and literature, there are two other mental processes that aid further development, and that, curiously perhaps, are somewhat opposed to each other. One is logic; the other is guessing. I think there was a bit of each behind my formulation of the 'survival' theory. I have outlined how I came to identify the concept of survival. Initially this was a hunch, or a guess, which I entertained for a moment while I *tested* the notion against my field notes and transcriptions, and against further data that I then collected. When it was shown to 'stand up', I systematically developed the typology – itself a further test of the validity and usefulness of the concept.

I then had to reason out why teachers behaved in that manner. From my observations of and conversations with teachers, one thing was clear: a set of circumstances one could envisage as a number of constraints, which acted as a check on their doing what they wished to do (i.e. teach) – such things as the high pupil-teacher ratio; the organization of schooling, which gave them a high proportion of recalcitrant pupils; examination requirements and few resources, which both restricted their options.

While this may account, at least in part, for their not being able to do what they wished to do, it does not tell us *why* they felt the need to keep up appearances in such a manner. However, I knew from my conversations with them that they felt under increasing pressure from parents, governors, inspectors – to become more 'professional', to gain examination results, to acquire more qualifications, to quell indiscipline, and to be *seen* to be doing these things. Growing accountability, therefore, was the next piece in the scenario.

However this still does not tell us why such a seasoned teacher as the chemistry master should go to such extremes as in the 'non-lesson' described earlier. Surely there is a point beyond which one will not go, either taking some action to try to change the circumstances, or moving elsewhere, or leaving the profession altogether? The answer to this, I felt, lay partly within teachers, partly within their situations. It is very difficult for teachers to change situations while there are high pressures and low resources, particularly, as in this case, in a traditionally authoritarian organized school. And it is difficult for them to leave. Teachers are the kinds of professionals who tie their energies and loyalties to the social system, and often their personalities become identified with the job they do. They become very highly qualified, after years of training. The further they go on in their careers, and the more experienced they become, the more specialized they become, and the more they identify themselves, their careers, achievements and prospects with teaching.

Why not move elsewhere? Because of another aspect of commitment: most have too many and too strong ties to the area where they live – family, mortgage, friends, hobbies – which all help to bind them to their job.

If these are the ingredients, how do they operate? Here I envisaged a pair of nutcrackers gripping a nut. One arm of the nutcrackers is the constraints and pressures, the other is the

155

teacher's commitment to job. The nutcrackers are being squeezed, the shell cracks, and the nut ('teaching') falls out. Only the pieces of shell are left, which teachers skilfully patch together to look as good as new. Its contents, however, have been lost.

One may refine the argument in several ways. Pursuing the survival metaphor, there are those who die or get killed off through dismissal or nervous breakdown. Some commit suicide through resignation. Some are bleeding to death, slowly losing the struggle for survival. Some are murdered, and come back as ghosts to haunt their murderers. (Riseborough (1981) describes a group of ex-secondary-modern school teachers who were demoted in status, below young, highly-qualified, newly-appointed staff of short experience, in a new comprehensive. They had lost their whole professional identities, and could derive satisfaction and esteem only through tormenting their tormentor – the headmaster.) Alternatively one can seek to formalize the theory by applying it to situations other than teaching. Wherever one finds those simultaneous pressures of constraints and commitment – in hospitals, the police force, the armed services, factories, universities, etc. – one might expect to find a survival problem.

This is a simplified version of the argument, the purpose of which is to demonstrate the logical progression from question to answer, to another question and answer, and so on until a coherent integration becomes possible.

Theoretically-based studies

The last two examples show some ways in which theory is developed from data, and how concept formation, models and typologies aid that task. However there are now sufficient ethnographic studies in education for us to think in terms of more theoretically-orientated studies from the beginning. We can conceive of this in several different ways. There is not much point in 'adding on to', 'illustrating' or 'replicating' existing theory (D. Hargreaves, 1981), but there is a need to move towards 'sensitizing' as opposed to 'descriptive' categories (Blumer, 1954; Bulmer 1979), and to develop and 'fill in' existing theory (Hammersley, 1979c).

From descriptive to sensitizing categories
Descriptive categories are those organized around common features as they are first observed or represented. Sensitizing categories are

more generalized, concentrating on common characteristics among a range of descriptive categories, which at first sight appear to have nothing in common, but which are revealed by comparison with other sensitizing categories. It is in this sense that the concepts behind the categories have careers (Denzin, 1970; see also Glaser and Strauss, 1967; Glaser, 1978; Becker, 1958). These are stepping stones to theory, and there are certain areas where we can make use of them. One example is in the area of pupil perspectives of school. There is now a considerable amount of data on these. Ethnographers interested in discovering how pupils represent the reality of school have found that they do not like teachers 'who are a load of rubbish', who are all straitlaced, who put them down, who do not know who they are (Marsh *et al.*, 1978); that they are opposed to excessive routine, regulation and restriction (Woods, 1979); that they like teachers who can 'have a laugh' with them, who are 'fair', reasonable, and understanding, but who can also 'teach' and 'control' (Nash, 1976; Gannaway, 1976; Delamont, 1976). Now several of these seem to have a common quality – the individual's concern with what they experience as dehumanizing institutionalization. It would appear that teachers also experience this in some form (Woods, 1979). We might hypothesize that some elements of conflict, at least between teacher and pupil, are rooted in the institution, and slant a future enquiry accordingly. Such an enquiry would immediately engage in 'theoretical sampling', where-in data collection is controlled by the emerging theory (Glaser and Strauss, 1967), exploring aspects of teacher and pupil role and school structure through teacher and pupil perspectives. Since such research is sectional rather than holistic, there might also be af-forded the luxury of a comparative study with two or more schools with contrasting structures.

This, then, is one example of a 'phase two' project; that is, one using existing ethnographic studies as a launching pad, more theo-retically conscious in the early stages, and engaging in theoretical sampling, hypothesis formation and testing. There is not the same need to 'muddle through', though it is important to stress that the existing theory is not accepted until the data is re-grounded in the new research situation. It is possible, of course, that new categories may be discovered and the existing ones unverified. That, then, simply adds to the baseline descriptive categorization. With more and more studies of this nature, however, this will happen less and less.

Another example of this kind of development is the area of teacher and pupil cultures. In the former, David Hargreaves (1980) has already done a kind of ideal-typical analysis, distinguishing three main themes in teacher occupational culture – competence, status, and relationships. This whole area is one replete with theoretical possibilities, for, as Hargreaves says:

> The teachers' culture is a significant but inadequately
> formulated 'intervening variable' between the macro and micro
> levels of sociological analysis, which we are currently seeking to
> articulate ... Between the experiential teacher dilemmas and the
> structural contradictions lies the mediating culture of teachers.
> (p. 126)

It is an area, therefore, worth examining for that reason, but there are other directions theoretical developments might take. We might discover, for example, that pupil cultures are also distinguished by their emphasis on these same three elements. They may be 'differentiated' and 'polarized' (D. Hargreaves, 1967; Lacey, 1970) in other ways, but it does seem likely that pupils of all social classes, genders, ages, races, nationalities, etc., are concerned with competence, whether it be in school work, meeting the norms of the peer group, or being a 'proper' person (*ibid.*; Willis, 1977); with relationships (B. Davies, 1982; Measor and Woods, 1984; Willis, 1977; Woods, 1979; Meyenn, 1980); and with status (D. Hargreaves, 1967; Measor and Woods, 1984; Bryan, 1980).

We must not, of course, commit the error of *post hoc* analysis; that is, impose categories on the data. However, one does not, in fact, have to search the literature very deeply to recognize their significance – they do, then, in a sense, 'emerge'. Further ethnographic work might 'fill in' some gaps in the data – with different kinds and ages of pupils, with different schools, and so on. In another direction, however, interesting possibilities would appear to be opened up in the area of formal theory (Glaser and Strauss, 1967), for the substantive categories of teacher competence, status and relationships appear to have formal properties by this comparison with pupils. They have a wider applicability than the particular circumstances of the teacher role and job; they have to do, it would seem, with human association in society, particularly in adapting to institutional life. This reflection might then lead us to examine different substantive areas that consider similar kinds of relationships, such as those that appear in Becker *et al.* (1968). We might speculate that these concerns are the product of the individual's struggle for identity in the modern world, and that their form and emphasis will vary, depending on a number of elements, such as economic and political factors determining resources and policy, institutional structure, environment, and so on. This in turn both suggests further areas for enquiry, and the potential usefulness of other theoretical traditions, in this case identity theory. In this way there is dialectical interplay between theory and data collection, precipitated by the initial theoretical cast of the study.

Developing existing theory

Another kind of 'phase two' study is to work from some existing already well-formulated theory, perhaps from a different field. Such a theory may help us understand our particular concerns in education to such a degree and no further, so that we must refine or develop the theory. Lynda Measor and I did this in our study of pupil transition (Measor and Woods, 1984). For this, Glaser and Strauss' theory of status passage (1971) was clearly relevant. We can easily identify several of the properties in their analysis, and by their relative strength and distribution gain some idea of the character of pupil transfer as a status passage. But our study of the phenomenon provides, we feel, further theoretical insights. In particular, the phases of these passages appear to have been inadequately specified (Van Gennep, 1960; V. Turner, 1969; Musgrove and Middleton, 1981), and the whole area of identity transformation or development in the process underwritten, as a result of previous concentration on social aspects. We may, therefore, be able to develop the formal aspects of this theory, taking into account not only material unearthed in our own study, but also related findings from recent studies of status passages in different substantive areas (Hart, 1976; Ditton, 1977; Oakley, 1980). Once we have identified these lacunae in the existing formal theory, they become a major focus of study.

In this example we began with the desire to improve our understanding of a particular educational phenomenon, which we believed to be of increasing *relevance* (owing to the growing compartmentalization of the pupil career). Initial data collection *mapped* the contours of the experience primarily from the pupil's perspective, and '*rediscovered*' the relevance of several of the properties contained in the *existing formal theory* on the subject. It also identified certain undeveloped areas of the theory, and attention then turned to *refining* some elements (in the area of phases) and *generating* other strands to the theory (in the area of identity transformation), these theoretical concerns now *guiding* later collection of data. It would be inappropriate to have assumed that this one substantive instance necessarily affected the formal theory greatly, but here we were able to take into consideration several other

159

recent individual ('phase one') studies in other substantive spheres, and thus to suggest that these new elements had *formal* properties.

Ethnography can contribute to certain theoretical areas as a corrective. Here, research may not be designed to test any existing theory, but material is discovered that raises questions about it and corrects certain aspects of it, without entirely invalidating it. Rather, it acts as a 'synthesizer'. A useful illustration here is within the field of pupil cultures, as previously discussed. Work here reflects developments, both within sociology and education, and reminds us that the *historical* element has to be taken into account in the construction of theory. In the 1960s D. Hargreaves (1967) and Lacey (1970) posited their differentiation/polarization model of two pupil sub-cultures, one pro- and one anti-school. These were linked to social class, but fostered by the school streaming structure. Differential norms and values were generated, to which individuals gravitated. This sub-cultural model was too restrictive for my own Lowfield study, which revealed a wider variety of responses, which underwent change along temporal and situational dimensions. I had recourse to the adaptational typology outlined in chapter 6, which was determined by reactions to official goals and means. All inmates are required to make a response to these, even if it is to reject both, but it assumes a priority which may actually misrepresent many pupils – and teachers. This was picked up by interactionists working closer to the fine detail of the lived moment. Furlong (1976), strongly criticizing Hargreaves for not taking pupil knowledge into account, developed his notion of 'interaction set', a more amorphous and transient grouping than a sub-culture, in and out of which pupils shaded; and Hammersley and Turner (1980) considered the pupil's adjustment to school primarily in terms of his or her own interests, revealing the problematic nature of 'conformist' or 'deviant' labels. Whether pupils conform, they argue, depends on whether the school has the resources to meet their interests.

Now I would argue that this represents a cumulative sequence, though not all the contributors to it might agree, and though the studies involved are pitched at different levels of generality and abstraction. It is distinguished again by the search for *balance*, and this particular series of studies does exhibit a certain roundedness. Theoretical purchase is immediately gained by selection of an *appropriate* area where there is a body of non-ethnographic theory available, in an area where ethnography can make a signal contribution. The ethnographic studies were undertaken first in a spirit of challenge and *critique*, focusing first on the deficiencies of previous theories and directing data collection toward their repair. This, in turn, created a new imbalance, which itself found one kind of rectification in the *synthesis* offered by Ball (1981), where he shows that the major bi-polar cultures still exist, but that a range of adaptations exists within them.

Attitudes towards theory

Throughout this book I have laid emphasis on the person and mind of the ethnographer. There is a considerable disciplining and conditioning involved – in establishing rapport, exercising patience, communing with conscience, recognizing critical cases, in interviewing, making notes, and so on. So, too, it is necessary to cultivate certain attitudes towards theory. I refer to two of them here – openness and creativity.

Openness

Ethnographers need to be more aware of and open to other substantive studies, both in their own area and in others, to other theoretical approaches and to other methodologies. There is limited usefulness in replicating studies and continually 'rediscovering' the same things. There are signs of this 'one-dimensional' approach, for example in the areas of 'negotiation' and 'deviance' (I include some of my own work in this, I hasten to add).

In the area of deviance we find, for example, 'deviance-insulative' and 'deviance-provocative' teachers (D. Hargreaves *et al.*, 1975); 'judgmental', 'explanatory/understanding', and 'fraternal' teachers (Grace, 1978); 'coercive' and 'incorporative' teachers (Reynolds and Sullivan, 1979). In negotiation, we have various metaphorical representations of forms of agreement as 'truce' (Reynolds, 1976), 'aided colonization' (Woods, 1979), 'negotiation' (Martin, 1976; Delamont, 1976; Woods, 1978; Ball, 1980; G. Turner, 1983), 'working consensus' (D. Hargreaves, 1972; Pollard, 1979), and 'avoidance of provocation' (Stebbins, 1970; A. Hargreaves, 1979; D. Hargreaves *et al.*, 1975; Bird *et al.*, 1981). The subject demands the kind of cumulative phase two work, spoken of earlier, which takes a bird's-eye view of these various studies, each for the most part contained within its own separate case-study, and which seeks to formalize the elements and properties of negotiation. If this were done in this particular instance, we might be forced to consider issues of 'power', for example, which some claim is underplayed in ethnography. Negotiation, of course, is all about power, but it rarely gets abstracted to any extent from the baseline description.

Further to this, the proliferation of studies in this area at phase one level causes one to wonder whether more cannot be done at source. Mutual research projects, shared research personnel, multi-site ethnography, research teams, are all ways of spanning the divides and overcoming the basically insulating effects of the method once it is under way. By advancing on some kind of team basis, we can economize on the basic steps of data collection, identification and saturation of categories and their properties and so forth, and more quickly arrive at the stage of sharper definition of concepts.

Such associations can be as loose or as tight as the people concerned wish to make them. Team research can pose problems, and indeed prove to be more counter-productive than productive, more 'draining' than 'stimulating' (Glaser, 1978, p. 139; see also Payne *et al.*, 1981, on ethnographic 'teams'). Team work may pose special problems within ethnography, for, as noted, not only is the nature of the research extremely personal, but also for that very reason it may attract strongly individualistic people. However, this can, and should, be allowed for.

There could be a range of alliances. At one extreme, we might have a fairly loose-knit organization where individuals or groups planned their work collectively, perhaps on different, but related, aspects of the same substantive or theoretical area, and where regular meetings, where data was pooled and ideas advanced, were built into the design of the research. At a more local level, the virtues of collaboration have been attested to by, for example, Glaser (1978, p. 29):

> *When it works*, its energizing potential is fantastic, each stimulates the other's thinking usually faster than a solo approach, each keeps the other on his toes and each can spell the other during periods of depression, decompression and lying fallow. A project can be done better and faster and finished more easily, since good collaboration takes over the solution of each other's problems during research such as 'can't write' or 'can't finish', 'can't interview such and such', 'can't face a certain aspect of the research' and so forth. One can conceptualize while the other talks data, thus working two levels at once with maximum energy. They can continually sensitize each other to the theory in the data.

Lynda Measor and I have had a taste of this during our research on pupil transfer (Measor and Woods, 1983, 1984). Lynda did all the field work, for a period of about eighteen months. During that time we met regularly and discussed the progress of the research, and it is fair to say, I think, that it 'evolved' between us. Several papers were produced, Lynda preparing the first draft, me the second, and both of us the third. We had, of course, by this time worked out our underlying theory by a process of dialogue and testing, but organizing the basic data around this theory is a huge task, let alone raising the conceptual level to dominance. Sharing the work certainly eased this task. Lynda took first turn at data organization. I would then edit this and suggest possible concepts and/or new categories and their properties. Lynda then told me which of these were sufficiently grounded in her data or were otherwise appropriate, and we would develop them together. She would also tell me which important points I had 'edited' out of her account, and we would ensure they were written back in more strongly. The eventual product was, I feel, stronger than if either of us had worked on it alone. It is, after all, a form of triangulation from source, rather than in the objects of the solitary researcher's attention.

In short, the collaboration aids in these distinct respects.

(1) *Refining* the categorization and conceptualization.
(2) As a check on *validity*, testing the strengths of data for conclusions drawn, and the strength of theory for the available data.
(3) Providing a broader basis for *comparative* work, since the total range of experiences and knowledge is increased enormously. This also can work for greater *balance* in outlook; in our case, for example, it helped to have both a female and male outlook. It is a useful corrective to *hidden biases*.
(4) Accomplishing *distance* from the data. This is not always easy for the field worker who has been intent on *immersion*. It also permits the field worker to indulge in that, not to the extent of 'going native' but at least to indulge in *participant* observation, which is hardly at all practised in current ethnographies.
(5) *Pacing* the work – allowing time to draw breath and recover after the totally exhausting work of data collection and initial analysis, without the sense of loss of impetus.
(6) *Generating ideas*, which are often sparked off in discussion.

As well as openness to others, which might allow for more coordinated work, we might be more open to other areas of substantive content. A. Hargreaves (1980) and Hammersley (1980) have both argued for more 'macro' concern on the interactionist ethnographer's part. However there is also another world within the individual, beyond the surface meanings. For example, symbolic interactionists have been drawn to focus on the world of subjective meanings, and have ignored the emotions and the subconscious. We shall obtain a very partial view of school life if we continue to do so, but we must, perforce, move into other theoretical areas if we are to consider them. Lynda Measor and I attempted to do this in our research on pupil transfer, where we uncovered a corporate body of pupil myths on the subject (Measor and Woods, 1983). To move towards an understanding of these, we drew on structuralist and functionalist approaches, and a Freudian analysis of the unconscious. However, this took place within an interactionist framework, and we tried, in the interpretation of the fantasy world of myth, to remain faithful to the pupil-life world as it was revealed to us by observation and interview. A condition of this kind of approach, we feel, is that data and analysis should be kept separate in presentation; in other words, the analysis should not obtrude on the data to the extent that it prevents other interpretations (see also D. Ball, 1965; A. Hargreaves, 1980).

Openness to other substantive and theoretical areas will also require openness to other methodologies. I indicated in chapter 5, for example, the usefulness of questionnaires. However, there are methodologies that complement ethnography more precisely, and which can assist in generating theory. One of these is the life history method, popular among the Chicago school in the 1930s and now promising to undergo a revival (Faraday and Plummer, 1979; Goodson and Walker, 1979; Goodson, 1980; Bertaux, 1981; Plummer, 1983). It is, in a way, a natural progression. As Goodson (1980, p. 74) has argued:

> Life history investigations set against the background of
> evolutionary patterns of schooling and teaching should provide
> an antidote to the depersonalized, ahistorical accounts to which
> we have become accustomed. Through the life history, we gain
> insights into individuals coming to terms with imperatives in
> the social structure ... From the collection of life histories, we
> discern what is general within a range of individual studies;
> links are thereby made with macro theories but from a base
> that is clearly grounded within personal biography.

This is not to say that the life history method is all promise and no problems. It has been criticized for its apparently atheoretical and unscientific nature. Of all techniques, it was the one that seemed most likely to produce the descriptive, journalistic, individualized, account, but, as Faraday and Plummer (1979) have argued, the selection of any research technique depends upon the general goals of the research. It would appear, for example, to be well suited to the exploration of the biographical arm of the coping strategies model discussed earlier, for it combines the various elements of the model within the life history, yet retains the traditional interactionist emphasis on subjective meanings, process, flux and ambiguity, and 'totality'. In such an instance, it begins with a firm base within theory, and might lead to a reformulation of it. Its chief theoretical contribution is likely to be exploratory, generating sensitizing concepts in new areas. While it will not provide general theories about social structures, it might illuminate those structures and the individual's relationship with them in a revealing way. As Faraday and Plummer comment, 'When one conducts a life history interview the findings become alive in terms of historical processes and structural constraints' (*ibid.*, p. 780). However they themselves prefer what they term 'ad hoc fumbling around' to generating theory in the streamlined way advocated by Glaser and Strauss, which they found too limiting. This was because their major concern was exploring a whole substantive area hitherto neglected in research. The technique is at its best, they conclude, 'when it is being used in an exploratory fashion for generating many concepts, hunches and ideas, both at the local and situational level and on a historical structural level, and *within* the same field, and in *relationship* to other fields' (*ibid.*, p. 785). The theoretical interest is preserved by 'systematic thematic analysis', whereby the sociologist blends the individual's own account with themes derived from theory (see also Glaser, 1978).

However, 'hunches' and 'ideas' do not appear in a vacuum. They may be stimulated by certain cues, and some research techniques might throw up such cues more than others, but there is another element – the most important instrument in ethnographic research upon which recognition of cue, formulation of idea, analysis of data and construction of theory depends – and that, of course, is the researcher. We can refine our methods as much as we like, but in the last resort, research – and particularly theory construction – will be as good as the people doing it. Its quality will depend not on the slavish adherence to technique but in the free exercise of the creative mind.

Creativity

There is some good advice in the literature on the cultivation of the power of insight, although discussion on this subject is often consigned to an appendix or is otherwise very limited. For example, in Glaser's book specifically on 'theoretical sensitivity' (1978) there are only two pages on 'creativity'.

The most comprehensive statement on the matter is still that of C. Wright Mills (1959). He urges total personal involvement, the cultivation of intellectual craftsmanship, the keeping of a 'reflective' journal (cf. the 'research diary'). He also draws a useful contrast:

> The sociological imagination ... in considerable part consists of the capacity to shift from one perspective to another, and in the process to build up an adequate view of a total society and of its components. It is this imagination, of course, that sets off the social scientist from the mere technician. Adequate technicians can be trained in a few years. The sociological imagination can also be cultivated; certainly it seldom occurs without a great deal of often routine work. Yet there is an unexpected quality about it, perhaps because its essence is the combination of ideas that no one expected were combinable ... There is a playfulness of mind back of such combining as well as a truly fierce drive to make sense of the world, which the technician as such usually lacks. Perhaps he is too well trained, too precisely trained. Since one can be *trained* only in what is already known, training sometimes incapacitates one from learning new ways; it makes one rebel against what is bound to be at first loose and even sloppy. But you must cling to vague images and notions, if they are yours, and you must work them out. For it is in such forms that original ideas, if any, almost always first appear. (pp. 232–3)

Are we in danger, in our concentration on certain aspects of method, of becoming ethnographic technicians, and of foreclosing on the possibilities of original thought? Again, the issue would appear to be one of balance. Most agree that the ideal–typical circumstance in which ideas emerge is a mixture of, on the one hand, dedication to the task, scrupulous attention to detail and method, and knowledge, and, on the other, the ability to 'let go' of the hold of this rigorous application, to rise above it, as it were, and to 'play' with it, experimenting with new combinations and patterns (*ibid.*; Denzin, 1970; Glaser and Strauss, 1967; Becker,

1970; Glaser, 1978; Weber, 1946). Certainly some of what I consider my better ideas, such as they are, come to me when I am actually relaxing from the task – walking the dog, gardening, driving to work, listening to music. I have to make an immediate note of these or they may vanish as quickly and mysteriously as they appeared, or some 'brilliant' ideas might be driven out by even more 'brilliant' ideas! Needless to say, many 'brilliant' ideas turn out to be not so brilliant when considered at length later, but a great number have to be rehearsed for a few of them to stick.

However, ideas never appear in a vacuum. The problem with all its ramifications has already been analysed and *keyed* into the mind. The mind, too, has been *'programmed'* with all the relevant materials to come up with a solution – other studies on the subject; certain theoretical formulations; a social scientific orientation which *disciplines* the production of ideas at the same time as they are stimulated; a host of past experiences; certain initial experimental attempts at putting things together. The mind is also *energized* in the sense that the problem nags and worries; there are, perhaps, curious anomalies in one's data, or they differ substantially from other studies in the same area, or one may feel intuitively, without being able to resolve it, that there is a relationship among certain apparently disparate elements, or some thoughts may have been 'pigeon-holed' for future reference during the data collection.

The achieving of this kind of psychological state has attracted some attention to specific techniques (see, for example, Denzin, 1970, pp. 68–74). We are advised to search for *negative* evidence (Becker *et al.*, 1961), to develop drive, curiosity, reflective consciousness and to 'de-stabilize' concepts (Sjoberg and Nett, 1968), to cultivate insights from personal experience (Glaser and Strauss, 1967). I wish to make a more general point, to do with our overall orientation towards our subjects of study. A distinction is sometimes made between scientific and novelistic ethnography. As social scientists we would want to identify with the former, and have been concerned to improve the scientific rigour of our work. In an influential article, Becker (1958) argued that qualitative research should become more a 'scientific' and less an 'artistic' kind of endeavour. Highly appropriate at the time, ethnography now stands to lose by such a separation, for theory can be aided by an artistic frame of mind. Popper observes that theories are 'the result of an almost poetic intuition' (1963, p. 192). Brown argues that 'The choice for sociology is not between scientific rigour as against poetic insight ... (but) between more or less fruitful metaphors, and between using metaphors or being their victims' (1977, p. 90). Brown advises cultivating 'aesthetic distance' for promoting 'perceptual and compositional activity' (*ibid.*, p. 53) and for sociologists to bracket their own world along with everything else. Nisbet (1962) argued in an essay on 'Sociology as an Art Form' that 'the science of sociology makes its most significant intellectual advances under the spur of stimuli and through processes that it largely shares with art; that whatever the differences between science and art, it is what they have in common that matters most in discovery and creativeness' (p. 544). He refers to 'processes of intuition, impressionism, iconic imagination ... objectification' (p. 545). His thesis is that art and science became divided in the nineteenth century, and they succumbed to myths: the one, that it involved 'genius or inspiration' and was concerned with beauty; the other, of rigorously controlled method and objective truth. But Nisbet argues both are concerned primarily with *reality*, and with understanding; both depend upon detachment. But it is the artist, or the artist in the scientist, that provides the 'leap of imagination'. He quotes from Rabinowitch:

> The artist is the most sensitive individual in society. His feeling for change, his apprehension of new things to come, is likely to be more acute than of the slower-moving, rational, scientific thinker. It is in the artistic production of a period, rather than in its thinking, that one should search for shadows cast in advance by coming events ... the revelation, in the framework of artistic production, of the mental attitudes which only later will become apparent in other fields of human endeavour.
> (quoted in Nisbet, 1962, p. 549)

And from Morse, that:

> Discovery in mathematics is not a matter of logic. It is rather the result of mysterious powers which no one understands, and in which the unconscious recognition of beauty must play an important part. Out of an infinity of designs a mathematician chooses one pattern for beauty's sake, and pulls it down to earth, no one knows how. Afterward the logic of words and of forms sets the pattern right. Only then can one tell someone else. The first pattern remains in the shadows of the mind.
> (*ibid.*, p. 550)

Likewise with sociology, argues Nisbet, ideas like Durkheim's theory of 'suicide' were derived not from data processing or logic but from a creative blend more typical of the artist. The message is a simple one: that science and art rely on the same kind of creative imagination; and that where art is defined out of science, the latter loses a great deal of its creative stimulation.

I am not arguing that we should not have a rigorous methodology, with due attention to matters of validity, access, ethics, data collection, etc., nor that we should not have tested and recognized techniques and routines. Rather that, as part of that methodology, we should give equal attention to the cultivation of mental states conducive to the production of theory as to the collection of data. One requires liberation, creativity and imagination: the other discipline, control and method. In some ways, they tend to work against each other, and where we put more emphasis on one, the other will suffer.

The first decade of ethnographic revival has inevitably been mainly concerned with exploration, establishment, credibility. The next phase must focus equally on the frames of mind, the circumstances, the resources that promote the creativity and originality that go into theory construction. Only then will ethnography achieve its full potential.

Chapter 8

Writing up

The 'pain' threshold

In the 'creative' activity of data analysis there is a critical point that falls as much within the communication of these ideas as in their generation. Ideas can be fleeting, hazy, ill-formed, fanciful, irrelevant, inconsequential. Often, it is only when we apply the iron discipline of writing to them that we come to realize this. Like the budding author in Piers Paul Read's *Polonaise* (1977, p. 131), 'The difficulty he faced with the white sheet of paper was not that he had no ideas, but that he no longer trusted his ideas to keep their shape as he gave them expression.'

Thus we might find what we thought a particularly useful concept rather difficult to grasp; or a seemingly beautiful, but light and airy idea only wafted further away as we try to seize it; or an apparently imposing edifice, encapsulating our research and all others in a totally new and discipline-shattering way, knocked over, like a castle of matchsticks, by a stroke of the pen. With others, we find, as we put on them the best constructions we can, a certain emptiness, banality, impossibility, inappropriateness, unoriginality. We may be forced back to a reconsideration of our data, perhaps to more data collection and re-categorizing, certainly to re-conceptualizing.

Failure, or a 'refusal' at this Becher's Brook of data analysis can be a disheartening experience. Perhaps this is why so many promising Ph.D. studies founder, why some research studies never get reported, and why some spend so long in data collection. It is not, however, an insurmountable problem. Charles Morgan has said of the artist, 'no one can be effectively an artist without taking pains ... This technical part of an artist's life may be learned, and the learning may be carried so far that it ceases to be narrowly technical and becomes a study of the grand strategy of artistic practice' (1960, p. 119). Thus there is a certain amount of craftwork in the creative enterprise. Additionally, it may be helpful to conceive of the problem not so much in terms of what you do to the data, but, again, what you do to yourself.

Pain is an indispensable accompaniment of the process. How often do we hear somebody admitting they 'sweated blood' in writing a certain piece; or stating that they know a certain stage in the research is near, and must be faced, but that they are 'dreading' and 'hating it'? This aspect of the research is best conceived as a *rite de passage*, a ritual, that is as much a test of self as anything else, that has to be gone through if the research project is to reach full maturity. If we do not feel pain at this point, there is almost certainly something wrong. Perhaps we are not progressing, and simply marking time on the spot, being satisfied with analysis at an elementary level which plays safe and avoids the risk of burning in the ring of fire, as well as the burden of hard work. While such reports may not be entirely without value, they may not be making the best use of their material. Researchers must be masochists. We must confront the pain barrier till it hurts.

We share this experience with all kinds of creative people. I recall hearing Philip Gardiner (a Norfolk artist) describing his experience of painting as 'tense and draining – but it has to be, I wouldn't have it any other way. It's very precarious, but it adds a certain lustre to life.' The biographical annals of composers, writers, poets, artists are strewn with similar accounts of self-imposed suffering.

Moral imperatives and mental conditioners

How, then, might we break out of this psychological state and render our chief research instrument more effective at this critical juncture? There is, firstly, a baseline of physical, mental and situational fitness without which it would be difficult to do this sort of work. I cannot write if I am tired, worried or ill, or if I am distracted. Nor does the creative urge in research and art necessarily go well with teaching. Research may benefit teaching, but the converse does not apply. As Hugh MacDiarmid has noted of art (in the general sense, and in the same sense that Nisbet, 1962, saw it as applying to sociology):

> To halt or turn back in order to try to help others is to
> abandon artistic progress, and exchange education for art.

171

> There is no altruism in art. It is every man for himself. In so
> far as he advances, the progress of others may be facilitated,
> but in so far as he is conscious of according any such
> facilitation, his concentration on purely artistic objectives is
> diminished. (1969, p. 45)

If peace is essential, so, too, is pressure. I have heard some writers
(novelists) say that their best work is done in situations where time
hangs heavy on their hands, but I have not found that always so.
Perhaps their pressure derives from a self-generating muse, whereas
I am very much a product of the Protestant Ethic. I need external
motivators. In fact the danger is that, given time, I sink into even
greater torpor. Certainly one must have time for analysis and writing, and research sponsors rightly stress the need to make due
allowance for it. But nothing concentrates the mind more wonder-
fully than schedules. We might bemoan them, but where a research
report is due, a publisher's deadline to be met, a paper prepared
for a certain seminar or conference date, then there is necessity
whipping the flaccid mind into activity. For this reason it pays to
contrive to have inserted in the research programme at strategic
points dates for the production of papers on some aspect of the
research. They must, of course, involve some investment of status,
and that means addressing a public. Thus status will be lost if the
schedule is not met. At the same time, it needs to be recognized
that there is a fine dividing line between a nicely crowded agenda
and overwork, the latter possibly having grave consequences for
the quality of product and personal well-being. Writing is like making sausages. The mincing machine works more efficiently and produces better sausages when the meat is being crammed in, but we
must take care we do not clog the machine or mince our fingers!

Schedules can be awesome and counter-productive if they ask
for too much in too short a time. The most serviceable, possibly,
are those that are staggered, that do not require a finished article
at a stroke, but permit degrees of sophistication. The leap from
data to presentation then need not seem too vast, and the perfec-
tionist instincts that many researchers have can be requited and
exploited in a legitimate way instead of adding to the difficulties of
the task. For there is a need to take risks in the early stages of
analysis, to 'play' with the data, to 'try out' certain configurations
and explanations. This experimentation requires feedback and
input from others. The ideal circumstance, of course, is the working
group, when it is freely acknowledged that all are concerned in
development.

Having internalized the moral imperative to write, I feel the need for some mental stimulants and conditioners. These are of two kinds, techniques and aspirations. Techniques are to do with the mechanics of communication. Here I might recall certain aspects of my training – 'Where to begin, how to end, how to orchestrate, how to be simple and direct ... these things are the armoury of writers' (Morgan, 1960, p. 132). And Morgan recalls his own indebtedness to his own former studies, for example Greek and Latin – 'For case, mood, tense, voice and a thousand refinements different from his own ... and while he fights his own battle for an elusive meaning, he may be fortified against the accursed blight of "It couldn't matter less" by the sound and memory of battles long ago' (*ibid.*).

The stimulation of mental agility no doubt varies greatly from person to person. I prefer at these times to read material other than sociology or education. To be sure, one cannot research in a vacuum, and a thorough knowledge of the relevant literature is assumed. However, academic research has a curious tendency to be all-consuming. There is so much of relevance to read, and which we feel we should know about. Thus if there is anything at all to spare we probably invest it in that further academic article or book that we just have not as yet had time to read. But while a certain amount of such reading is essential for research context, it may not serve us very well as models of presentation. For some, of course, it may inspire. Others may find forcing themselves to embrace a wider field of literature and art productive in terms of mind-stimulation and models for writing.

For power and economy of words, for mental leaps, comparisons and metaphors, I would recommend poetry (see also Brown, 1977; Harris, 1976). For strength of description, powers of observation, ability to bring off a point, give shape to an episode, form to a story, sustained development and integration, social commentary, human insight and sheer inventiveness, I would go to a novel or to drama.

A critic made this comment about Virginia Woolf's *To the Lighthouse*:

> It is a book that has deeply influenced me. I might be walking down the street involved in a series of thoughts which probably don't seem to have any connection – the brilliance of Virginia Woolf is that she discovered there were connections and, more important, she could make sense of them and write them down.

This is essentially the same kind of creativity involved in research.

Music and art are also helpful in this respect; they can calm the frenzied mind and reduce pain. Edward Blishen played a recording of Schubert's Octet obsessively whilst engaged in his *Adaptations*. Schubert 'can't have imagined that, 130 years after it was written, this enchanting music for the chamber would be used as a lenitive by a literary oddjobman' (1980, p. 38).

What all these forms of art have in common is:

(1) in their timeless, eternal beauty, a kind of absolute validity;
(2) a perfection of form – their various parts all hang together and follow one another almost inevitably;
(3) a sense of growth – as point follows point, it is not simply a matter of addition, but greater depth to the message; and
(4) human creativity – they are among the highest achievements of people.

All this is neatly illustrated in the play 'Amadeus' by Peter Shaffer. Salieri, in wonderment at some new Mozart compositions, exclaims 'Displace one note, and there will be diminishment; displace one phrase, and the structure will fall.' As he looked at the manuscripts he realized that he 'was staring through those ink-notes at an absolute beauty'. Mozart himself realized his worth. 'Too many notes!' complained the emperor. Replied the composer, with absolute certainty: 'There are just as many notes, your majesty, no more, nor less than are required.'

In all these respects, works of music, art, etc., serve as worthy models, in their mental processes, for our ethnographic work. All forms of art have the same properties. William Trevor, for example, himself a former sculptor, likens his story-telling to moulding and chipping away at a sculpture. It is what the writer David Lodge is alluding to when he says, 'Every word must make an identifiable contribution to the whole.' Structuralists argue that there are basic common properties among these various different areas (see also Hammersley and Atkinson, 1983). Though 'transfer of training' theory was not popular a few years ago in the debate over the usefulness of Latin as a school subject, Levi-Strauss, for example, believes that the receipt by the brain of musical messages can serve as a model for the receipt of all other kinds of cultural message. For example, he argues that melody and harmony illustrate the structural linguist's distinction between sequence and content. Interestingly, Levi-Strauss himself is often described as an artist as well as a scholar, and 'his style remains a baroque combination of order and fantasy' (Sperber, 1979, p. 24).

There is a further point – that whatever we select to consider in the area of art will reflect our own personal concerns and make-up, and encourage reflectivity. Thus it not only helps put our research on a broader plane of people's affairs, but helps give it depth. Ethnographic work is extremely personal. To a greater extent than other forms of research, it allows a working out of one's own destiny within the context of 'public issues'. In other words, it offers insight into problems and anomalies one may have experienced in the past in a structured way aligned to general human experience, and thus avoids the excesses of self-indulgence.

Cranking-up

These models are the Rolls-Royces of the artistic world. When I come to address myself to writing up research, I am reminded of my first car, an ancient Morris 1000, which had to be cranked up before it would start. It was rather erratic in its running (largely, I eventually discovered, because of the tendency for its tappets to seize up), and boiled over on occasions, but it usually got there in the end, though not very quickly.

The 'cranking up' is a necessary preliminary. Analysis is multi-layered – it does not all take place on the same mental plane. Writing is such a different activity from other responsibilities of teaching and academic life that we are not usually in the right frame of mind, nor do we fall into it naturally; it has to be artificially induced. We might regard it as another one of those 'challenges' and as potentially very rewarding intellectually. We might persuade ourselves that we actually enjoy writing, though any intellectual reward or enjoyment usually comes afterwards, certainly not at the beginning. 'Writing-up' research is nothing like the delightful essays we used to do at junior school, or the cathartic bits of biography, diary or magazine articles we may compose from time to time, which have a stronger measure of self-indulgence and journalese about them. Academic writing is a strongly disciplined activity, and we have to gear ourselves up for it.

I might have to set anything from a day to a week aside for 'cranking up'. I might find that I have two or three clear days that I can give over to making a start on writing, to generate a bit of impetus that may then be carried on over the next two to three weeks. This is an average time for getting to grips with a writing project, and in general I find I have to devote all my attention to it during that period if I am to master it. I am very unsociable and rather ill-tempered during this time. Some of us may actually have to appear to undergo profound personality changes in order to do the work. Unlike Dr Jekyll, however, we have no magic potion.

I find it is done almost by default. That is, I always delude myself into thinking that I am actually going to commence writing on those first days. I rarely do, for what happens is confrontation and engagement with the pain barrier. Part of this is to do with forcing oneself into psychological overdrive. What these initial two to three days consist of, then, might be a reconsideration of all the research material, a continuous sifting and re-sifting, clearing out the debris, identifying the strengths, aligning the material towards them, checking on key associated work, re-classifying, having one or two attempts at an introduction, and, if that fails, putting together one of the more complete, coherent and interesting sections. If the latter works, it can snowball and provide a comparatively easy passage. More typically, it is only the beginning of the struggle.

What one is doing, then, in these early stages is, first, undergoing a process of 'psyching up' to writing pitch (a process attended by some disorder and discomfort), and, second, going through the initial stages of preparing one's material for presentation. The cranking-up process is partly systematic and consolidating, partly disorderly and adventurous, as one searches for new configurations. This latter indicates a third activity therefore, one of trying to develop new insights. It comes from reading and re-reading field notes, transcripts, summaries, categories; examining comments made along the way, perhaps in a research diary, made at the time 'for future reference'. One tests out a few more ideas, seeing what they look like on paper. Diagrams are useful in trying to show inter-relationships. The wastepaper basket fills up rapidly. Robert Graves was told by an early mentor that his 'best friend was the wastepaper basket' and this, he later discovered, was 'good advice'.

At the end of the first day, therefore, all that may have been produced is a side of A4, which will probably be at once discarded the following day, but a great deal of mental preparation and ground clearing of data will have been done. I have a standard 'production rate' of five written pages, or a thousand words a day. I think this is a kind of writer's norm I have somehow internalized, and it seems to be about right when I am working properly. The quality may be variable, especially to begin with, but I do not worry about that at this stage, as long as the brain is being oiled into gear and some ideas are beginning to come. The 'quota' stands as some tangible and identifiable product of the work of the day. While this is a stage for throwing ideas around in the mind and testing out alternative constructions, the acid test for them is whether they retain their potential value in communication. The quota is a reasonable amount to provide for such a test – long enough to require sustained and coherent thought and to reflect fairly large-scale organization, and short enough to tackle in a day without exhausting front-line concentration.

Protestant Ethic (P.E.) person also internalizes time regulation. When I was schoolteaching, this was beautifully controlled externally by the 'nine to four' and 'termly' requirements; you knew when you were working and when not. As an academic, management of time is more personal, but I find I am still governed by P.E. standards. The ritual of sitting down to work at 9 a.m. and working through to 12 or 12.30, and then a further two hours in the afternoon, is a good mental discipline. Without this moral impulsion behind the ritual I doubt whether I would ever get round to writing at all. However, it is a curious thing that, while I keep to the ritual, 'off-duty' hours can be vastly more productive. Thus, winter evenings, weekends, late at night and occasionally early in the morning are all comparatively high productivity times. P.E. standards dictate that these are 'free time', and the psychology of it is that I cannot make a mess of them, or it does not matter if I do. I am consequently more relaxed, and usually therefore more productive. Periods before holidays are also useful. Holidays must be earned, and, if a project is unfinished, will not be enjoyed. There is, too, a strong practical impulsion, for a partially finished project means that 'cranking up' has to commence again on the same piece, after the 'limbering down' of the holiday – hardly the best use of scarce resources.

Having got cranked up, successfully engaged a gear and begun moving, I will at various points meet a roadblock. I take comfort, however, from the fact that this happens to the best of authors. In one of his novels, Tchekhov agonized for days over how he was going to get one of his heroines across the threshold of a house. Conrad had terrible torments. He sometimes wished to be a stone breaker, because 'There's no doubt about breaking a stone. But there's doubt, fear – a black horror, in every page one writes' (Karl and Davies, 1983). Edward Blishen speaks of a highly capable novelist of his acquaintance who, after writing 'a hundred splendid pages would be overtaken by literary dread at its worst' – fear of reviewers, and fear that 'the narrative had come to a halt' (1980, pp. 118–19). He would beg Blishen 'to tell him frankly if I thought his skills were in decline ... And at the end, always, as I made the noises necessary to keep him writing, he'd ask, "Does it move? It does move, doesn't it?"' The moral here is that we need good

177

friends, mentors, trusted colleagues whom we can rely on for good advice and moral support. This kind of therapy does not rule out the equally valuable constructive criticism one looks for from colleagues, which at times might be quite trenchant – though that is addressed to a different problem.

Writers develop their own psychological boosters. John Mortimer (1983, p. 9) has his study plastered with his own playbills. 'I've never been strong on confidence. When the page is blank and you fear, as I regularly do, that it may never be filled again – it does help to look up and think at least I wrote *that*!' For those of us who have not got that far, we must have recourse to basic elements of character – confidence in one's ability to pass the threshold; patience, in not expecting too rapid a return and in tolerating difficulties and hold-ups; stamina and determination, to keep at the task, exploring all avenues and employing all one's resources in countless configurations to find a way ahead. At such junctures we might recall Masefield's optimistic lines (1932):

> Therefore, go forth, companion: when you find
> No highway more, no track, all being blind,
> The way to go shall glimmer in the mind.

though it is as well to bear in mind the old adage that the 'light at the end of the tunnel may be an oncoming train!'

There are strategies one can bring to bear on blockages. The first thing is to analyse the problem. Is it because you are tired (even though perhaps you have not reached your quota)? The answer, clearly, is rest, or a change of activity. Is it because of a lack of preparation or inadequate groundwork, so that you really do not know what you want to say? This would require a reconsideration of data, more reading perhaps, and certainly more preliminary thought. Or perhaps you have an uneasy feeling that the account is going up a blind alley or that what seemed like the right direction in planning, now in writing turns out to be a mirage. There is no alternative but to return to the beginning of the faulty line. The important thing is not to get consumed by the blockage, but to master it.

Otherwise, there are numerous little ploys that I am sure we all use to avoid such blockages. Gazing out of the window at the panoramic vista ('I will lift up mine eyes unto the hills from whence cometh my help'), drinking numerous cups of coffee (as much for the breaks as for the caffeine), pacing the room, listening to a cheerful thrush, examining distant activity on the allotments through binoculars (Damn! The coalman is getting ahead of me again!), conversing with the dog, explaining a point or making a speech to an imaginary audience (C. Wright Mills, 1959, recommended this), holding a conversation in one's head, taking a walk around the garden, playing the violin ... and so on. Thomas Keneally has a snooker table in his study for such moments. Some recommend a bout of strenuous exercise, almost as if thrashing the ennui out of one's system – squash, swimming, running. One headmaster I knew used to keep a punchbag in his office for 'insoluble problem' times.

However, one needs to distinguish genuine blockages from self-induced ones. Work-avoidance strategies are particularly subtle in writing activities. In a study of student methods, Bernstein (1978, p. 30) describes the 'creativity fritter'.

> It is best to wait until you are bursting with ideas or are sufficiently motivated, even if the motivation is guilt due to unsuccessful previous application of fritter techniques. This is therefore the let-it-brew-for-a-while fritter (closely related to this is the I'll-lie-down-and-think-about-it fritter; the possible danger in this tactic is, of course, very clear; listing all things people are designed to do horizontally, studying is one of the lowest on the list).

We might take heart again from the fact that even the best writers 'fritter'; indeed they excel at it. Coleridge wrote to a friend, 'To-morrow morning, I doubt not, I shall be of clear and collected spirits; but tonight I feel that I should do nothing to any purpose, but and excepting Thinking, Planning and Resolving to resolve – and praying to be able to execute' (letter to John H. Morgan, 1814). William Cowper similarly:

> Difficult (I say) for me to find opportunities for writing. My morning is engrossed by the garden; and in the afternoon, till I have drunk tea, I am fit for nothing. At five o'clock we walk; and when the walk is over, lassitude recommends rest, and again I become fit for nothing. The current hour therefore which (I need not tell you) is comprised in the interval between four and five, is devoted to your service, as the only one in the twenty-four which is not otherwise engaged (letter to the Rev. William Unwin, 1781).

Work-avoidance strategies may indicate a genuine need for relief, or an only-too-human reaction to steer clear of pain. We might at least recognize them for what they are. As for blockages, one might try to head them off by ensuring a stream of options. Pen and paper should be carried at all times. Ideas may be sparked off by auto-suggestion when watching television, listening to the radio, cooking a meal, digging the garden, and should be noted down before forgotten. I find driving in the car a particularly productive situation, and here a recording machine is helpful. When writing, I often find the mind playing with future possibilities at the same time as concentrating on the point in hand. Even as I write, I scribble down a key word at the bottom of the paper to remind me of them, lest they be lost.

If a blockage is unavoidable and immovable, I go elsewhere to some other part of the analysis where the going is easier. This helps recovery of fluency and confidence and helps salve the P.E. conscience as it fills out more of the quota, or I may go back over what I have done filling out a point here and there and further rationalizing my plan. I shall then return to the blockage later, with new-found impetus. The whole report, paper, article or book is then put together later like a film at cutting and editing stage. I rarely write an article sequentially. The introduction is usually written last, for only then will I be sure of what the article is about. My final handwritten manuscript will be a mass of deletions and inserts, some written overleaf, some on extra pages, which themselves will have inserts, deletions and, perhaps, extra pages. A secretary once described my manuscripts as like a game of Monopoly – 'Go to . . .' 'Do not . . .' 'Go back to . . .' 'See over . . .', with lines, arrows, bubbles, etc.

If all else fails, the blockage may lead to discarding that particular element, or at least pigeon-holing it for future reference. However, it is as well to bear in mind that these are likely to be the most gratifying, worthwhile and celebrated aspects of the work if the problems are overcome. They should not be set aside lightly.

Planning

I recall in my school days the requirement to 'plan' an essay in rough. It was a one-off activity. You did your plan – you 'thought' – and then you followed it and 'wrote'. Planning in writing up research is immensely more complicated. The former is secondary work, and not particularly creative. The latter is a search for new formulations, and almost by definition cannot be planned in advance, for the creative process continues into writing up. In fact it may be *the* most creative part of qualitative work, and at times it is difficult to distinguish between planning and writing.

However, like patios and paint, as I have found over the years, you cannot apply the finish successfully without a good foundation. One's whole research, of course, involves planning, but in qualitative work, data collection ranges in a free and relatively uncommitted way. Plans for the final product usually begin to take shape during initial analysis, beyond which I find four main planning stages:

(1) a preliminary, partly systematic, partly randomized, speculative scheme;
(2) a provisional working plan;
(3) a re-worked plan at first draft stage, which may be repeated in subsequent drafts; and
(4) a final tidying up plan.

Their nature is as follows.

Speculative scheme

The initial scheme attempts to combine the solidity of the work already done with more speculative attempts to theorize and conceptualize. One must be heavily selective, reducing the data to a manageable size for the presentation vehicle in mind. Ideally, the plan should present an all-inclusive, see-at-glance picture of all the most important features of the research. This facilitates seeing what relates to what, and in what way various elements might hang together. Weak, unsupported elements are discarded. Data is marshalled to support others, and examples chosen. At the same time this fairly mechanical work is accompanied by 'brainwaves' – attempts to see the data in a new light. I will make plenty of notes at this stage, scribbling down these brainwaves as and when they come to me. I shall end up with a file of these, which I duly go through on an appointed 'planning' day. They will be annotated and classified, added to as further thoughts occur, and reduced as I find similar points repeated. The preliminary plan may be fairly detailed, and certainly the more thoroughly it is done, the easier the passage into writing, even though that particular plan may soon be radically altered. For it is performing another function – preparing the mind. It is not only giving it a grasp of the whole enterprise but forcing it to concentrate on the mechanics of construction. In the next stage, 'writing' will combine with this to produce the more lasting plan.

Writing up

Provisional working plan

The provisional working plan is abstracted from this. It consists, in essence, of a number of major headings, with sub-headings where appropriate, and an indication of the content (and where it is to be found) to be included under them. I may have a special chart for points I wish to emphasize in the conclusion. The latter is not easily written, yet is one of the most important sections. One solution, therefore, is to carry forward an ongoing plan of the conclusion, to which notes are added as writing proceeds.

All the notes and data headings are systematically reconsidered to check for omissions or misrepresentations. Then the working plan is re-examined for order and for connecting links. These are not too strong at this stage, for the working plan will inevitably be changed once writing commences. In qualitative work especially, it is important to carry this divergent cast of mind through almost to the end product.

Re-worked plan

A re-worked, 'realized' plan emerges in writing the first draft. The preliminary plan will not be slavishly followed, for improved ideas will emerge as you begin to write. Some sections may prove very productive, others less so. In fact, any overall plan may be suspended temporarily while promising lines of thought, themselves with several branches, are investigated. If they prove productive, they may be afforded greater prominence within the scheme, and others relegated. The first draft may thus have a kaleidoscopic quality about it which is stitched together to provide an element of coherence and continuity, and which may bear little resemblance to the preliminary plan. This coherence, however implicit, should be real, and available for strengthening in subsequent drafts. However, what you may find yourself doing at this stage is indulging the development of the component parts. You have a notion of the finished product, but its eventual quality depends on the quality and strength of its component parts as well as the way they are put together. You cannot make a Rolls-Royce out of Morris 1000 parts.

182

Final plan

It follows that there must be a further plan, where the linkages, development and explanation are strengthened, and the material, possibly, again re-ordered. It sometimes pays to set the first draft aside for a while to 'mature'. Returning to it with a fresh mind, it is easier to spot strengths and weaknesses. Also new resources are brought to bear, in the form of new thoughts, more 'focused' research and reading, and, most importantly, the reactions of others. Also, by this stage, the pain barrier has been overcome, and the tidying up can be done with greater confidence and equanimity. You have successfully externalized the product, and can now relax and 'chip away' at its improvement, deleting here, adding a further word of explanation there, finding a more mellifluous and accurate phrase perhaps, re-ordering, tightening up, fitting it in to the general framework of research to which it relates, adding references, drawing conclusions.

At this stage the severest tests are applied. What is missing here? What is wrong with this argument? What does it need to strengthen it? How else could this material be interpreted? How could this be criticized? What prejudices am I indulging? What do I really mean by this? Here there is a nice quote – but is it really needed? Here are some impressive sounding sentences – but what are they saying? There are some good points in this paragraph – but do they really relate to what goes before and after? Though in some ways easier to do than initial composing, in some ways it is still quite hard to summon up the resolve to rewrite sections once they have been typed. Nonetheless, it has to be done.

The twin principles here, I think, are that one must plan at each stage, but also maintain flexibility. It is not only important to have some sense of the overall scheme – we cannot just sit down and start writing – but equally important to realize that as the intensity of mental involvement with the data increases at each stage, so the previous plan may be amended or discarded. William Walton said he had not wanted to do 'Facade' at the time. His comment later was, 'One sometimes happens to do something very good by mistake.' This is equally true of writing. One must aim for a productive tension between constructive planning and anarchic, but potentially highly productive, freedom.

With all these stages of writing and levels of thought, it is helpful to the psychological management of one's output to have several projects, or aspects of a project, under way at the same time, all at different stages (see Glaser, 1978). Malcolm Bradbury, for example, has various exercises in different typewriters around his house. It is comforting to be in the final stages in one, and to have the option of 'chipping away' at a second draft for another, when one is working up inspiration for assaulting the pain barrier with a third. If they are related, they might 'feed off' each other; and certainly allow for ease of switching between psychological states, thus maximizing the use of one's time and energies. This, however, calls for careful scheduling – over-production can lead to under-achievement.

Common failings in first (and sometimes later) drafts

In countering pain and meeting the difficulties of writing up, there is a natural tendency to have recourse to some false solutions. This is another reason why it is so difficult to produce a finished paper in one or even two drafts. Among these are the following.

The 'straw person'

There is a strong temptation to work on a principle of contrasts. Thus, in an attempt to highlight one's own argument and increase its purity and force, one may construct an apology of an opposing one which does not really exist. It is a kind of bastardized ideal type, drawing on the evils of certain positions and glueing them together into a Frankenstein's monster of a case. The straw person typically draws on the work of a number of people and in itself is recognizable as nobody.

Another similar form of misrepresentation, is to seize on only those points within one person's position that serve the present purpose, ignoring their context which may well modify those points. This is error enough in itself, but the major sin is inadequately contextualizing one's own work within the field. Of course, people who disagree with the representation of their position and one's analysis also, on occasions, shout 'Foul! Straw person!' when it is real flesh and blood.

Over-claiming

This often accompanies a straw person. One gets carried away by excitement and enthusiasm as ideas emerge, and in attempting to make the most of the argument in the strongest terms, one over-states the case. It is often only when the product is seen in type that this is recognized. The initial exuberance has faded, and a more rational evaluation can take place.

It is worth noting that there are pressures on us to over-claim. It has often been remarked that only positive research gets reported. We need to make our research tell and count. We are therefore looking for opportunities to 'excel'.

Under-claiming

This derives from an unwarranted modesty or failure to perceive possibilities. The report may be written 'down' in an inconsequential way, set in a rather lugubrious context with the disadvantages of the method stressed over the advantages, and the weaknesses rather than strengths stressed in conclusion. By oversight, there may be missed opportunities, unspotted connections and relevances. Here especially one stands to gain from the comments of others.

Utopianism

This is an imaginary state of ideal perfection. It is not necessarily a fault if recognized for what it is. At times, however, Utopian suggestions are put forward as practical possibilities. The research then becomes predicated on an other-worldly base and loses credibility. As in the case of the straw person, however, there might be arguments as to what is Utopian and what is not.

A form of Utopianism leads, on occasion, into mysticism. Unwilling to commit thoughts to the impurity of the printed page, we may cloak them in obscurity and advance them as an 'ongoing exploration of minds'. Unfortunately it is a journey without end, on which we are likely to be lone travellers. As C. Wright Mills (1959, p. 243) notes, 'the line between profundity and verbiage is often delicate, even perilous'. At times, too, we may indulge in excessive jargon. We may fall into this in straining to show some theoretical richness in our work, but it is the strain that shows not the theory. I am reminded of Shakespeare's character who 'draweth out the thread of his verbosity finer than the staple of his argument'.

185

Writing up

Sloppiness

This is too casual writing, showing inadequate thought during analysis and planning. There might be wild claims without proper evidence, ambiguities, inconsistencies, *non sequiturs*, contradictions. Many of the latter can be ironed out in later drafts, but if the general structure has not been adequately conceptualized, there is no alternative but to start again.

Over-zealousness

I have argued for a productive tension between planning and freedom. Too much of the latter leads to sloppiness, too much of the former to over-zealousness. The ideal situation is where the free-ranging mind can produce ideas that are then subjected to methodological rigour. It is difficult to work the process the other way round. Too much concern with the proprieties of method and *le mot juste* at this early stage can lead to a barren product. It is like batting immaculately for a whole session yet scoring no runs, or rigorously scrubbing some clothes - the product ends up scrupulously clean, but threadbare. Ideas must be allowed space and time to germinate. They will quickly rot if they are no good, but they will certainly never take root if not sown and cultivated.

Over-exactness

This is too neat an account. There is pressure on us - from research sponsors, from publishers, from the academic world at large - to be meticulously tidy, to present our work in ordered packages, duly itemized, sectionalized and sequenced. However, qualitative data above all is not like that. The problem is how to convey the sense of flux, process, messiness, inconsistency, ambiguity, which is the very essence of everyday life. This is difficult to do whilst also trying to derive some theoretical order from the material. It is easy to slip into a previous, inappropriate, presentational framework, and make categories and types too sharp and distinct, and the account rather too foursquare. The greatest danger of this comes when seeking to use earlier models or theoretical constructions. An extreme example of this I saw recently involved a 4×4 matrix where the author had felt pressured to produce a type for every square. The result was to make a nonsense of the matrix, for most of the types could have gone anywhere.

186

Theoretical inadequacy

Common forms of this among ethnographic research include the following.

Exampling
All that is done is to provide further illustrations of somebody else's concepts or theoretical constructs. Unless deliberately set up as a replication study, or seeking to develop formal from substantive theory, there is little worth in this. What should be done is to re-examine the material carefully to tell us how it advances understanding in these areas. More appropriate, if one knew the research was going to involve these theoretical areas, would be a prior consideration of them on the Popperian lines already suggested. How might they be tested, falsified? What considerations do they omit? How adequate are they as representations of the data?

Theoretical lag or mismatch
Some of us have had to be dragged kicking and screaming, or yawning and rubbing our eyes, into the proper season of ethnography. A good illustration of this 'lag' is the 'characteristics' model noted by D. Hargreaves (1977) attending much of the early 'interactionist' work in schools, as opposed to a more purist 'process' model. The characteristics model was a hangover from psychological approaches, especially interaction analysis, which had certain affinities with ethnography.

Theoretical 'lag' may come about through one's own biography. Steeped in certain methods and approaches by training and experience, we may find it difficult to make a complete break and view the world otherwise.

Under-theorized description
Ethnography is description by definition, but it is description that is theoretically informed (see Hammersley, 1980). The description I have in mind here is little more than a presentation of the data as it stands, with little attempt to analyse, explain, draw out common features across situations, identifying patterns of behaviour, syndromes of factors, and so forth. Of course, marshalling the data is an appropriate step in research analysis, but it comes at an earlier stage.

Conclusion

The point where rich data, careful analysis and lofty ideas meet the iron discipline of writing is one of the great problem areas in qualitative research. While true to some extent of all kinds of research, it is more of a difficulty in qualitative approaches because of:

(1) the emphasis in them on the investigator as the chief research instrument, which tends to make such problems appear more personal than they really are;

(2) the nature of the research as process – an open-ended ongoing dialogue between data collection and theory, where the search for ideas militates against early foreclosure; and

(3) the necessity, in view of this, to regard the 'writing-up' process as an important inducement to the production of ideas, as well as to their communication.

The disjuncture produces pain, which I have argued is the inevitable corollary of the rites of passage we must go through in our quest for a fully matured product. Regarding it like this externalizes and demystifies the problem, making it less personal. Further analysis then reveals the patterned nature of the complexities involved, which renders them susceptible to treatment. I have made suggestions, from my own experience, of the form that this 'craftwork' might take – the cultivation of amenable situations; pandering to the Protestant Ethic (if a 'P. E. person') one minute with schedules and quotas, and outflanking it the next with productive use of 'free' time; calculated risk-taking; giving special attention to models of excellence in areas, perhaps, outside that of the research, such as literary or other artistic work; 'cranking up' to the appropriate mental state, and undergoing apparent personality changes; meeting 'blockages' in similar analytical style and applying to them a range of techniques; maintaining flexibility in the complicated planning procedures without loss of rigour or impetus; and recognizing some common errors that attend our first efforts at writing.

Such are the strategies that go towards the attempts to produce 'a new song, played skilfully with a loud noise' (Psalm XXXIII). An essential part of the apparatus, however, is a healthy scepticism and a recognition of our ultimate imperfection, that we never quite make the song 'new' enough, or play with sufficient skill, or make a 'loud' enough noise. For if we thought otherwise, we might never produce anything. As the poet said,

And what is writ, is writ, –
Would it were worthier!

188

Bibliography

Adelman, C. (1985), 'Who are you? Some problems of ethnographer culture shock', in Burgess, R. G. (ed.), *Field Methods in the Study of Education*, Lewes, Falmer Press.

Atkins, M. J. (1984), 'Practitioner as researcher: some techniques for analysing semi-structured data in small-scale research', *British Journal of Educational Studies*, XXXII, 3, pp. 251–61.

Atkinson, J. M. (1977), 'Coroners and the categorization of deaths as suicides', in Bell, C. and Newby, H. (eds), *Doing Sociological Research*, London, Allen & Unwin.

Atkinson, P. (1984), 'Words and deeds: Taking knowledge and control seriously', in Burgess, R. G. (ed.), *The Research Process in Educational Settings; Ten Case Studies*, Lewes, Falmer Press.

Atkinson, P. and Delamont, S. (1977), 'Mock-ups and cock-ups: The stage-management of guided discovery instruction', in Woods, P. and Hammersley, M. (eds), *School Experience*, London, Croom Helm.

Ball, D. (1965), 'Sarcasm as sociation: the rhetoric of interaction', *Canadian Review of Sociology and Anthropology*, 2, 3.

Ball, S. J. (1980), 'Initial encounters in the classroom and the process of establishment', in Woods, P. (ed.), *Pupil Strategies*, London, Croom Helm.

Ball, S. J. (1981), *Beachside Comprehensive*, Cambridge, Cambridge University Press.

Ball, S. J. (1982), 'Competition and conflict in the teaching of English: A socio-historical analysis', *Journal of Curriculum Studies*, 14, 1, pp. 1–28.

Ball, S. J. (1983), 'Case study research in education: Some notes and problems', in Hammersley, M. (ed.), *The Ethnography of Schooling: Methodological Issues*, Driffield, Nafferton.

Ball, S. J. (1984), 'Beachside reconsidered: Reflections on a methodological apprenticeship', in Burgess, R. G. (ed.), *The Research Process in Educational Settings: Ten Case Studies*, Lewes, Falmer Press.

Barnes, D. (1976), *From Communication to Curriculum*, Harmondsworth, Penguin.

189

Bartholomew, J. (1974), 'Sustaining hierarchy through teaching and research', in Flude, M. and Ahier, J. (eds), *Educability, Schools and Ideology*, London, Croom Helm.

Becker, H. S. (1958), 'Problems of inference and proof in participant observation', *American Sociological Review*, 23, pp. 652–60.

Becker, H. S. (1970), *Sociological Work*, Chicago, Aldine.

Becker, H. S. (1977), 'Social class variations in the teacher–pupil relationship', in Cosin, B. R. *et al.* (eds), *School and Society*, 2nd edition, London, Routledge & Kegan Paul.

Becker, H. S. and Geer, B. (1960), 'Participant observation: The analysis of qualitative field data', in Adams, R. N. and Preiss, J. J. (eds), *Human Organization Research: Field Relations and Techniques*, Homewood, Illinois, Dorsey Press.

Becker, H. S., Geer, B., Hughes, E. C. and Strauss, A. L. (1961), *Boys in White*, Chicago, University of Chicago Press.

Becker, H. S., Geer, B., Riesman, D. and Weiss, R. S. (eds) (1968), *Institutions and the Person*, Chicago, Aldine.

Bell, A. E. (ed.) (1977), *The Diary of Virginia Woolf Vol. 1, 1915–1919*, London, Hogarth Press.

Bell, J. and Goulding, S. (1984), 'Students planning investigations in educational management', in Bell, J. *et al.* (eds), *Conducting Small-Scale Investigations in Educational Management*, London, Harper.

Berlak, A. and Berlak, H. (1981), *The Dilemmas of Schooling*, London, Methuen.

Bernstein, S. (1978), 'Getting it done – notes on student fritters', in Lofland, J. (ed.), *Interaction in Everyday Life*, Beverly Hills, Sage Publications.

Bertaux, D. (1981), *Biography and Society: the Life History Approach in the Social Sciences*, Beverly Hills, Sage.

Beynon, J. (1983), 'Ways-in and staying-in: Fieldwork as problem solving', in Hammersley, M. (ed.), *The Ethnography of Schooling: Methodological Issues*, Driffield, Nafferton.

Beynon, J. (1984), 'Sussing-out teachers – pupils as data gatherers', in Hammersley, M. and Woods, P. (eds), *Life in School*, Milton Keynes, Open University Press.

Beynon, J. (1985), *Initial Encounters in the Secondary School*, Lewes, Falmer Press.

Bird, C., Chessum, R., Furlong, J. and Johnson, D. (1981), *Disaffected Pupils*, Brunel University, Educational Studies Unit.

Blishen, E. (1966), *Roaring Boys*, London, Panther.

Blishen, E. (1980), *Shaky Relationships*, London, Hamish Hamilton.

Blumer, H. (1954), 'What is wrong with social theory?', *American Sociological Review*, 19, pp. 3–10.

Bogdan, R. C. and Biklen, S. K. (1982), *Qualitative Research for Education: An Introduction to Theory and Methods*, Boston, Allyn & Bacon.

Bowles, S. and Gintis, H. (1976), *Schooling in Capitalist America*, London, Routledge & Kegan Paul.

Brown, R. H. (1977), *A Poetic for Sociology*, Cambridge, Cambridge University Press.

Bruyn, S. T. (1966), *The Human Perspective in Sociology: the methodology of participant observation*, Englewood Cliffs, N.J., Prentice Hall.

Bryan, K. (1980), 'Pupil perceptions of transfer between middle and high schools', in Hargreaves, A. and Tickle, L. (eds), *Middle Schools*, London, Harper.

Bulmer, M. (1979), 'Concepts in the analysis of qualitative data', *Sociological Review*, 27, 4.

Bulmer, M. (ed.) (1982), *Social Research Ethics*, London, Macmillan.

Burgess, R. G. (ed.) (1982a), *Field Research: A Sourcebook and Field Manual*, London, Allen & Unwin.

Burgess, R. G. (1982b), 'The unstructured interview as a conversation', in Burgess, R. G. (ed.), *Field Research: A Sourcebook and Field Manual*, London, Allen & Unwin.

Burgess, R. G. (1983), *Experiencing Comprehensive Education: A Study of Bishop McGregor School*, London, Methuen.

Burgess, R. G. (ed.) (1984a), *The Research Process in Educational Settings: Ten Case Studies*, Lewes, Falmer Press.

Burgess, R. G. (1984b), 'Keeping a research diary', in Bell, J. *et al.* (eds), *Conducting Small-Scale Investigations in Educational Management*, London, Harper.

Burgess, R. G. (1984c), *In the Field: An Introduction to Field Research*, London, Allen & Unwin.

Burgess, R. G. (1985a), 'The whole truth? Some ethical problems of research in a comprehensive school', in Burgess, R. G. (ed.), *Field Methods in the Study of Education*, Lewis, Falmer Press.

Burgess, R. G. (1985b), 'Key informants and the ethnographic study of education', in Burgess, R. G. (ed.), *Qualitative Methodology and the Study of Education*, Lewis, Falmer Press.

Cicourel, A. V. (1968), *The Social Organisation of Juvenile Justice*, New York, Wiley.

Corrigan, P. (1979), *Schooling the Smash Street Kids*, London, Macmillan.

Davies, B. (1982), *Life in the Classroom and Playground*, London, Routledge & Kegan Paul.

Davies, L. (1984), *Pupil Power: Deviance and Gender in School*, Lewes, Falmer Press.

Davies, L. (1985), 'Ethnography and status: Focusing on gender in educational research', in Burgess, R. G. (ed.), *Field Methods in the Study of Education*, Barcombe, Falmer Press.

Dean, J. P. and Whyte, W. F. (1969), 'How do you know if the informant is telling the truth?', in McCall, G. J. and Simmons, J. L. (eds), *Issues in Participant Observation*, Reading, Mass., Addison-Wesley.

Delamont, S. (1973), 'Academic conformity observed', unpublished Ph.D. thesis, University of Edinburgh.

Delamont, S. (1976), *Interaction in the Classroom*, London, Methuen.

191

Delamont, S. (1981), 'All too familiar? A decade of classroom research', *Educational Analysis*, 3, 1, pp. 69-83.

Delamont, S. (1984), 'The old girl network: Reflections on the fieldwork at St Luke's', in Burgess, R. G. (ed.), *The Research Process in Educational Settings: Ten Case Studies*, Lewes, Falmer Press.

Delamont, S. and Hamilton, D. (1984), 'Revisiting classroom research: A continuing cautionary tale', in Delamont, S. (ed.), *Readings on Interaction in the Classroom*, London, Methuen.

Denscombe, M. (1980), '"Keeping 'em quiet": The significance of no noise for the practical activity of teaching', in Woods, P. (ed.), *Teacher Strategies*, London, Croom Helm.

Denscombe, M. (1983), 'Interviews, accounts and ethnographic research on teachers', in Hammersley, M. (ed.), *The Ethnography of Schooling*, Driffield, Nafferton.

Denzin, N. (1970), *The Research Act in Sociology: A Theoretical Introduction to Sociological Methods*, London, Butterworth.

De Waele, J.-P. and Harré, R. (1979), 'Autobiography as a psychological method', in Ginsburg, G. P. (ed.), *Emerging Strategies in Social Psychological Research*, London, Wiley.

Dexter, L. A. (1956), 'Role relationships and conceptions of neutrality in interviewing', *The American Journal of Sociology*, LXII, 2, pp. 153-7.

Ditton, J. (1977), *Part-time Crime: an Ethnography of Fiddling and Pilferage*, London, Macmillan.

Douglas, J. D. (1970), *Understanding Everyday Life*, Chicago, Aldine.

Edwards, A. D. and Furlong, V. J. (1978), *The Language of Teaching*, London, Heinemann.

Eldridge, J. (1980), *Recent British Sociology*, London, Macmillan.

Elliott, J. and Adelman, C. (1975), 'Teachers' accounts and the objectivity of classroom research', *London Educational Review*, 4, pp. 29-37.

Esland, G. (1971), 'Teaching and learning as the organization of knowledge', in Young, M. F. D. (ed.), *Knowledge and Control*, London, Collier-Macmillan.

Faraday, A. and Plummer, K. (1979), 'Doing life histories', *Sociological Review*, 27, 4.

Flanders, N. A. (1970), *Analyzing Teaching Behaviour*, New York, Addison-Wesley.

Ford, J. (1975), *Paradigms and Fairy Tales*, London, Routledge & Kegan Paul.

Fothergill, R. A. (1974), *Private Chronicles: A Study of English Diaries*, London, Oxford University Press.

Fuller, M. (1978), *Dimensions of Gender in a School*, unpublished Ph.D. thesis, University of Bristol.

Fuller, M. (1980), 'Black girls in a London comprehensive school', in Deem, R. (ed.), *Schooling for Women's Work*, London, Routledge & Kegan Paul.

Fuller, M. (1984), 'Dimensions of gender in a school: Reinventing the wheel?', in Burgess, R. G. (ed.), *The Research Process in Educational Settings: Ten Case Studies*, Lewes, Falmer Press.

Furlong, V. J. (1976), 'Interaction sets in the classroom: Towards a study of pupil knowledge', in Hammersley, M. and Woods, P. (eds), *The Process of Schooling*, London, Routledge & Kegan Paul.

Galton, M. and Simon, B. (eds) (1980), *Progress and Performance in the Primary Classroom*, London, Routledge & Kegan Paul.

Galton, M., Simon, B. and Croll, P. (1980), *Inside the Primary Classroom*, London, Routledge & Kegan Paul.

Galton, M. and Willcocks, J. (eds) (1983), *Moving from the Primary Classroom*, London, Routledge & Kegan Paul.

Gannaway, H. (1976), 'Making sense of school', in Stubbs, M. and Delamont, S. (eds), *Explorations in Classroom Observation*, London, Wiley.

Ginsburg, M., Meyenn, R. J. and Miller, H. D. R. (1980), 'Teachers' conceptions of professionalism and trades unionism: An ideological analysis', in Woods, P. (ed.), *Teacher Strategies*, London, Croom Helm.

Glaser, B. G. (1978), *Theoretical Sensitivity: Advances in the Methodology of Grounded Theory*, University of California, Sociology Press.

Glaser, B. G. and Strauss, A. L. (1967), *The Discovery of Grounded Theory*, London, Weidenfeld & Nicolson.

Glaser, B. G. and Strauss, A. L. (1971), *Status Passage*, Chicago, Aldine.

Goodson, I. (1980), 'Life histories and the study of schooling', *Interchange*, 11, 4.

Goodson, I. (1981), 'Becoming an academic subject; Patterns of explanation and evolution', *British Journal of Sociology of Education*, 2, 3.

Goodson, I. and Walker, R. (1979), 'Putting life into ethnography', paper presented at SSRC *Ethnography of Schooling* Conference, Sept. 10th–12th, St Hilda's College, Oxford.

Grace, G. (1978), *Teachers, Ideology and Control*, London, Routledge & Kegan Paul.

Greer, W. (1983), 'Interviewing as conversation', unpublished paper, Milton Keynes, The Open University.

Griffin, C. (1985), 'Qualitative methods and cultural analysis: Young women and the transition from school to un/employment', in Burgess, R. G. (ed.), *Field Methods in the Study of Education*, Lewes, Falmer Press.

Griffiths, G. (1985), 'Doubts, dilemmas and diary keeping: Some reflections on teacher-based research', in Burgess, R. G. (ed.), *Issues in Educational Research: Qualitative Methods*, Lewes, Falmer Press.

Hammersley, M. (1977a), 'Teacher perspectives', units 9–10 of course E202, *Schooling and Society*, Milton Keynes, Open University Press.

Hammersley, M. (1977b), 'School learning: The cultural resources required by pupils to answer a teacher's question', in Woods, P. and Hammersley, M. (eds), *School Experience*, London, Croom Helm.

193

Hammersley, M. (1979a), 'Towards a model of teacher activity', in
Eggleston, J. (ed.), *Teacher Decision-Making in the Classroom*,
London, Routledge & Kegan Paul.

Hammersley, M. (1979b), 'Data collection in ethnographic research',
block 4, part 3 of course DE304, *Research Methods in Education and
the Social Sciences*, Milton Keynes, Open University Press.

Hammersley, M. (1979c), 'Analysing ethnographic data', block 6, part I,
of course DE304, *Research Methods in Education and the Social
Sciences*, Milton Keynes, Open University Press.

Hammersley, M. (1980), 'On interactionist empiricism', in Woods, P.
(ed.), *Pupil Strategies*, London, Croom Helm.

Hammersley, M. (1984), 'The researcher exposed: A natural history', in
Burgess, R. G. (ed.), *The Research Process in Educational Settings: Ten
Case Studies*, Lewes, Falmer Press.

Hammersley, M. and Atkinson, P. (1983), *Ethnography: Principles in
Practice*, London, Tavistock.

Hammersley, M. and Turner, G. (1980), 'Conformist pupils?', in Woods,
P. (ed.), *Pupil Strategies*, London, Croom Helm.

Hargreaves, A. (1977), 'Progressivism and pupil autonomy', *Sociological
Review*, August.

Hargreaves, A. (1979), 'Strategies, decisions and control: Interaction in a
middle school classroom', in Eggleston, J. (ed.), *Teacher Decision-
Making in the Classroom*, London, Routledge & Kegan Paul.

Hargreaves, A. (1980), 'Synthesis and the study of strategies: A project
for the sociological imagination', in Woods, P. (ed.), *Pupil Strategies*,
London, Croom Helm.

Hargreaves, A. (1981), 'Contrastive rhetoric and extremist talk', in
Barton, L. and Walker, S. (eds), *Schools, Teachers and Teaching*,
Lewes, Falmer Press.

Hargreaves, D. H. (1967), *Social Relations in a Secondary School*,
London, Routledge & Kegan Paul.

Hargreaves, D. H. (1972), *Interpersonal Relations and Education*, London,
Routledge & Kegan Paul.

Hargreaves, D. H. (1977), 'The process of typification in the classroom:
Models and methods', *British Journal of Educational Psychology*, 47,
pp. 274–84.

Hargreaves, D. H. (1978), 'Whatever happened to symbolic
interactionism', in Barton, L., and Meighan, R. (eds), *Sociological
Interpretations of Schooling and Classroom: a Reappraisal*, Driffield,
Nafferton, pp. 7–22.

Hargreaves, D. H. (1980), 'The occupational culture of teachers', in
Woods, P. (ed.), *Teacher Strategies*, London, Croom Helm.

Hargreaves, D. H. (1981), 'Schooling for delinquency', in Barton, L.
and Walker, S. (eds), *Schools, Teachers and Teaching*, Lewes, Falmer
Press.

Hargreaves, D. H., Hester, S. K. and Mellor, F. J. (1975), *Deviance in*

Classrooms, London, Routledge & Kegan Paul.

Harris, A. (1976), 'Intuition and the arts of teaching', unit 18 of course E203, *Curriculum Design and Development*, Milton Keynes, Open University Press.

Hart, N. (1976), *When Marriage Ends: A Study in Status Passage*, London, Tavistock.

Henry, J. (1963), *Culture against Man*, Random House, New York.

Hicks, D. (1981), 'Bias in school books: Messages from the ethnocentric curriculum', in James, A. and Jeffcoate, R. (eds), *The School in the Multicultural Society*, London, Harper & Row.

Hitchcock, G. (1983), 'What might INSET programmes and educational research expect from the sociologist?', *British Journal of Inservice Education*, 10, 1, pp. 9-31.

Hopper, E. (1971), 'A typology for the classification of educational systems', in Hopper, E. (ed.), *Readings in the Theory of Educational Systems*, London, Hutchinson.

Hunter, C. (1980), 'The politics of participation - with specific reference to teacher-pupil relationships', in Woods, P. (ed.), *Teacher Strategies: Explorations in the Sociology of the School*, London, Croom Helm.

Jackson, P. W. (1968), *Life in Classrooms*, New York, Holt, Rinehart & Winston.

Karl, E. R. and Davies, L. (eds) (1983), *The Collected Letters of Joseph Conrad, Volume One: 1861-1897*, Cambridge, Cambridge University Press.

Keddie, N. (1971), 'Classroom knowledge', in Young, M. F. D. (ed.), *Knowledge and Control*, London, Collier-Macmillan.

King, R. A. (1978), *All Things Bright and Beautiful*, Chichester, Wiley.

King, R. A. (1984), 'The man in the Wendy House: Researching infants' schools', in Burgess, R. G. (ed.), *The Research Process in Educational Settings: Ten Case Studies*, Lewes, Falmer Press.

Lacey, C. (1970), *Hightown Grammar*, Manchester, Manchester University Press.

Lacey, C. (1976), 'Problems of sociological fieldwork: A review of the methodology of "Hightown Grammar"', in Hammersley, M. and Woods, P. (eds), *The Process of Schooling*, London, Routledge & Kegan Paul.

Lacey, C. (1977), *The Socialization of Teachers*, London, Methuen.

Lambart, A. M. (1976), 'The sisterhood', in Hammersley, M. and Woods, P. (eds), *The Process of Schooling*, London, Routledge & Kegan Paul.

Lindesmith, A. R. (1947), *Opiate Addiction*, Bloomington, Ind. Principia Press.

Llewellyn, M. (1980), 'Studying girls at school: The implications of confusion', in Deem, R. (ed.), *Schooling for Women's Work*, London, Routledge & Kegan Paul.

Lobban, G. (1978), 'The influence of the school in sex-role stereotyping', in Chetwynd, J. and Hartnett, O. (eds), *The Sex Role System*, London,

Routledge & Kegan Paul.

Logan, T. (1984), 'Learning through interviewing', in Schostak, J. F. and Logan, T. (eds), *Pupil Experience*, London, Croom Helm.

Lortie, D. C. (1973), 'Observations on teaching as work', in Travers, R. M. W. (ed.), *Second Handbook on Research on Teaching*, Chicago, Rand McNally.

MacDiarmid, H. (1969), *Selected Essays of Hugh MacDiarmid* (ed. Duncan Glen), London, Cape.

MacLure, M. and French, P. (1980), 'Routes to right answers: on pupils' strategies for answering teachers' questions', in Woods, P. (ed.), *Pupil Strategies*, London, Croom Helm.

McNamara, D. (1980), 'The outsider's arrogance: The failure of participant observers to understand classroom events', *British Educational Research Journal*, 6, 2.

Marsh, P., Rosser, E. and Harré, R. (1978), *The Rules of Disorder*, London, Routledge & Kegan Paul.

Martin, W. B. W. (1976), *The Negotiated Order of the School*, Toronto, Macmillan.

Masefield, J. (1932), *The Collected Poems of John Masefield*, London, Heinemann.

May, N. and Rudduck, J. (1983), *Sex-Stereotyping and the Early Years of Schooling*, Norwich, The Centre for Applied Research in Education.

Mead, G. H. (1934), *Mind, Self and Society*, Chicago, University of Chicago Press.

Measor, L. (1985), 'Interviewing in ethnographic research', in Burgess, R. G. (ed.), *Qualitative Methodology and the Study of Education*, Lewes, Falmer Press.

Measor, L. (1985), 'Sex education and adolescent development', unpublished paper, Milton Keynes, The Open University.

Measor, L. and Woods, P. (1983), 'The interpretation of pupil myths', in Hammersley, M. (ed.), *The Ethnography of Schooling*, Driffield, Nafferton.

Measor, L. and Woods, P. (1984), *Changing Schools: Pupil Perspectives on Transfer to a Comprehensive*, Milton Keynes, Open University Press.

Merton, R. (1957), *Social Theory and Social Structure*, Chicago, Free Press.

Meyenn, R. (1980), 'School girls' peer groups', in Woods, P. (ed.), *Pupil Strategies*, London, Croom Helm.

Miller, S. M. (1952), 'The participant observer and over-rapport', *American Sociological Review*, XVII, pp. 97-9.

Mills, C. W. (1959), *The Sociological Imagination*, New York, Oxford University Press.

Morgan, C. (1960), *The Writer and His World*, London, Macmillan.

Mortimer, J. (1983), 'Wig, pen and wisdom', *Radio Times*, 27 August-2 September.

Murdoch, I. (1980), *The Sea, The Sea*, London, Panther.

Musgrove, F. and Middleton, R. (1981), 'Rites of passage and the meaning of age in three contrasted social groups', *British Journal of Sociology*, 32, 1, March.

Nash, R. (1976), 'Pupils' expectations of their teachers', in Stubbs, M. and Delamont, S. (eds), *Explorations in Classroom Observation*, Chichester, Wiley.

Nias, J. (1981), 'Commitment and motivation in primary school teachers', *Educational Review*, 33, 3, pp. 181–90.

Nisbet, R. (1962), 'Sociology as an art form', *Pacific Sociological Review*, Autumn.

Oakley, A. (1980), *Women Confined: Towards a Sociology of Childbirth*, Oxford, Martin Robertson.

Oakley, A. (1981), 'Interviewing women', in Roberts, H. (ed.), *Doing Feminist Research*, London, Routledge & Kegan Paul.

Parker, H. J. (1974), *View from the Boys*, Newton Abbot, David & Charles.

Patrick, J. (1973), *A Glasgow Gang Observed*, London, Eyre Methuen.

Payne, G., Dingwall, R., Payne, J. and Carter, M. (1981), *Sociology and Social Research*, London, Routledge & Kegan Paul.

Player, J. (1984), 'The amorphous school', in Goodson, I. F. and Ball, S. J. (eds), *Defining the Curriculum*, Lewis, Falmer Press.

Plummer, K. (1983), *Documents of Life*, London, Allen & Unwin.

Pollard, A. (1979), 'Negotiating deviance and "getting done" in primary school classrooms', in Barton, L. and Meighan, R. (eds), *Schools, Pupils and Deviance*, Driffield, Nafferton.

Pollard, A. (1980), 'Teacher interests and changing situations of survival threat in primary school classrooms', in Woods, P. (ed.), *Teacher Strategies*, London, Croom Helm.

Pollard, A. (1982), 'A model of coping strategies', *British Journal of Sociology of Education*, 3, 2.

Pollard, A. (1984), 'Goodies, jokers and gangs', in Hammersley, M. and Woods, P. (eds), *Life in School: The Sociology of Pupil Culture*, Milton Keynes, The Open University.

Pollard, A. (1985a), 'Opportunities and difficulties of a teacher-ethnographer: A personal account', in Burgess, R. G. (ed.), *Field Methods in the Study of Education*, Lewes, Falmer Press.

Pollard, A. (1985b), *The Social World of the Primary School*, London, Holt, Rinehart & Winston.

Popper, K. (1963), *Conjectures and Refutations: The Growth of Scientific Knowledge*, London, Routledge & Kegan Paul.

Porter, M. (1984), 'The modification of method in researching postgraduate education', in Burgess, R. G. (ed.), *The Research Process in Educational Settings: Ten Case Studies*, Lewes, Falmer Press.

Prendergast, S. and Prout, A. (1984), 'The natural and the personal – reflections on birth films in school', paper given at conference on *The Affective Curriculum*, St Hilda's College, Oxford.

Read, P. P. (1977), *Polonaise*, London, Pan.

Redfield, R. (1953), *The Primitive World and its Transformations*, Ithaca, N.Y., Cornell University Press.

Reynolds, D. (1976), 'The delinquent school', in Hammersley, M. and Woods, P. E. (eds), *The Process of Schooling*, London, Routledge & Kegan Paul.

Reynolds, D. and Sullivan, M. (1979), 'Bringing schools back in', in Barton, L. and Meighan, R. (eds), *Schools, Pupils and Deviance*, Driffield, Nafferton.

Riseborough, G. F. (1981), 'Teacher careers and comprehensive schooling: An empirical study', *Sociology*, 15, 3, pp. 352–81.

Robinson, P. E. D. (1974), 'An ethnography of classrooms', in Eggleston, J. (ed.), *Contemporary Research in The Sociology of Education*, London, Methuen.

Rosser, E. and Harré, R. (1976), 'The meaning of disorder', in Hammersley, M. and Woods, P. (eds), *The Process of Schooling*, London, Routledge & Kegan Paul.

Rudduck, J. (1984), 'A study in the dissemination of action research', in Burgess, R. G. (ed.), *The Research Process in Educational Settings: Ten Case Studies*, Lewes, Falmer Press.

Rutter, M. *et al.* (1979), *Fifteen Thousand Hours*, London, Open Books.

Scarth, J. (1985), *The Influence of Examinations on Curriculum Decision-Making: A Sociological Case-Study*, Ph.D. thesis, Department of Educational Research, University of Lancaster.

Schutz, A. (1962) *Collected Papers*, The Hague, Nijhoff.

Shulman, L. (1984), 'Teacher education and educational research', paper given at conference on *Research in Teacher Education*, University of Leicester.

Sikes, P., Measor, L. and Woods, P. (1985), *Teacher Careers: Crises and Continuities*, Lewes, Falmer Press.

Silvers, R. J. (1977), 'Appearances: A videographic study of children's culture', in Woods, P. and Hammersley, M. (eds), *School Experience*, London, Croom Helm.

Simon, B. and Willcocks, J. (1981), *Research and Practice in the Primary Classroom*, London, Routledge & Kegan Paul.

Sjoberg, G. and Nett, R. (1968), *A Methodology for Social Research*, New York, Harper & Row.

Smith, D. (1973), 'Distribution processes and power relations in education systems', block I of course E352, *Education, Economy and Politics*, Milton Keynes, Open University Press.

Smith, L. H. and Geoffrey, W. (1968), *The Complexities of an Urban Classroom*, New York, Holt, Rinehart & Winston.

Sperber, D. (1979), 'Claude Lévi-Strauss', in Sturrock, J. (ed.), *Structuralism and Since*, Oxford, Oxford University Press.

Spradley, J. P. (1979), *The Ethnographic Interview*, New York, Holt, Rinehart & Winston.

Spradley, J. P. (1980), *Participant Observation*, New York, Holt, Rinehart & Winston.

Stanworth, M. (1983), *Gender and Schooling: A study of Sexual Divisions in the Classroom*, London, Hutchinson.

Stebbins, R. (1970), 'The meaning of disorderly behaviour: Teacher definitions of a classroom situation', *Sociology of Education*, 44, pp. 217–36.

Stebbins, R. (1981), 'Classroom ethnography and the definition of the situation', in Barton, L. and Walker, S. (eds), *Schools, Teachers and Teaching*, Lewes, Falmer Press.

Stenhouse, L. (1975), *An Introduction to Curriculum Research and Development*, London, Heinemann.

Stenhouse, L. (1984), 'Library access, library use and user education in academic sixth forms: An autobiographical account', in Burgess, R. J. (ed.), *The Research Process in Educational Settings: Ten Case Studies*, Lewes, Falmer Press.

Turner, G. (1983), *The Social World of the Comprehensive School*, London, Croom Helm.

Turner, V. W. (1969), *The Ritual Process*, London, Routledge & Kegan Paul.

Van Gennep, A. (1960), *The Rites of Passage*, London, Routledge & Kegan Paul.

Wakeford, J. (1969), *The Cloistered Elite: A Sociological Analysis of the English Public Boarding School*, London, Macmillan.

Walker, R. and Adelman, C. (1972), *Towards a Sociography of Classrooms*, Final Report, London, SSRC.

Walker, R. and Wiedel, J. (1985), 'Using photographs in a discipline of words', in Burgess, R. G. (ed.), *Field Methods in the Study of Education*, Lewes, Falmer Press.

Waller, W. (1932), *The Sociology of Teaching*, New York, Wiley.

Wax, M. and Wax, R. (1971), 'Great tradition, little tradition and formal education', in Wax, M.L., Diamond, S. and Gearing, F. (eds), *Anthropological Perspectives on Education*, New York, Basic Books.

Webb, E. J., Campbell, D. T., Schwartz, R. D., and Sechrest, L. (1966), *Unobtrusive Measures; Nonreactive Research in the Social Sciences*, Chicago, Rand McNally.

Webb, J. (1962), 'The sociology of a school', *British Journal of Sociology*, 13, pp. 264–72.

Weber, M. (1946), *Max Weber's Essays in Sociology* (Gerth, H. H. and Mills, C. W. eds), New York, Oxford University Press.

Westbury, I. (1973), 'Conventional classrooms, "open" classrooms and the technology of teaching', *Journal of Curriculum Studies*, 5, 2, November.

Whyte, W. F. (1955), *Street Corner Society*, Chicago, University of Chicago Press.

Whyte, W. F. (1982), 'Interviewing in field research', in Burgess, R. G. (ed.), *Field Research: A Sourcebook and Field Manual*, London, Allen & Unwin.

Willis, P. (1977), *Learning to Labour*, Farnborough, Saxon House.

Wolcott, H. (1975), 'Criteria for an ethnographic approach to research in schools', *Human Organization*, 34, 2.

Woods, P. (1978), 'Negotiating the demands of schoolwork', *Journal of Curriculum Studies*, 10, 4, pp. 309–27.

Woods, P. (1979), *The Divided School*, London, Routledge & Kegan Paul.

Woods, P. (1981), 'Strategies, commitment and identity-making and breaking the teacher role', in Barton, L. and Walker, S. (eds), *Schools, Teachers and Teaching*, Lewes, Falmer Press.

Woods, P. (1983), *Sociology and the School*, London, Routledge & Kegan Paul.

Woods, P. (1984), 'Teacher, self and curriculum', in Ball, S. J. and Goodson, I. (eds), *Defining the Curriculum*, Lewes, Falmer Press.

Woods, P. (1985), 'Ethnography and theory construction in educational research', in Burgess, R. (ed.), *Field Methods in the Study of Education*, Lewes, Falmer Press.

Wright, N. (1977), *Progress in Education*, London, Croom Helm.

Yablonsky, L. (1968), *The Hippie Trip*, New York, Pegasus.

Young, J. (1971), 'The role of the police as amplifiers of deviancy, negotiators of reality and translators of fantasy', in Cohen, S. (ed.), *Images of Deviance*, Harmondsworth, Penguin.

Youngman, M. B. (1984), 'Designing questionnaires', in Bell, J. *et al.* (eds), *Conducting Small-Scale Investigations in Educational Management*, London, Harper & Row.

Zimmerman, D. H. and Wieder, D. L. (1977), 'The diary: diary–interview method', *Urban Life*, 5, 4, pp. 479–98.

Name index

Subject index